KARAMOJO SAFARI

W. D. M. BELL

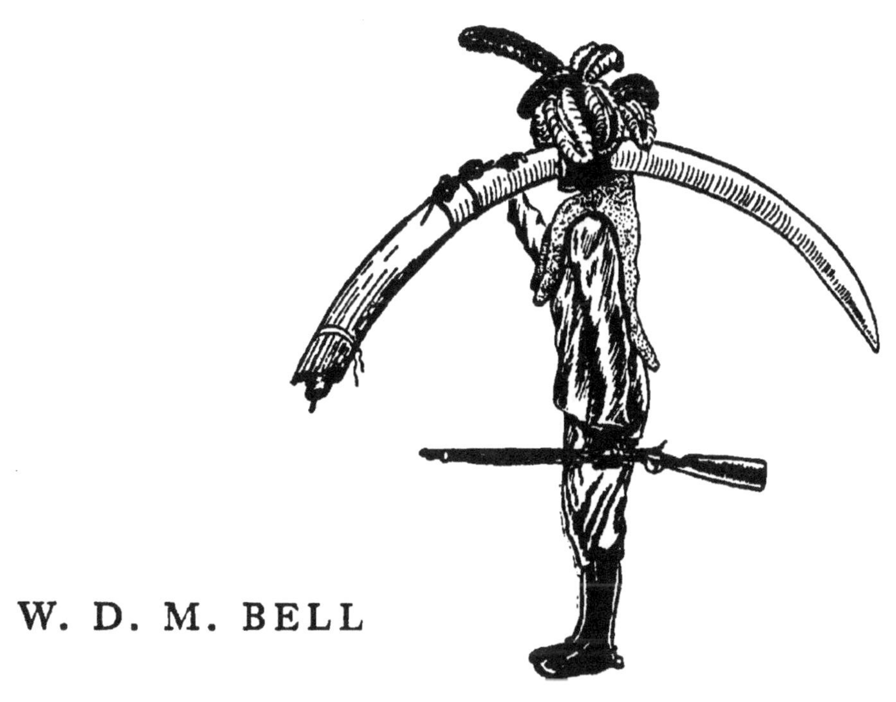

KARAMOJO SAFARI

HARCOURT, BRACE AND COMPANY
NEW YORK · 1949

A PATHFINDER BOOK REPRINT EDITION
Complete and Unabridged

Printed in the United States of America

ISBN: 979-8-8691-2209-4

TO MY AFRICAN COMPANIONS

INTRODUCTION

IT IS too much like the monkey walking ahead of the elephant when the circus parades through town for me to write an introduction to Karamojo Bell. He is far too great a man. I was surprised to find that he is still alive; his name is such a legend in Africa. Whenever you start to talk about elephants, his name comes up: he is synonymous. His first name has long ago been replaced by the name of the wild territory he hunted them in. The big hunters in East Africa will call your attention to Bell, not because he has killed so many elephants, but because he has understood them so well, and loved them. *"He knows!"* they will tell you. And there will be real affection in their voices.

This combination of the professional killer and the artist-adventurer is not so rare as one might think; a man must have something of the poet in him to become a great hunter. That is what gives them their awareness of the undertones, the subtleties of the African scene, and their ability to understand the ways and whims of the big animals they are hunting on it. It is a matter of record that practically all the great hunters of Africa have ended up by becoming mystics. They were halfway to being that before they went there: it was something inside themselves which called them to Africa. They came and they saw, and they stayed. The life of every one of them is an epic, could they but tell it. Bell has.

So far as I know, the elephant is the only animal which will try to help a wounded comrade from the scene of death. If an elephant is shot, and does not fall, other members of the herd will frequently get on either side of him to hold him up. Many an elephant has been killed who has lingered behind, trying to help a wounded elephant to his feet by lifting him with his tusks. When you know things like that, you begin to feel a great love for elephants.

Ten years ago, I made a detour on a drive I was making from coast to coast across Africa, to drop in and see a brigadier I had lain beside in hospital in the wartime Egypt of 1918. He was a colonel of the 8th Gurkhas then. He had since been the game warden of Tanganyika; and I dropped in to borrow his double-barreled .400 so that I might kill a lion. I found him sitting in the little bungalow he had built for himself out on the beautiful mountain of Ngong, where all the Masai medicine men once came from. He had a book by Bell before him. "Ever read that?" he asked.

I told him no, adding that I had no desire whatever to kill an elephant: it would be such effrontery.

He smiled: "Well, my boy, I'm not talking about you killing elephants. I'm talking about *Africa,* the real Africa—and this book is full of it. It's splendid."

This time, when I was back in Kenya, I drove out to see my old friend again. There he was, a bit grayer, but still sitting before the same book. "Ever read that?" he asked.

I laughed: "You asked me that ten years ago!"

"But have you *read* it?" he persisted.

I shook my head. He opened the book, put his finger on one or two of Bell's drawings: "Do you see that?" he said, tracing the line from eye to ear where Bell's sketch shows just where to place the deadly brain shot. "That man knows more about elephants—and what it is like to be out on safari—than any man who ever handled a high-powered rifle. I'm surprised at you."

Karamojo Bell is the first man who ever took a high-powered rifle to East Africa. You will probably find him the most endearing man on elephants, and Africa, that ever handled pencil or pen. And now, having introduced him, I want to get out of Karamojo Bell's way as quickly as possible.

NEGLEY FARSON

This is a true story of a journey into Karamojo some fifty years ago when it was an unknown part of Africa. Indeed, even today with the aid of modern transportation, it is but little known.

At the time dealt with in this book, the author was the first white man seen by the natives. Needless to say, the conditions then prevailing can never occur again.

KARAMOJO SAFARI

PROLOGUE

WHEN I first arrived in Africa in 1897, an era of exploration was coming to an end. The scramble for territory, with its attendant penetration and occupation of new countries, was drawing to a close. The map of Africa, at any rate, was colored, and its boundless territories portioned out to the various powers concerned. All this penetration and occupation had been carried out mostly by large military expeditions fully armed with rifles, machine guns, and, in some cases, with cannon—all without even consulting the original and native owners.

These owners of the soil were mostly savage and primitive peoples. Generally speaking, they knew nothing of trade or even of money. Consequently, when large bodies of foreign men armed with rifles appeared suddenly on their tribal boundaries, they fought to defend their meager stocks of foodstuffs from the invaders. The result was a foregone conclusion: rivers of native blood were shed.

All these expeditions were armed with black powder weapons, adequate enough to kill humans but poor performers against the prolific game herds that then literally swarmed on the African prairies and in the forests. These herds that could so easily have fed the expeditions were completely ignored; all rations had to be drawn from native herds and from native gardens, with the natural consequence that they had to be paid for in bullets.

Now Africa is an immense continent, and although the result of all these occupations looked well on the map, actually there were huge territories still untouched—some as large as France. Into one of these countries it was my lot to penetrate and live for five years without the killing of a single native. There were, of course, moments of hostility and even of danger. But it never came, that decisive killing that so often started the bloodletting.

It was the advent of the modern rifle that made this possible. Smokeless powder, magazine fire, and, above all, the solid nickel-covered bullet made the difference. Where elephant, rhino, and buffalo had hitherto simply repelled the soft leaden bullets of the former invaders of their centuries-old sanctuaries, the solid nickel-jacketed bullet of the .303 now reached their vitals, whether brain or heart, and laid them low. Suddenly, meat food—Africa's greatest lack—became abundant through the miraculous properties of a firearm without smoke and of small bore. From the role of Public Enemy Number One, the invader suddenly assumed the mantle of General Provider of Meat for everyone. Tons and tons of meat were provided in a single encounter with elephant. The natives got the meat and the invader got the bones—as they called the ivory—so everyone was happy.

The first rifle I used in Africa against anything larger than a rabbit was a single-shot falling block .303. It had a side lever and was a poor extractor, but was light, handy, beautifully sighted by Fraser of Edinburgh, and, of course, had the lovely snappy pull-off that distinguishes this system above all others. The release-shudder at pull-off was at its minimum as the internal hammer and striker were, of necessity, of very small dimensions and weight. But, alas, all these desirable features were washed out by impossibly poor extraction. This was in the days of cordite-loaded cartridges, and when these had been well baked in a tropical sun, the pressures used to rise enough to rupture the cases—and there you were, disarmed until you got to work with a ramrod. I was unlucky enough to find a .450 single-shot Winchester, falling block with outside hammer, in the possession of a Greek trader. It used a very long tapered case and burned a lot of black powder behind a light lead bullet. It was in poor condition externally but pretty good inside, and, what mattered most, it would extract. So, showing my beautifully blued and handsomely stocked .303, a trade was soon effected. All would have been well had it not been for the fact that all the ammunition I got with this rifle had that ghastly failure, the hollow copper-point bullet.

All this was in East Africa, now called Kenya. Lion, rhino, and game of all kinds were in great abundance on all sides. The country had been quite untouched by the rare Swahili and Arab safaris then using the Mombassa-Uganda trail, most of the big trading caravans using the Dar-es-Salaam-Ujiji trail.

Lion were then very numerous and bold. Although their natural food—zebra and antelope of all kinds—simply covered the landscape, there were the old lion with worn teeth and dulled claws to be reckoned with. Owing to the unfortunate custom of some of the tribes of throwing out their dead to be devoured by vultures by day and hyenas and jackals by night, many of these failing lion found it much easier to chase off the bitterly protesting hyenas from some festering corpse than to stand the ordeal by chase of the living quarry.* From corpse

* The author follows the hunter's preference for the use of the singular form when referring to game animals—lion, elephant, buffalo, etc. Non-game animals retain their customary plural forms.—ED.

to living being was but a short step and, as these were generally unarmed women, an easy one.

When used on the smaller antelope and gazelle, such as Thomson's, Duiker, Klipspringer, Oribi, or Impala (our preferred meat for the pot), the copper-point .450 bullet was very effective. In fact, too much so. It simply blew up and destroyed almost half the back: a messy business. Naturally the neck shot was used when the range would allow a fair chance of a hit.

One morning, just as the boys were giving the donkeys their last chance of a drink before a long and thirsty trek, one of them came running back to say there was a lion at the water hole. Here was a tryout for the .450. The lion had left the water hole and my first glimpse of him was as he stood in a patch of unburnt grass, only his head showing and about forty yards distant. Thinking to blow his head off, I let him have it. To my astonishment he lowered his head and started a most unholy growling and lashing about. I could not get in another shot before he darted back into some thick bush.

I was now joined by a native hunter with a muzzle-loader. The growling had ceased and the native said he was dead. We approached the patch of bush, I in the lead. On reaching the edge of the patch, it was obvious that visibility was nil. Not a sound from the lion. The patch was quite small, so we knew he could not be far away. However, my Scottish caution made me think to climb a handy tree for a look-see before going in.

Hoisting my rifle up across two branches, I was in the act of drawing myself up when there was a roar and a yellow streak right through and under my legs as I jerked them up. Seizing the rifle as I dropped to the ground, an exasperating target presented itself—the lion overhauling the native hunter so that I could not shoot. Next instant the native fell and the lion shot clean over him, braked hard with all four legs, and turned to follow the native who was up and off at a tangent. As the lion turned, I got in a shot on the shoulder. This halted the chase and evidently sickened him as he limped off into the bush again. Up came the undaunted native and we held a consultation.

By this time I had lost a considerable part of the confidence in my rifle with which I had commenced the affair. However, my companion seemed quite unshaken; indeed, he said he often dodged them by falling down like that and said we must get all the people at the camp to help. Whereupon he left me.

Surprisingly enough, he returned with half a hundred boys armed with clubs, pangas (large bush knives), axes, and whatnot. Forming ourselves into a line, we then advanced into the densest kind of bush, everyone shouting and whacking away with his knife while two or three native drums enlivened the proceedings. I seemed to be the only scared person there.

By the grace of Diana, the lion was immobilized by his wounds from attempting any rush at us, although still full of fight. Had he done so, someone would have inevitably become a casualty. As it was, we soon finished him off, and the post-mortem began.

The first shot had struck below his left eye, had shattered the lower jaw, and some pieces of lead had lodged in the upper palate while others had penetrated into the neck. But all were so small and lacking in energy as to be almost harmless. Some pieces were actually flattened out on the underside of the brain box. Certainly this bullet had prevented any tooth work—always such an important part of the lion's offensive armament—but it should have, by all laws of ballistics, laid the animal flat out. It was end-on when it hit, and had the bullet been a solid lead one, I think it would have carried on into the neck and so proved fatal. The shot in the shoulder had expended its energy in making a ghastly mess of the large muscles on the outer side of the foreleg but had not shattered the bone, nor had any of the particles had sufficient force to penetrate the lungs or any other vital part.

I had learned a valuable lesson and lost no time in re-arming myself. My next rifle was a .303 Lee-Metford ten-shot using the round-nosed bullet weighing 215 grains. The powder was at that time cordite. It was a mass-produced military affair but had been given a civilian fore-end and stock and sporting bead fore-sight with open V backsight. It retailed round about seven pounds in Britain. The ammo I got with it was now all solid-jacketed stuff, so I was away to the other extreme, having now no bullets that would open up at all. This meant that extremely careful shooting would be required as in those days such modern stuff as .303 could not be got except at the Coast, which was two months' foot journey away. With this rifle and bullet I soon found that, provided one got an end-on shot—either end would do—one could kill all the necessary meat animals with due economy of ammo. Sometimes, too, it was possible to kill two antelope with one bullet, broadside-on, of course.

Thus armed, I embarked on my first elephant-hunting safari.

There were forty-odd boys to feed and meat had to be got for trading native flour. And, in addition, elephant had to be slain for their ivory to make at least the expenses of the expedition, buffalo for their meat and hides for making sandals, and giraffe for their meat, fat, and hides to trade off to the natives for making shields. Then all the common antelope, hartebeest, topi, and eland had to be killed for meat and skins, the eland being used to make donkey saddles for packing flour, water bags, and of course ivory teeth when, and if, we got any. That .303 certainly had some work to do.

I never have liked our .303 action; it is so rough and unfinished-looking when compared with the beautifully polished products of the world-famous Springfield, Steyr, or Mauser factories. But I must in fairness say that it almost never let me down. I say "almost" because there were times when, through careless loading of the magazine, a cartridge would fail to feed up to the chamber. Sometimes the nose tilted down, sometimes the magazine failed to push the case up enough for the bolt head to catch a hold. These occasions were extremely rare and luckily never happened at very awkward moments. As for that loose-fitting rattletrap bolt, nothing would stop its functioning. During the short rains when elephant are subjected to fierce sun between heavy rain showers and flies are fierce and mud plentiful, the vegetation through which the hunter has to work his game is copiously drenched with liquid mud. Some of this dries between showers and clouds down on your rifle action as you pass along. I have had Mauser actions with their tighter-fitting bolts rendered almost useless through gritty mud, while the break-open double rifle under these conditions is a complete washout.

I am writing of the days when there were no restrictions on game hunting. And, indeed, there were almost no hunters except the old original natives with their pitfalls, falling spears, foot snares, spears, bows and arrows. How different it all is now when a year's license costs fifty pounds for one elephant and another hundred pounds for a second one, and when you are not allowed to kill enough meat to feed your boys and they have to be fed from tins, where, in my day, countless thousands of animals milled around and tons of beef on the hoof were always in sight. To sum up the .303 on that first safari, it brought me in sixty-three head of bull elephant, average weight of tusk 53 pounds; it killed two lion that had pestered the transport animals; it fed myself and some fifty boys, including my personal ones; and it provided shoe leather for all hands besides all the other uses to which meat and hides are put under safari conditions. And all without any serious failure. The solid round-nosed, very moderate velocity 215-grain bullet was certain death either for the body shot or for the brain shot. Naturally the latter is the choice of the man who wants to recoup the expenses of his safari and leave a bit over for future expeditions. I was most certainly in that category.

The day's work then became not so much a matter of picking out the largest tusker from a bunch of bulls but rather a matter of how to maneuver so that the whole lot was laid low. In diligent pursuit of this ideal it soon became obvious that the body shot would not do. When thus hit, the animal would flinch and give forth a shattering bellow and would straightway launch out into headlong flight even when mortally wounded. It did not continue long or far, but this was enough to set off all the others: a poor show. A hit in the brain was a very different matter. Frequently the animal dropped suddenly and quite silently to its knees. The huge ears continued to wave about as before and there were no groans or other signs of distress; in fact, to all appearances the animal was still alive and tranquil but had unaccountably lost stature. Its companions, closely bunched into the shade of some large tree, merely raised their heads and trunks, questing mildly the reason for the sudden noise, thus presenting easy targets for further brain shots. All the success or failure hangs on the first shot, for should this be taken at a moving or swaying animal and be fatal to that one, it will fall sideways and may stampede the others by so doing—not always, but sometimes.

In course of time I acquired a long-barreled .256 Mannlicher, stocked and sighted (iron sights but extremely refined) by Gibbs of Bristol. I did not use this rifle on elephant; I don't know why unless it was that I had only soft-nosed bullets. It was not until later that I got a .256 Mannlicher-Schönauer and used it on elephant. I used the long Gibbs—a most beautiful rifle—entirely for meat-getting. And what a deadly weapon it was. I have known it lay out a score of antelope from one ant-hill stance in the cool air of morning or evening. When, in course of time, my safari grew to a strength of over one hundred boys and their wives and their followers, all to be fed on the proceeds of one rifle, it can be imagined what shooting had to be done and how rich the game stock on the ground must have been. Not only the needs of the stomach but the need for footwear, for hides for donkey saddles, thongs, and buffalo and giraffe hides for trading flour from the natives all had to be provided by the rifle.

Just to give an idea of this sort of thing, the donkey headman demands four hundred skins for donkey saddles. This was when we had some three hundred and fifty tusks buried and were about to begin the "Shuka" (retreat). Or the headman comes and says he is running out of flour with one hundred and fifty mouths to feed and the nearest money-market two hundred miles away. This particular trouble was generally cured by nine or ten giraffe; failing them, a score or so of zebra or, more rarely, by a dozen buffalo. That Gibbs certainly had a full-time job to do. I don't think that even now a better rifle could be found for that particular work. It was a round-the-clock rifle. It projected a long heavy bullet at a very respectable speed. Pressures were low enough to obviate much trouble from the cases, and it performed well at long ranges as, for example, on giraffe. These, of course, present an enormous target well raised above intervening bush and may be easily killed at five hundred yards. I never tried at greater ranges than that.

At the same time I got the .256 I also acquired the first rifle I had made especially for me—a .275 (7 mm.) Mauser by Rigby of London. It was still in the days of the round-nosed bullet, and luckily for me the ammo was good, sound, reliable, German DWM stuff, powder, case, cap, and bullet. This was the hottest combination one could possibly have, although I knew it not at the time. Without fault or hitch, misfire or hang-fire, that little rifle slew some eight hundred bull elephant besides scores of buffalo, a few rhino, and an occasional lion. Never once did a soft-nosed bullet pollute that perfect barrel.

There was one peculiarity about this .275 bullet: it was the only bullet that I ever heard whining away after killing a large bull elephant with the brain shot. It may have been merely coincidence, but the fact remains that I never heard that whine from any other bullet and I used .256, .303, .318, .350, .450/400, and .416 for similar shots, admittedly on many less numerous occasions.

The boys had strict orders to bring me any bullets they

might find when hacking out the tusks or when exploring the interior of the carcasses for fat which, when rendered down, they mixed with their millet porridge and drank. As time sped on I collected in this way a most interesting box full of used bullets of all calibers.

As my experience with the brain shot increased, I began to study the possibilities of reaching the brain of those exasperating elephant that so often presented their fleeing sterns as targets. I noticed that sometimes they sort of tacked away, presumably so they might see their pursuer out of the corner of their eye. There seemed to be nothing to stop a bullet from reaching the brain except the mass of the neck muscles. These would have to be traversed by the bullet at a fairly acute angle. Not only the muscle but the hide itself would present a very sloping entry for the bullet. Luckily the neck skin is not so heavy as in other parts, and it seemed to be a shot worth trying.

If the ground is clear enough, what you do is this. Say, for example, you have closed with three bull elephant tree-browsing gently along. You range alongside without difficulty. You kill the first one with an easy shot to the brain. You get a fast one into a head that turns inquiringly toward the sound of the shot, and he goes down. But the third one flees, you after him. As he goes, his head swings slightly from side to side so he can see what is after him. The great ears are back but not flat on the side of the neck and the pace is hot—to begin with, anyway— round about twenty miles per hour, no matter what the terrain may be like. If it is thorn bush or high grass, you simply have no choice: you must follow his trail. But if it is open bush, you may be able to range off a bit to one side while still keeping your station behind him. If you can do this—and you must be fairly speedy—the shot comes a lot easier. It consists of a sudden stop on your part, just as you see the head begin its sideways movement, and a lightning shot directed toward the center of that enormous skull. Only with perfect timing can this shot be brought off—a difficult shot for a novice.

Of course sometimes it fails. The timing may be a fraction out or the bullet may be deflected. And in this connection the otherwise incomparable 7 millimeter bullet came under suspicion in my mind. There began to arise those times when one felt everything was all right and yet a failure was registered. I began to use a .318 bullet of 250 grains with long parallel sides—like an enlarged .256 bullet in fact—for these slanting-through-the-neck shots. At once the inexplicable misses ceased.

As prosperity descended upon me, resulting from my hunting, I began to arm myself with rifles of various calibers embodying my own fancies and requirements. Among these there arrived for me in Central Africa, after many months of travel and many difficulties, a very refined little Mannlicher-Schönauer .256 with a goodly store of solids. I meant to try it out as an elephant gun. It weighed five pounds empty by dint of some machining-away of the action and cutting-down of the barrel.

Of all the weapons I have owned, this was certainly the most beautiful. The stocking, bluing, and sighting had been done by an artist—Fraser of Edinburgh. A genius in his own line, it was a terrible loss to all riflemen when he died quite young. He taught me how to watch bullets in flight with the naked eye and what a devastating bar to close shooting flinch can be. He taught me that, even from a gunmaker's rest, flinch can spoil grouping and, in fact, that flinch was the worst enemy of the aspiring rifleman.

After many years' experience I am inclined to think he was right. Let us analyze a very common case. In Africa a man may often be heard to say that he aimed for a certain spot on an elephant's head from forty yards' distance and the rifle failed to kill. Apart from the fact that he should not have been shooting at any spot on the elephant's head but at the brain itself, how many men will put their *first* shot, under conditions of fatigue and intense excitement, into a four-inch group from a heavy rifle— say a .465 or .470—at even so short a range as forty yards? This forty yards, by the way, will often be found to be nearer fifty. Even in cold blood I have seen men flinch so that their shots were barely in a twelve-inch circle at fifty yards, shooting off-hand of course. The truth of the matter is, these heavy calibers are so unpleasant to fire and the cartridges are so large, heavy, and expensive that people do not fire them often in practice and so do not know how unreliable and inaccurate their first shot is going to be. Remember, you are not allowed a sighter, and you can hardly bring yourself to fire two or three practice cartridges in camp for fear of disturbing game.

I shall never forget the unpacking of that .256 in the wilds of the African bush, the ripping open of that tin-lined case that looked so incredibly small. There, wrapped in greaseproof paper, lay the oily little rascal. Out in the hot sun it was but a moment's work to strip off the mercurial grease Fraser used for protecting his steelwork on tropical voyages. What a thrill just to handle it.

As it happened, we were in the midst of good elephant bush, fruit was heavy on the trees, and the great game was in the midst of the tree-browsing season. So there was every chance of contacting a few bulls. Examining the cartridges for the .256, I noticed that they bore the genuine Steyr mark and should therefore have been the best for use in their own rifle. I noticed also that the bullets were held in the neck of the case by pressure only. Knowing nothing to the contrary, I thought this was all right. And so it was—for a time.

In Africa, where situations may arise with great suddenness, one carries the magazine full of solids for an emergency and loads single cartridges into the breech, solid- or soft-nosed as occasion demands, thus keeping the full magazine for anything demanding fast action. Examining each case, as I always did, I filled my belt. Finding no faulty cases, I strode joyfully off into the bush, twirling around that dandy little gun.

Well, luck was in and we came on a party very intent on working a wild orchard of heavily laden trees. Underfoot all grass had been burned off and was now replaced with numbers of wild, sweet-smelling flowers. Their scent, mingled with elephant dung, urine, and the buzz of countless insects, seemed to make a quivering jelly of the air, quite intoxicating to the hunter. The elephant were rather scattered and on the move from tree to tree, so they did not give the rifle the chance that a slumbering group all bunched together would have afforded. Nevertheless that little .256 laid them low with a shot apiece—all brain shots. Was I delighted? Here was the perfect rifle—strong enough for the heaviest game and yet small enough for the tiniest antelope, or for shooting the heads off guinea fowl.

There was one survivor from that first encounter. The .256 and I legged it after him. In a surprisingly short run he brought us among another lot, also somewhat scattered, and all listening intently to what the rather flustered new arrival had to tell them. Whether he had not much to say or whether they disbelieved what he told them, I don't know, but at any rate they were not alarmed enough to take flight and only stood around listening from time to time and, occasionally, evacuating.

I had killed twelve good bull elephant with one shot each in the brain from all angles except the stern quartering shot when a large bull elephant was seen in open bush. The ground was so clear that I actually sat down to take the shot forty paces distant from the animal—a most exceptional thing to happen. Usually there is something intervening and almost always the shooting is off-hand in Africa. I made absolutely certain of that grand bull and squeezed off. Click! A misfire! Waiting a few seconds in case it was only a hang-fire and feeling good about the absence of flinch, for it is only when there is a misfire or a hang-fire or no cartridge in the chamber that one knows about this, I opened the bolt and extracted the misfire. Here is where I made the fatal mistake. With my eye on the elephant I tried to push in another cartridge. It failed to enter the chamber, and looking down, I saw that the misfire had extracted all right! Having no wad between bullet and powder, the granular stuff had spilt into the action. But that only required shaking to get it out. What did matter was that the bullet was now firmly fixed in the throat of the barrel by my disastrous attempt to shove in another cartridge.

I have thought since, wise after the event, that I should have found another case and shoved it onto the lodged bullet and all might have been well. I don't know. What I did was this, while that seven-hundred-dollar bull browsed sedately along. First I tried hitting the butt with my fist, then on my thigh, all the time eying the elephant and trying not to alarm him. Then I tried thumping the butt on the ground. At the third bump the old rascal cocked his enormous ears and listened. After a while he recommenced his browsing. Now I had to clear out and get that gun fixed somehow. Withdrawing quietly a few hundred yards, I thumped the butt sharply against a tree trunk. Nothing would move that bullet, so the search for a rod to push it out began. Now caliber .256 is mighty small when it comes to finding a branch long enough and straight enough to do the job. I could find only short lengths to enter the barrel, and so, of course, when finally the bullet was pushed out, the barrel remained full of bits of stick which obstinately resisted any efforts to shake them out. However, I reloaded and returned to the still unsuspicious elephant, who had moved on perhaps a quarter mile while all this was going on.

This time I thought I had better take him in the body as I expected there might be some deflection of the bullet by all those pieces of bush. And deflection there certainly was, for, at the shot, he launched himself into a flight straight for the Nile some three hundred miles distant. For all I know, he may have reached it nonstop because I gave up after about fifteen miles. I have never seen an elephant before nor since so determined on changing his locality. Not once did he stop for a shower—as they so often do—or even slacken his gait in the least. Nor did he keep looking back by swinging his head from side to side. Whether he had got the bullet in a tender part or whether the pieces of rod had tickled him will never be known.

For several years after this affair I stuck firmly to the 7 millimeter for elephant. Always loaded with solids, it was inevitable that one should have occasion to shoot up lion. Once when a lioness chased a boy, while her cubs scuttled away, and sometimes when they might have stampeded our donks and cattle, I found the round-nosed solid entirely satisfactory, especially for end-on shots.

For some years I continued to use the five-shot 7 milli-meter Mauser with a ten-shot .303 as a sort of reserve. I always had hopes that sometime somewhere I would find a bunch of bull elephant so foolish as to stand around while I shot them down and numerous enough for the ten-shot rifle. Needless to say, I never found them so trust-ing. The nearest I ever came to realizing my dream was when a small native boy and I caught a bunch of bulls in an acute-angled bend of the upper Nile in pouring rain. It was in the middle of the big rains—the best time to hunt if you can stick it and if you can persuade your boys to stick it. It is tough work; the grass is immense—from eight to twelve feet high—biting bugs of all sorts are a plague, rivers are swollen, raging torrents, and tornadoes are of daily occurrence. During this season the African is bound to his village—he hates the wet and cold—and game roams unmolested right up to the village confines.

This is how it happened. We were camped close to the Nile with a lot of ivory in but with precious little food. Across the river were some native villages where millet flour could be got for meat. On the morning of this particular day it was deluging in solid sheets when the headman reported the flour ration finished. Would I kill some meat to trade for flour? Now we had been killing elephant right along, and I, reluctant as any African to face the continuous shower bath of the high grass, ob-jected, pointing out that it was only a few days since our last killing and that the boys must still have lots of meat.

To this the headman replied that meat, even when smoked, cannot be kept dry and therefore cannot be kept good. Cursing them all, I said I would try to get a hippo.

Now the wily hippo is greatly prized by the Africans, and if he ventures on land in the daytime in the dry season, he soon finds himself full of spears in spite of his inch-and-a-half-thick hide. So he does not so venture. But in the heavy rains and especially while rain is actually falling, out he comes. With this in mind I thought to catch one or two quite near camp and accordingly looked round for a companion. My eye lit on a small Lumbwa herd boy and I beckoned him over.

At the age of twelve or so, before they start any woman-palaver, these Africans are as sharp as needles. They know a lot about the bush, cannot lose themselves, and make charmingly keen and intelligent hunting companions. Telling him to park his spear, short sword, and knobkerrie—his usual armament for the defense of our sheep and goat herd—I gave him a short .318 to carry, more to jolly him along than for any use I might have for it. Taking a long .318 myself and, of course, the cartridge belt holding thirty-five rounds of solids, we slipped shuddering into the sea of dripping grass following the river bank.

The rain was coming down in that tropical way that reduces visibility to about one hundred yards, so when we saw some glistening backs showing silvery through the rain curtain, we took them to be hippo out from the river and in shorter grass. Instead they were bull elephant in long grass, only the tops of their backs showing above it.

This was thrilling. There were five of them. The downpour drowned all lesser noises and the wind was up and down the mast. At about eight paces—one could not see

the vitals until then—the first one got it. For some unknown reason the others came directly toward the shot,
possibly because we stood between them and the higher
ground away from the river. Of course this coming head-
on toward the rifle is the kind of thing the experienced
hunter dreams of. For one thing, the frontal brain shot
is the easiest for the bullet; that is, it encounters very
little bone opposition, and when they have their heads
down, as in flight, it is one of the easiest for the hunter.
If you ground the one making straight for your stance,
you have cleared your position, as it were, and the two on
either side do not move over so as to run you down. You
have therefore two more fast shots at the right- and left-
hand ones, a shot at the third when abreast of you, and
another oblique shot behind the ear of the fourth as he
will have already passed you.

The two survivors went no distance at all, and we
caught them listening motionlessly for their three companions who had so unaccountably ceased to exist. One
we killed with an easy shot, but the other gave no chance
at all, his nerve being completely shattered by this time.
Without troubling to cut off the tails—they would have
been too heavy for the lad anyhow—we weaseled after
that fleeing rascal in a most unpleasant shower from the
surrounding grass. When really alarmed, elephant—and
others, too—are attacked by uncontrollable "squitters,"
and we were the sufferers. But what did that matter? For
in a half-mile rush he led us to an incredible scene.

Just here the upper Nile makes an almost right-angled
bend. In the bend on the west bank, where we were, there
is a bed of papyrus reeds, then a piece of harder level
ground, then, overlooking the whole terrain, a rocky out-
crop. And that is exactly where we arrived.

Looking down from our perch, we saw that the level ground this side of the wall of papyrus was a seething mass of elephant. Counting roughly, there were over fifty, and, more incredible still, they were all bulls. The show of ivory was more impressive than real as the tusks were well washed by the rains and showed up larger than they really were. It seemed to me that there was no escape for them. Either they must overrun us or take to the river and swim for it.

I now loaded up the short .318 hitherto carried by the little boy. I thought if they decided to come our way it would be needed. Then I started the works. The range could not have been greater than forty yards—almost an ideal distance. To begin with they were completely flustered and milled around any old how. When five or six had foundered, one took the lead and came determinedly up the hill, pushed along by a solid wall of massive foreheads, and, of course, just as I was reloading. Here came the break-out. Grabbing the short .318, I began the belated defense of our position. The leader was about half-way up the slope when he got it. The others came on gallantly as four more of their leaders fell. That was enough; the rest turned back just when victory was in their grasp. My rifle was empty and the long one had only one cartridge in it. Another five yards and they would have overrun us and been free in a few million square miles of bush.

As it was, the demoralized survivors slouched off, some into the papyrus and some into the river itself. Those in the reedbed were soon lost to sight as far as shooting was concerned. The dozen or so that took to the river turned back when they found the water creeping up their sides. All except one: he swam away in great style, almost submerged, with his trunk up like a periscope, and landed on the opposite bank in face of a crowd of highly excited natives who had been watching the whole affair. He landed right in the native gardens and was last seen by us careering madly through the fields, pursued by a crowd of native farmers.

Turning to the battlefield, we counted fifteen carcasses. Eleven were so close together that one could step from one to the other without touching ground. With the four back in the bush that made nineteen, the biggest day I ever had and the easiest. But not the biggest ivory. They were young and middle-aged herd bulls, tired for the moment of their slippery-sided lovebirds perhaps and having a bachelor dander-round. Their ivory was long, but so were the hollows. Consequently the weights were poor. Although all of them had two tusks, the total for the nineteen was but little more than 1,400 pounds, giving an average weight of about 37 pounds per tusk, whereas away eastward on the headwaters of the Pibor I once killed nine bulls yielding a total of 1,463 pounds for the day. Even then one of them had a tusk on one side broken off short at the lip so that there were really only seventeen tusks. That gives the very fine average of 81 pounds. That was a 7 millimeter day.

It was quite impossible to carry eighteen whole tails—one having fallen on his tail into a hippo trap—owing to their weight, so we cut off the very tips only. Even these weighed a considerable amount, so slinging them on thongs cut from the edge of the ear where the skin is thin and hanging a bunch from each end of a bush stick, we struck out for camp as best we could, cold, weary, drenched to the bone, but triumphant.

CHAPTER 1

A LONG ironstone ridge stretched across the horizon. At one end of it appeared a square earthenwork fort, its flagstaff jutting abruptly into the sky. At the other end of the ridge, huddled in confusion, lay the native town, while away in the blue distance the lower slopes of Elgon lay shrouded in haze, its summit hooded by a deep layer of cloud. This was Mumias, the starting point of all safaris to the countries far to the north of Elgon.

At the time of which I write—some fifty years ago—Mumias was the farthest outpost in this direction of the British flag. There lay nothing between it and the distant Sudan and Abyssinia. None of the intervening tribes were in any way under any sort of control. Most of the natives had never seen a white man; none of them had any knowledge of money other than beads, brass wire, iron chain, and the like. All were nude people, scornful of clothes and wearers thereof. Living at perpetual war with their neighbors, they were expert spear fighters, and their contempt for firearms made them rather difficult to deal with. From argument to spear thrust was a matter of little moment to them, and they had successfully brought off some startling massacres of whole trading caravans by inborn treachery and native cunning.

All caravans to Karamojo, the general term for the

countries north of the Turkwel River, went fully armed. For mutual protection a large number of petty traders would combine their forces and resources, appointing one man to be leader of the whole. By an intricate system of bookkeeping each shareholder was apportioned his share of the profits at the final division when each shareholder would have to settle up with the Indian and Arab Shylocks who had advanced the money necessary for fitting out. These Shylocks abounded in Mumias and seemed to do extremely well, their business system being soundly grounded on such a basis that if one client paid, ten others might die or default and there would still remain a profit.

Ivory was the aim and object of every enterprise, its acquisition, by fair means or foul, the goal of every safari. Formerly, slaves for the Coast and the Persian Gulf had absorbed all energies, but now the unreasonable and stern opposition of the British rule had rendered it almost impossible to carry on.

Once a trading safari had crossed the Turkwel River on its journey north, white rule ceased and black rule took over. Safaris were laws unto themselves. They had their own methods of penetration of hostile tribes, of disciplining their numerous followers, and of enjoying life to the utmost. Time was of no object whatever—two years, three years, what did it matter? They carried with them great numbers of women, acquired in slaving days mostly, and they still had great numbers of male slaves also. It is true that about this time they began to find it profitable to send their slaves out to enroll for labor with whites and to pouch their wages on payday, but nevertheless many remained for safari work. I have seen boys draw a year's pay from me and carry it forthwith to their owner, who would graciously return one fifth of it as a present. I have had the owner of some of my boys come to camp and demand the wage money they had earned and, when the tally showed that they had spent some of it, storm and rave about killing them off and replacing them on my staff with other slaves. It seems extraordinary that these boys should have continued to carry their hard-earned wages to their masters when they could have freed themselves by applying at the nearest post. Yet it was so, and the reason would seem to lie in the fact that they were not really slaves as we understand the word. A "Tajir's" household was really a community where everyone had a share of whatever might come along. In times of plenty the head shared everything with his followers; in times of adversity he had to support them somehow. They took his name when they became Mohammedan, and if they served him well, he would finally provide them with a wife.

At the commencement of the ivory trade great profits were made. The tusks were still lying about in the bush where they had lain for years. In many cases, of course, the annual grass fires had damaged the outer skin, but ivory is tough stuff. The price was then about eight shillings the pound at the base. The natives knew nothing about money and traded freely what they contemptuously called "elephant bones" for a few pennyworth of iron, brass, or copper wire or for a string of kauri shells or a handful of beads. At every camp in the bush all hands would be sent out to search the surrounding country for ivory. Frequently they were rewarded. Of course, all this was "dead" ivory, but it was so abundant that no one turned his thoughts to the living stores of the precious stuff. There was still the small annual crop of tusks from the native traps, but the amount was very small when compared with the pick-up of "dead" tusks.

This was a period of great excitement among all concerned. Profits to the "Tajirs" were immense, and they were buying new women right, left, and everywhere, their outcasts being eagerly absorbed by their women-hungry satellites. For the natives, too, it was a time of hectic doings. Every man had seen "bones" lying about somewhere, any favor from the girls could be had for the pretty beads, and how splendid they themselves looked in their brightly polished iron collars, made from the trade wire, and their iron chain belts. What a figure they cut at the dances, and no longer had they to give quite so many cattle, sheep, goats, and donkeys for a wife.

Soon, however, this supply began to run dry. Prices soared. Where handfuls of beads sufficed formerly, calabashes now had to be filled therewith, and presently sheep and other livestock were demanded in exchange for the rapidly diminishing supply of "bones." Finally cows became the only sure medium of producing the coveted tusks. The "dead" ivory was exhausted.

Hitherto relations had been friendly between trader and native. Peaceful and unexacting, the safaris had penetrated many tribes, welcomed for the beautiful trade-stuff they brought with them. But when cows became the medium of barter, relations became rapidly worse. To the blacks of those parts a cow or heifer is what gold is to the whites, the great procure-all. But cattle are hard to come by for the trader. They are too dear to buy and no native will part with them for any consideration whatever. There is only one way of procuring them—superior force.

Always the safaris had carried firearms for self-defense. Occasionally they were tried on the numerous elephant met with on their wanderings, but with little result other than a great expenditure of ammunition. None of the natives had possession or knowledge of firearms, their first contact with them arising when tracking for the Swahili hunters. And it was very largely due to this contact that the idea started, and became commonly held by the natives, that these "fire tubes" simply made a big smoke and a rude report and that, although the bullet might certainly catch you and let the fire into you, thereby killing you, all you had to do was to duck when you saw the smoke and the bullet would pass harmlessly overhead. The prevalence of this idea caused much bloodshed in the ensuing raids, the natives showing an utter contempt for the Swahili gunmen, whereas they treated me and my firearms with the utmost respect and even awe. Where safaris of three hundred guns feared to go, we, with nothing more than a few old Sniders and my own personal rifles, came and went as we would.

So far, then, the native man had cognizance of three methods of acquiring the precious white "bones": firstly, the pick-up of "dead" ivory; secondly, his own snaring and trapping of elephant; and thirdly, the blasting into elephant of enormous quantities of lead from the "fire tubes" of the traders. They stood in the above order of merit in his mind. With my arrival in the country, however, he was about to be compelled to rearrange his ideas on the efficiency of "fire tubes" when dealing with elephant. Hitherto he had seen the Swahili and Mnyamwezi hunters approach quite close to their victims, discharge heavy loads of powder and bullets—the latter well medicated by the medicine men and the former raising huge volumes of smoke—throw down their pieces of ordnance, and clear out as fast as their legs would carry them. On their cautious return to the scene nothing but perhaps a little smoke still hanging in the air would be found. From all this evidence the native had concluded that firearms were of little account.

With my advent, bearing as I did such modernities as .303, .275, and .256 rifles, it quickly dawned upon the native mind that this was a different show altogether. Here was something that made hardly any smoke; moreover, the bullet arrived as soon as the bang! Yet the hole in the fire tube was minute and the bullet long and burning bright. When an elephant was hit it simply collapsed, finished. What on earth could it be? Medicine! Magic! So the simple-minded savage summed up the situation. The brain shot struck them as especially uncanny, for no weapon they had ever heard of could penetrate the bony structure guarding an elephant's brain. Spears or arrows could not do so. The only weapon of theirs that might have led them to surmise the presence of such a vulnerable spot in the head was the falling spear trap. Very rarely an elephant would be pierced to the brain by the heavily weighted and poisoned shaft and would then of course drop stone dead beneath it, but no one would be there to see the extraordinary occurrence and it would all be put down to the power of the poison.

To sum up the situation, I was the first white man to dwell among these people, the first man of any sort to devote himself exclusively to hunting elephant, and the first to demonstrate the extreme deadliness of modern firearms. To these facts I owe it that for years I roamed among these truculent tribes, flogged them when they were too naughty, fined them, made them return raided cattle sometimes, and prohibited the killing of women in their raids, this being considered the most unreasonable prohibition of them all. I was then some twenty years of age, but old warriors with half a century of raids and bloodshed behind them called me "father." They used to be convulsed with laughter when I had any of them, perhaps a man double my own age, beaten in ceremonious style by the headman of the safari. They never resented these beatings and, indeed, they hardly felt them. A man would kill another man, they argued, but would only beat a child; therefore this crazy "red" man-child, as they thought me, evidently looks upon us, great hulking warriors, as his children. Were it otherwise, he would surely kill us with those infernally dangerous guns of his. These were the sort of thoughts that passed vaguely through their unanalytical minds, I think. At any rate, whenever I had someone beaten up for bathing in our drinking water or other misdemeanor, there would be roars of laughter, the victim himself laughing heartiest of the lot.

What a nervous organization was theirs! What heroic, or rather stoic, indifference to pain. They simply did not feel anything. A flogging that would prostrate, if it did not kill, a civilized white man left them entirely indifferent. Spear thrusts received in forays they supported through miles and miles of thirsty desert in spite of formidable loss of blood and entire lack of dressings or medical knowledge. A native with a flap of lung appearing and disappearing through a gaping wound under the arm walked quietly up to a white doctor and raised the arm for his inspection. One glance and: "Take him away! Nothing can be done. The lung is involved!" That man was about again in three weeks' time.

Nature is kind to her not too clever children. So long as they remain truly hers, she endows them with splendid health, tremendous stamina, and intense endurance; dense hair, good eyes, perfect teeth set wide apart, and the digestive ability to extract all the nourishment their diet affords; thick skulls and a smooth thick hide heavily pigmented to filter the sun's rays; a nervous system which defies everything, including description. It successfully withstands defeat in battle and consequent ruin, famine, loss of children, wives, husbands, homes, and wealth. Nothing prevents sleep, nothing disturbs digestion. And greatest gift of all—a sublime capacity for enjoying life: that is the inheritance of those who conform to her laws. For those who cannot do so, there is but one thing— death. Weakly or ailing children pass out. Deficiencies or defects developed in later life are detected and lead either to death in battle or to ostracism, which amounts to sterilization. Sometimes this latter very necessary social regulation is attained through ridicule alone. A wondrous thought! Where nudity rules, who dare bear about with them the results of excess or indulgence?

Now in my years of contact with savages I have always felt a sort of resentment against fate or whatever you like to call it. I was a quite average sort of person physically. I had average muscular development, could run, walk, jump a bit, and swim a bit. I had an all-absorbing passion for hunting elephant which amounted to mania and which enabled me to endure fatigue and discomforts that would otherwise have resulted in boredom. Yet I was always demonstrably inferior to my native companions in everything that counted for success in our joint enterprise. I felt the sun's rays beating my very life down whilst they merely had a headache. Fatigue would seize upon me and sometimes bear me to the very depths of despondency, as when no further response to my mind's urgent demand for just one more burst of speed to bring me on terms with some fleeing monster would come from my tired and aching body, while my sun-resisting companions would slide away ahead with consummate ease over the terrible terrain, every now and then to look back at me in surprise that I did not come on. Of this I am convinced: they drew from the sun or sky some energy denied my clothed body. They started off in the morning without food or even the thought thereof. At night they ate their frugal meal of native whole-meal flour with some elephant meat, and that seemed to energize their bodies for a further twenty-four hours, whereas I was often too tired to eat and sometimes too tired to sleep.

On the other hand, I possessed and carried to the hunt the result of centuries of intelligent application of nature's laws to the problem of causing death. My rifle was a weapon streets ahead of anything the black man could produce, ingenious as he is in his use of poisons and traps, spears and arrows. And moreover, my mind was more capable of appreciating the necessity of introducing my tiny death-dealing bullet into such parts of the pachydermatous anatomy as to produce the desired result in the quickest and least fuss-producing manner. In the melee of a mix-up at close quarters in thick stuff with a numerous herd of elephant my mental equipment enabled me not only very largely to overcome fatigue and exhaustion but also to control those nervous impulses which become so insistent in such moments. I had a much more detached outlook at such moments than my companions. They became wildly excited, generally demanding of me the immediate shooting of the closer animals irrespective of size and with no forethought as to what the ultimate bag might become. Their distractions became so great as to completely outweigh the advantage their presence on the scene undoubtedly supplied, so that in time I came to leave them well behind and to approach alone or with Pyjalé only. We were on our way to his country now and I was looking forward to seeing him again.

This man was a great find. He was a fine specimen physically although not so tall or heavy as many of his tribesmen. But he had "savvy" equal to that of most whites. He never bothered me with excited comments at awkward moments nor did he do any dodging about or hurried retreating. Never did he suddenly shout "look out!" as some silently foreshortening elephant darkened the sky above us. Rather would he jab the imminent trunk with one of his spears, and the resulting roar would bring round my rifle to flatten the astonished aggressor with a touch to the brain. He was always there when you wanted him, always silent, and could track like a bloodhound. He always marked where each beast fell and could bring the ivory-cutting gang straight to the spot. A marvel was Pyjalé! A paragon!

CHAPTER 2

I DO not propose to deal with my first efforts in hunting. It will suffice to say that they were immediately successful. What I propose to describe is my fourth safari into Karamojo. All truculence and opposition had by then been overcome. The natives were all on the friendliest terms and elephant were still extremely numerous.

The fitting-out of a safari for a year's sojourn in the wilderness away from all sources of supply requires careful preparation. Money in the form of coin or notes would purchase nothing. A millionaire might have starved for want of the necessary trade medium with which to purchase a cupful of flour. Therefore trade goods in the form of beads, brass and iron wire, iron chain, and the like had to be purchased. Donkeys had to be acquired to carry them. Saddles had to be made and dozens of other items required attention. Boys I already had: a loyal gang of ruffians prepared to follow me anywhere. Rifles and ammunition likewise I had in sufficient numbers.

Our preparations for the bush were somewhat different from those of the traders in ivory. Ours was a hunter's safari, first and last, but at the same time it was necessary to provide some sort of transport for the precious tusks. Now elephant tusks are extremely awkward things to carry by pack animals. They are long and curved in several directions so that only the shorter ones may be handled by donkeys. The very long ones, weighing from 100 pounds upward, require porters for their carriage. Porters require food rations consisting of banana flour or Matama flour, and on waterless stretches they require to have drinking water laid down in canvas bags at convenient distances. Each man carries a tusk weighing say 115 pounds, a rifle with eleven pounds of ammunition, a pound or two of grilled elephant meat, his own little personal trinkets such as a snuff horn, some mysterious objects in the way of "Dawa" (medicine), and a sleeping mat. All these are stuffed into the hollow end of the tusk, the whole thing weighing from 120 pounds up to 170 or more pounds in the case of very large tusks. Of course they are picked men, these tusk carriers. They get double rations and are enormously proud of their job. The best are from the Mnyamwezi tribe. They carry on the shoulder and acquire great horny pads from the pressure of their almost red-hot burdens. They work themselves elaborately colored bead garments and mount ostrich feathers and giraffe manes, lion manes, and leopard skins all over themselves. Whenever a very large tusk comes to camp, there is a rush to secure it; the bigger and heavier it is, the more they like it.

These men are of the greatest value to the safari and must be carefully looked after. They must have regular rations of some sort of grain besides unlimited meat. Salt must be carried for them, tentage must be provided, and if mosquitoes are bad, each man must have a net. Then their hammered copper cooking pots, all their paraphernalia and that of their wives has to be carried by donkeys, besides flour rations for months away from food centers, for often the best elephant country lies two or three hundred miles from a place where food may be traded for glass beads and iron, brass, and copper wire.

The native donkey is a grand little animal in his own dry country and will cheerfully carry his load day after day on nothing but what he can pick up in the few hours of daylight left after reaching camp. At night, of course, the poor fellows have to be rounded into a thorn zeriba which always occupied the center of the camp. Surrounded as it was by the tents and camp fires, it helped to prevent a stampede or the entry of hungry carnivora.

The donkey strength used to be about one hundred and eighty, and this allowed about sixty or eighty animals being loaded each day on the basis of one day on, one day off. Only thus could backs be kept whole and condition maintained. They were of mixed sex, and until castration quietened them a bit, the noise from fifty or sixty jacks braying simultaneously was inconceivable. Coast men were found to be the best at donkey work, and fifteen of them would load up the sixty animals, starting their labors about 2:30 A.M., and be ready to push off at dawn, 5:30 A.M., with the rest of the safari. As time went on ivory would come in and the shorter tusks would require to be loaded onto the donkeys. In order to hold the points and hollow ends so as not to gall the animals, raw hides had to be provided in great numbers. This was easy, of course, and great numbers of hartebeest, topi, and eland were shot, the meat all being used for food. The tusks were then securely sewn and lashed into the fresh hides so that they were securely held when the skin dried and shrank onto them. They would then give no trouble until the rains commenced.

We now had thirty-two tusk carriers and fifteen donkey men. To these must be added six camp guards or "askaris" (soldiers) as they were pleased to call themselves. These were old fellows who had been with me for years and who well merited what passed with them as a soft job. In reality it was nothing of the sort. They carried no load, it is true, but if anyone fell out and could not make the pace, they had to shoulder his load to camp. They were responsible for the rear of the safari and for its safety at night. They also helped in pitching camp, and in the tornado season when a howling gale with floods of rain would be bombarding my tent, these devoted fellows would be found sitting drenched to the skin on the tent guy ropes. At night they had to keep a good fire going and to patrol the donkey boma besides keeping prowling hyenas and jackals from the camp generally. They were astonishingly good shots at night and nothing could move and live within the radius of light from the fires.

Then there was my personal retinue: Swédé, my head boy, who first joined me a tiny soft-eyed little tot about three feet high, but who had now become thickset and much married; then Suliemani, the cook, also with me a long time, also much married, hard-eyed, a great wit, and of cannibal parentage; then cook's mate, second and third boys, gunbearer, headman, second headman, and innumerable followers; then, of course, the natives had their wives. We were not just travelers from one point to another; we were nomads of the desert places, and we fully intended that our sojourn in the wilderness should be as pleasant as we could make it. Altogether we would number well over one hundred.

My personal tents comprised two of the very best: rotproof canvas, double fly with red or buff lining, perfectly fitting groundsheets, bathroom behind and veranda in front, large-size tent bed, Jaeger rugs, linen sheets, mosquito nets, rifle rack by bedside, canvas bath, long easy chairs, pajamas, cases of soap, heaps of fresh linen washed every day, personal clothing, khaki shorts, cotton singlet and shirt, socks and various sorts of shoes. A slop chest had to be carried as no shop of any sort where money could be used would be met with until our return twelve or fourteen months hence. Therefore tobacco, cloth of various kinds, needles and thread (for, of course, these foolish followers of mine considered they were above the naked savage and thought they had to clothe themselves), sugar and tea (they were acquiring all our silly habits), and matches and candles all had to be carried. A clerk from among the donkey boys would be appointed to keep the book and would diligently and laboriously note down every purchase in what he and we fondly supposed to be Arabic characters until at the end of the safari we found that neither he nor any Arab yet born could make head or tail of it. But what did the consequent loss of several hundred rupees matter against the laugh we had as he puzzled his head over it, licking and biting his pencil stub, catching a syllable here and there in his mangled manuscript and trying to rhyme it with something that would emerge as a word?

All these preparations for a safari take an interminable time, and whilst waiting for the various supplies and animals, I had leisure to observe some of the doings of contemporary trading safaris which were also preparing for their ventures into the "Barra," as they call the wilderness.

There were great preparations afoot for a marriage feast. The whole town was excited about it. One of the "Tajirs," or rich men, was about to take to himself a "bint" (maiden) daughter of one of the local Nubian settlers. It would therefore be an affair of importance.

From this tribe the finest fighting men have been recruited from time immemorial. Mexico, Turkey, and Egypt all have experience of their fine soldierly qualities. And the reason I think lies largely with their marriage customs. On the principle that only the strong deserve the fair, they have evolved a set of customs which insures that only strong men in their prime can marry young women. To this end the girl children, while still of tender age, are operated on in such a fashion that they grow up sealed women. There is no possible chance for promiscuous philandering. Then when a suitor appears on the scene, it is up to him to show to all concerned not only that she is a worthy bride but also that he is a fit husband. Should he fail to consummate the marriage within seven days, he forfeits both bride and the dowry he has paid over to the parents. The actual ordeal a hopeful bridegroom has to go through would daunt the stoutest heart, one would think. Custom insists upon the bride's resisting the bridegroom's advances with all her power, at the same time denying him any adventitious aid in his project. For seven days and nights they are under close observation. The woman is by nature extremely robust and powerful and she is never married at a tender age. In her resistance to siege she kicks, bites, scratches, and shrieks. Meanwhile, a mob of friends eat, drink, and dance at the bridegroom's expense. The poor man is faced with ruin as the only alternative to success in his matrimonial venture.

Periodically he is spurned forth into the dance-melee between the rounds of what can only be regarded as a fight for a bride. Each time he emerges unsuccessfully from the fight, his friends seek to stir him to greater efforts by a process of flagellation carried into effect with hippo-hide whips upon his half-naked body, whereupon he rushes back to his waiting bride on the principle of choosing the lesser of two evils. Not only does this custom insure the suitability of the man but it also gives the girl an opportunity of escaping from an obnoxious partnership, for should she really detest the man, there is slim hope of his gaining her.

Now for some obscure reason these Nubi "bints" exercise a powerful attraction on the more effete Coast natives, Arabs, Persians, and the propertied class of trader. Just why this should be so is not at once apparent. Certainly the "bints" are not beauties, in our eyes at any rate. They have the attraction that good health always gives and the attraction that a bulldog's lack of beauty also gives. But they are squat and fleshy, pretty dark in the skin, and quarrelsome. I think the reason why they attract the blasé, much-married harem-owners probably lies in the fact that they have only to be shown a man once and they are certain to have a child. At any rate, of the first child's sireage the harem-owners may feel tolerably certain. Of course it is ridiculous to suppose that any of this well-worn gentry could undergo such an ordeal as is cheerfully faced by the Nubi man. He has to supplement his lack of physical force with the aid of dollars. Everyone concerned is lavishly bribed.

In the case of my own men there was also much marrying. It was fortunate that their tastes in women were more easily satisfied. A chance meeting in the Suk (market place) with any well-tried mount, the purchase of a cloth or two, and there they were, man and wife. Once out in the "Barra" it was pretty certain that her service would be satisfactory.

There used to be much controversy among white men

on this subject of carrying women on safari. Almost everyone was against it. Imbued as they were with the idea that women are delicate creatures, unfitted for the hardships of safari life, they were firmly against their presence on such expeditions. They would argue that jealousy and quarreling would arise, that sickness would take its toll, and that it meant so many more mouths to feed. In reply to these arguments I would draw their attention to the classic case of a certain expedition. A soldier in charge of an expeditionary force refused to allow women a place upon it, with the result that there was a mutiny entailing tremendous bloodshed for its suppression. And what happened was that the women of the mutineers not only assisted their menfolk in the battles by carrying ammunition but actually seized the rifles from their dead and continued the fight themselves.

Any question of their physical fitness for safari work is simply ridiculous. It shows an utter lack of knowledge of the African. The women are ever so much stronger and more enduring than the men. It must be so when one comes to think that not only must they till the soil, fetch and carry firewood and water, cook, build the huts, grind the corn, express oils from seeds and nuts, weave mats, make pottery, brew beer, and do a thousand and one other things, but they must find time midst this frightful array of tasks to have the annual baby. And on top of it all they must preserve a placid and equable temper, for their menfolk anyhow. They can and do relieve themselves upon their female neighbors, putting just as much energy and vim into it as they do into their other tasks.

After considering all this, can anyone reasonably argue that a person capable of filling the role of "African wife" is unfit physically for marching unloaded with loaded men? Should they fall sick, we had donkeys to carry them. If they had children on the way, it was only a matter of retiring to the bush with a friend for an hour or so. With regard to the food question, although a more generous ration had to be served out, they cooked the food properly and thus repaid it tenfold in the improved condition and tempers of all concerned. But the one obvious and indisputable point in favor of their presence was that so long as the men were satisfied at home, there was no inducement for them to seek the native women, thereby eliminating the most frequent cause of feud and bloodshed. Besides all this, they were a cheery element in camp life. They were not beauties, it is true, but they were not she-men, unpleasant to look upon. They all bore about them those signs of strong feminity so soothing to male eyes, although their actual features might have let them down badly in a beauty contest.

Time is rightly credited with working wonders, and so even the preparations of an African safari are finally completed. The best way to hasten this is to take the bit in one's teeth, shut one's ears to all pleadings, and give the order to march, at the same time seizing one's rifle and starting off. Thus you bring to your Africans' dilatory minds the fact that the long-contemplated start is indubitably upon them. That the Bwana has himself left means that he must be followed. There seems nothing for it but to get down to it. Meanwhile you escape the harrowing details of Musa's loss of his wife, how she has deserted him, taking with her the cloth he so recently purchased for her, and a thousand other excuses for one more visit to the town. Then you halt at some convenient site for camp not too far distant from town because, although you have been preparing to start for the last three months, no one is really ready and there will be a constant night-long traffic from camp to town. You must now refuse to hear all complaints; every attempt to engage your sympathy for some tale of woe must be sternly denounced as "Kilele" (noise); otherwise you will take root and grow hoary upon the spot.

If you have resolutely carried out these instructions, you may set off next morning with about half the outfit. Never mind! If you have, as you certainly ought to have, a good headman (I had two), he will bring on the stragglers. Then, in a few days, instead of chaos there will reign orderliness and method in your movements.

We are off at last!

CHAPTER 3

TO SEE the first start-off is harrowing to the safari leader. The animals are raw and generally missing. Many of the boys are also missing, having a last swill of beer. Others are chasing the sweethearts who have promised to accompany their temporary husbands, who have taken an advance for the purchase of clothes, and whose hearts have failed them at the last moment. Bad talk by the traders has been going about among our crowd. Prophecies of violent endings for a certain number of our following, put forth by those mischievous "malimus," have had some effect. They do this as they have no desire for the presence of a white man in their trading territory. There are desertions, and as everyone has had three months' advance of wages, it is important to bring them back. Luckily this is not so difficult as it might seem. Every African is a born policeman and extremely loyal to his employer. He will side with his own safari against everyone, including his own relations, and he will soon hunt down any deserters. As an instance of his efficiency in this connection, I will cite an example. It was outside Mombassa and in camp that three hundred rupees were stolen from a box in my tent. At once news of the theft was sent to the police, who held out very little hope of my ever seeing the money again. But a few of my own boys said they would like to have a try. I sent them off with many misgivings, I must confess, and warned them that they were not now out in the bush and that no force was to be used. In an incredibly short time they returned with a stranger who certainly had two hundred and forty rupees on him, new boots, and new clothes. In due course we ran him into the police station where he was committed for trial and the money was handed over to the police. The magistrate gave him six months and the gear and money were handed back to us, but whether he was really the thief or whether his luck was just out I have often since wondered.

Somewhere about 3:00 P.M. we finally get ourselves into some sort of motion. Only occasionally is this motion in the right direction. Donkeys are fresh and buck off their saddles in all directions. Everyone throws down his load and chases them. A jack gets a string of cooking pots wound round his hind legs and stampedes the whole lot just as we get going once more. This time he reaches the herd of trade cattle, mostly frisky little heifers. They scatter to the wide, their Masai and Lumbwa herders cursing the sweating donkey men who follow them as they fly toward the horizon, over a plain littered with torn tents and foundering pots, in pursuit of the disappearing tails of their charges. Finally, evening draws down and we have accomplished three miles. Animals and equipment are somehow gathered together into some sort of camp, and we rest, our sides sore with laughter.

Next day a very similar state of affairs prevails, but daily the safari improves and starts are earlier, distances covered rising to ten and fifteen miles a day. We now pass through Kakamega where gold has been recently found. Nothing do we know of it, however, and presently we reach the last village before plunging into the true

"Barra" or wilderness. A halt of a few days is called, for here we must try to load up as much Matama flour as we can. There will be nothing procurable except meat between this and Mani-Mani, the large settlement in Karamojo some twenty days' march farther north. While trade goods are displayed to attract flour sellers, I set off with the long Gibbs .256 to shoot meat for the safari. A fair number of hartebeest and a few roan and oribi are secured and their meat proves most popular with the native housewives.

During the few days' halt I visited the cave dwellers on Mount Elgon. They are supposed to be the survivors of the tribe that once inhabited the Uasin-Ghishu plateau and left so many ruined stone-built dwellings all over that lovely country. They are poor little devils, inhabiting these caves through fear more than for any other reason, I think. They seem to live by trapping bush animals and gathering honey, swapping their stuff for grain and beer with the Kakamegas. Of course I inquired of them about elephant. They pointed to the north and said I might meet with some three or four days farther on. I climbed with them to about eight thousand feet, mostly in bamboo, but saw no traces of elephant.

More fully loaded than ever, we staggered forth, our path winding along the lower spurs of Elgon where they jutted out into the plain. We were well elevated above the general level of the plain and got enchanting views of game herds in the distance, giraffe being in great numbers. Between the larger spurs cold clear streams of water debouched from the mountainside out into the hot dazzling plain, convoyed by tall, dark green mountain-forest trees for a considerable distance. The grass had been burned off, and the seepage from the mountain had caused a lovely growth of fresh green verdure on which it was easy work to provide food for all concerned, covered as it was with hartebeest and oribi. Bush buck were in good number also, but the meat of this buck is not popular among tribes whose country is not inhabited by it, and even then its meat is taboo to many, so it was seldom we bothered with it.

The procedure in the morning was as follows: Half an hour before sunup (6:00 A.M.) I was called with tea and biscuits, fresh shorts, socks, and hunting shirt. I would be off by sunup or a little before, accompanied by a boy carrying a calabash of cow's milk. I would race away as fast as possible so as to lose all sound of the following safari. Then the true joy of the hunter's life would seize and hold me until such time as the sun became oppressive. Constantly you are in sight of game of some sort. In the cold damp air of the early morning buffalo would still be in the open, perhaps sunning themselves or wandering slowly toward their forest haunts, where they would rest during the day, and taking a few last mouthfuls of the sweet dew-laden grass that would provide such a pleasant aftermath when they came to chew the cud in the dim cool cathedral of their midday refuge. Almost certainly oribi, those neat and agile little buck, would be sprinting about, always in pairs and perhaps faithful to each other so long as life does last, like the mallard at home is said to be. In Africa it would not be a very lengthy penance should they dislike each other, for enemies are numerous and life is short. Then wart hog with their ugly faces and dear little babies, all in line-ahead and all with their tails up and curled in matchless imitation of mother; giraffe, standing and staring spellbound at the khaki-colored apparition or swaying and lurching off toward the safety of the wide-open plain; and, of course, always the expectation of finding a huge elephant track appearing dark in the surrounding glisten of dew-laden grass.

Before reaching elephant country proper, it was essential to provide everyone with sandals. Once across the Turkwel River all the country is covered with thorn trees of every variety, ranging from the long, straight, darning needle sort to the small, curved fishhook, wait-a-bit kind. As much of our work would be in the bush with no paths other than game tracks, everyone had to have some sort of footgear. I had several dozen pairs of shoes, but I never found perfect gear for this work. Every form of shoe hurt and blistered the feet. The most one could do was to powder the washed socks thickly with boracic powder and carry on. Canvas shoes with rope soles were, I think, the best of a bad lot. Running shoes were pleasant on soft ground, but the spikes bored into one's feet on hard ground. Football boots I tried, but they galled most frightfully. Crepe rubber soles and soft leather uppers were good when they appeared on the scene. In African thorn country there are three main sources from which come good sandals: the belly pieces of the elephant, the hide of the buffalo, and the hide of the giraffe. Elephant hide is the most supple but takes in moisture sooner than buffalo or giraffe hide, and the latter two require a terrible amount of beating to render them amenable to the flexing of the human foot so necessary if galling is to be avoided. Buffalo provide ornamental tails for fly swatting, and giraffe give many feet of mane with great upstanding hair of a rich chestnut color seven or eight inches long. This, cut into suitable lengths and joined round the head, provides pleasant shade for the eyes and face of the wearer, leaving the top of the skull unprotected.

This does not matter to the African; all he desires is ornamentation. The tails of giraffe, with their long black hairs springing from a single knob, are also very much prized for their ornamental value. The meat of all three is excellent, and it may be noted that no marrow is obtainable from the leg bones of fully adult bull giraffe. With these matters in mind, the long .256 was kept well to the fore, with the result that we formed camp by one of Elgon's perfect streams a few hundred yards from the massive carcasses of one bull and four cow giraffe. The donkeys and cattle rolled in the sweet short grass and filled themselves to the bursting point.

The safari was now in decent working shape and, after its few days of lazy marching on full rations, was in splendid trim. The season was dry, and bright sun and pleasantly cool breezes were the order of our days. There was an inevitable elation of Africans at the sight of quantities of meat, and there were many inquiries as to whether the beasts were fat. The tents were pitched incredibly quickly. The donkey boma was run up in no time, and everyone seized knives and baskets and rushed off to the butchery, the women tying their oldest and skimpiest rags round their bulging hips, singing and dancing all over the place.

While this merry scene took place upon the edge of the plain, I sloped off upstream by myself for one of those solitary rambles that are, to my mind, of the very essence of hunting. I know no joy like it. Carrying my elephant rifle, a sweet little .275 Rigby Mauser, I followed up the line of forest bordering the stream and soon was beyond all sound from the camp. Here was primeval Africa with all its possibilities. What might I find?

Presently I saw the faint beginnings of an elephant

path. Soon it became clearer and better defined until, when near the beginning of the mountain slopes, it was quite clear of vegetation and smooth as a pavement with the edges as well defined. As a rule these paths are only frequented by the aged and cow-sick bulls, carrying ivory of a length in inverse ratio to that of their tempers. So far the surface of the path was quite free from those corrugations that so delight the hunter's heart, made as they are by the rugged soles of this ponderous game. They look for all the world as if made by crepe rubber but magnified eight times or so.

What a glorious sensation it is to follow along an unfamiliar elephant path. Round every bend one half expects to see some colossal monster barging slowly along, while one's ears are tuned expectantly to catch the rumble of a ponderous belly. All I actually heard, however, was the chattering of monkeys. The thought that I should soon be among the elephant consoled me. At any moment now I might cross the track of some solitary bull.

Quite close to the edge of the main forest and just as the path began to climb more steeply toward the densely wooded ravines of the mountain, a well-defined path converged from the right. On closer inspection there were the precious corrugations, faint because of the hardness of the dry surface but quite unmistakable. Later in the day when the sun mounted higher they would not be so easily seen, partly because the sun would be higher and shadows would disappear and partly because the dry season breezes would have blown the dust about, obliterating them.

It soon became apparent that the tracks were those of two good bulls. The queer sensation of these moments now rushed over me. It is as if all one's senses had been half asleep and had just awakened fully. Speed, hearing, and sight become intense. The feel of the rifle in one's hand sends a thrill through the body. I sprang forward on the trail, but I did so more silently than before.

Soon one huge dropping, then several more close together, told their tale. They were not traveling fast; the distance between droppings was small. They had paused in the act, as the droppings were almost unbroken. They had passed about two hours ago: the outside was oxidized and cold, but the centers were bright yellow and still warm. Their smell is as delicious to the hunter as that of stables to a horsy man.

Soon one sees where monkeys have been to them, picking out the unchewed tamarind seeds. Here they must have passed well after sunrise, for monkeys are rather like their human counterparts and hate to get going in the chill of the morning. The path still hugs the stream, with occasional diversions where the grade is too steep. The forest becomes denser, damper, and darker. There is a lot of undergrowth and visibility is not more than a few yards. One might run into them now, but it is probable that two such old hands will seek the very depths of the forest for their midday siesta. One should go silently as a shadow now, not so much because of alarming the quarry as of preventing one's own ears from catching the dull ear flappings, belches, belly rumblings, or leaf-stripping sounds that will indicate their proximity. Chances are against one's seeing them before hearing them. If some unusual sound or faintest air taint from the hunter has warned these fantastic beasts, they may either crash away or you may almost bump into a massive leg in no way distinguishable in the half-light from the scores of other dark upright objects in the near foreground.

The excitement is intense. I always used to wonder why. I had killed many elephant and had passed through many such experiences, and I always thought that I should have attained a much cooler state. But no! Never could I prevent my pulse from beating faster. I think it is because nothing is ever the same. Anything may happen at such close quarters. Where the game is in full sight the whole time, as out on the open plain for instance, you can at least see what is happening. But in such stuff as the present you really know nothing of what is going on. It is possible to be close on the heels of elephant all day long and wondering why you never come up with them, until time at last bears to your reluctant mind the conviction that they are hearing you and simply flitting along before you as silently as shadows.

The greatest aid to silent going is bare legs. Bare feet also would be a further refinement and advantage, but I never could attain to the latter. With the former, however, a very fair degree of silence can be obtained; you feel freer and avoid so much sound-producing contact with the bush.

I was now expecting at any moment to hear my quarry. But there are many noises apparent to tense ears at such moments. Only experience can differentiate between those made by monkeys, pig, bush buck, or elephant. At last a great but subdued sigh struck my ear. Luckily there was no apparent wind in these forest tunnels. I peered breathless in the direction whence it seemed to come. A gentle trickle, trickle, plop, confirmed the sigh. They were not more than fifteen paces in front of me. I peered and peered, stooping here and there, trying to catch a glimpse of some movement. How infernally dark it was. I glanced along my rifle. Yes, the wart-hog ivory bead of my foresight stood out nicely. I began a stealthy approach, not because I wanted to be nearer (on the contrary, about thirty yards is the range I would choose) but because I could still see nothing—not even a foot when I looked along under much of the undergrowth. There was nothing for it but to go in still farther. It was no good leaving the path in order to find more open ground; the best chance lay along the path.

A wall of foliage seemed to be hiding what I so ardently desired to see. It had given way and closed in behind scores of elephant, yet it showed no sign of wear. It was as opaque as ever. It must be parted. Gently I pressed the branches aside. Then quite close to my face was an unusually dark patch. Slowly it assumed the outline of some part of an elephant, but what part was a mystery. This was devilish work. They, or rather it, for the other was still completely invisible, was far too close. You cannot envisage the locality of the vitals at such close quarters on such extensive monochrome surfaces; you cannot tell at what angle the animal stands; and yet, if you retreat one step, all is lost to sight. And to add to the delicacy of the situation, at any instant they may wind you, crash right over you, or disappear in a whirl of agitated bush.

After a few intolerable seconds, there was a movement of the bush on my right and a small, brightly lit-up gray triangle appeared in a shaft of sunlight and disappeared again, with very little noise except a faint rustling. It was part of an ear and its owner was gently fanning himself. He might have been ten paces to my right front, whereas the other was directly in front and his nearest part might have been six paces distant. I judged from a movement in the bush that I could feel with my left hand that this was caused by his tail and that he was approximately stern-on to me. I could do nothing to him in that position that I could rely upon, so I had to retreat and come up some other way. I dared not wait for one of them to turn; they were dozing and it might be an hour before one of them did so. There was nothing for it but to try from a different angle. Withdrawing as silently as possible, I came in from a small detour well to the right. At about fifteen paces I was rewarded with the sight of a dark patch shutting out all light and approximating to the outline of an elephant broadside-on but, of course, still too much intercepted by bush for any shooting. Creeping on a little farther, I could make out a fair amount of ear but I could not find the ear root and the eye so necessary for calculating the position of the brain. The heart shot was quite out of the question, its position being smothered by green stuff.

Then came my reward, just as I was getting desperate. Up through the foliage came the tip of a trunk, feeling and curling about like some huge snake and unpleasantly close to me. The head swung round toward me, the trunk wrapped itself round a succulent branch, and at the stripping pull the whole apparition of the head appeared as if a curtain had flown aside, and I placed a bullet just right and down he fell, kneeling, without a sound, the only quiver that of his still beating heart. At the shot his companion threw up his head but did not otherwise move. He was facing the shot elephant at the instant of death and, I suppose, continuing to see him, he had no other thought than to remain listening. Hurriedly pushing a little toward the dead elephant, I came into instant view of the live one and got in a frontal brain shot, to my very great joy, as it was neither an easy position, the head being high and the range close, nor was it a moment over which to waste even a split second. Wiping the sweat from my streaming brow with curved forefinger, I took a view of the ivory after noticing automatically the quivers and jerks only produced when the brain has been pierced. Both of them carried satisfactory teeth, the first one round about 70 pounds each and the second one a whole tooth of about 90 pounds and one broken one of about 50 pounds.

Seating myself on a convenient foot, I produced a black shag of tobacco and rolled myself a cigarette, inhaling the welcome fumes while thinking to myself what a capital affair the whole thing was. It was a good start; I had hardly dared to hope for elephant this side of the Turkwel River. How very fortunate I had been that nothing had alarmed my victims while I had been so close to them for such a length of time. I thought I would just pace off the distances and found that the first beast had been killed at eleven paces, as near as I could make it, and the other at seven.

Now I must hurry off to get the cutting-out gang so that they might finish the job before dark. It would be a lengthy business as there were no natives to help them denude the heads of the troublesome skin and gristle surrounding the bone sockets holding the tusks. The natives are obliged to do this before they are permitted to attack the carcass. Once the skull is cleared, heavy axes soon liberate the tusks, but it is delicate work and requires experienced boys. I had a gang of eight adepts who once succeeded in stripping the tusks from nineteen bull elephant in one day, but on that occasion they had the assistance of several hundred natives. These eager butchers not only cleared off all the tissue but actually severed each gigantic head from its body, thereby lightening my boys' task enormously.

Cutting off the great tails, I join them together with a bush rope, sling them over my shoulder, and beat it for camp at a steady trot, filled and glowing with satisfaction. My entry is greeted in silence as I stride through the busy throng. They are rather awed, I think. They have heard no shot, seen no sign of elephant, and my cartridge belt shows but two gaps in the glistening row.

It might be asked why I bothered with the cumbersome tails. Well, it is firstly a sign of ownership. Secondly, it is much more impressive to throw down a dozen tails than to boldly announce that you have killed twelve elephant. And thirdly, spoken numbers convey but little to the African mind. The natives must see tokens corresponding to the number. If you want some tusks brought from a cache, you have to give them a piece of stick for each tusk in the pit so that, as they unearth them one by one, a stick is placed on each. If you tell them to go and cut out the tusks from eleven elephant, they might return with the tusks of only ten or even nine. But if they have seen eleven tails come into camp, the tusks of eleven elephant will be brought in. Moreover, it acts as a check on the bag. Without it you might easily imagine you had more down than was actually the case. Lastly, it is customary.

The headman comes up as I throw the tails down in front of my tent. He receives orders for the cutters-out to be ready and for as many as may want elephant meat to accompany me. Then I stick my head deep into a bucket of what seems icy cold water, letting it stay there as long as possible. Swédé soon has tea ready, and Suliemani, the cook, produces a meal of rice and curried oribi

liver while pandemonium breaks loose in the camp. Everyone appears to be going for meat although the camp is already simmering with huge meat-drying operations from
the giraffe. Great slabs of giraffe hide lie about ready to
be cut into sandal sizes. Two women are filling a gigantic
giraffe bladder with beautiful golden fat. Bare shank
bones lie about ready to be grilled for the white delicious
marrow they contain. I notice that some deluded fellow
has brought in a bull shank. When he comes to toast it,
the knowing ones will congratulate him on the feast he
is going to have and will pretend to wish to be invited to
join in it. Then, when the poor fellow begins to wallop it
to try to crack it, someone will eagerly bring him one of
the heavy axes. Finally he will succeed in breaking it
when it is brittle with fire, and instead of a gush of
white and marbled fat, he will look ruefully at a solid
bone or, at the best, a tiny white string no thicker than a
pencil. There will be a roar of laughter.

My meal finished, we set off for the ivory. Looking
back, it seems as if the whole camp is coming too. Surely
they do not want more meat. But elephant meat is a
favorite with the Wanyamwezi and elephant fat their
great delight. Camp will not be deserted as the donkey
boys are Mussulmen and will not touch elephant meat;
anyhow, the camp askaris will look after things.

Soon we reach the scene and business begins on the
tusks. On the carcasses, too. In a very short time they
have the whole gralloch spread about. Rivulets of water,
thick with chewed leaves and grass and mixed with blood,
flow about. Great explosions throw columns of ferment-
ing vegetation high in the air when some wag stabs
a taut intestine with his knife. Shrieks of laughter when
anyone is caught in the shower. Two or three burrow deep

into the yawning cavity in the search for fat, emerging with their bodies reeking with blood and grease. Someone throws a long gyrating piece of fat to his woman in the background. On its way it is intercepted by someone else's woman. Immediately there is a fierce fight. What a din! With everyone loaded up, we begin the retreat to camp. Here everything is most home-like. The evening is drawing down, and under a thick canopy of savory smoke from the grilling meat, the place looks almost fairy-like, from a distance anyhow. I do like women about a camp. They are noisy and quarrelsome, troublemakers often, no doubt, but they do give an air of domesticity. And they are ornamental, too, in a way—when carrying water pots on their heads, for instance. How leisurely and graceful they are, what poise and balance. Instead of seeking these effects from costly corsetry, our women would do well to parade about with a five-gallon jar of water balanced on their heads. We would see fewer round backs and necks sticking out at the wrong angle if they did so for a few moments each day from childhood up.

Now I have a hot bath. The evenings are chill and I change to pajamas. Then my evening meal, after which I take my long chair out to the camp fire. By this time the ivory has been scrubbed clean at the brook and is now laid out beside the tarpaulin-covered heap of donkey saddles. I take a look at the tusks and note how nice they look with their deep rich tones no longer concealed with blood and muck. From now on the lane of tusks should extend to a greater length day by day as we penetrate farther into the Barra, until it will present quite a little walk in itself as I promenade along the dull glowing tops. And finally there will be two rows, I hope.

Presently Swédé appears with a kettle of boiling water

and the cleaning rod, tow, and oil. Rifle cleaning is a task of love. Thereafter I sit in contemplation, swinging my rifle idly about. The mere feel of it is a never-ending pleasure: so small, so neat and light, and yet so deadly. I cannot help thinking how supremely lucky I am. All my troubles are now well behind me. White men with their ridiculous civilization lie far from me. No longer need I be a slave to money. Thank goodness all the natives before me are still quite ignorant of that fearful bondage. The few remaining tokens thereof are stowed away in one of the boxes and will not see the light of day for at least a year. No letters will find us; no newspapers can disturb the tranquillity of our days with their sensations and anxieties. We are off into the blue!

All the same, what about the poor donkeys and this mass of meat my merry men propose to load them up with? Shrink as it will, certainly there will remain several tons of it by morning. I shall have to be early astir to see that there is no overloading. And early it will be, for now everyone is in splendid condition. After the evening meal there is a capital singsong. The camp chronicler has already strung together three verses alluding subtly to the incidents of the safari. They have to be interpreted to me as their points quite escape me although I speak the language. One of the verses concerns poor Swédé's recent matrimonial venture, how when his obdurate wife had finally surrendered, he had encountered the wide highway where he had paid for and expected the narrow path. Roars of laughter, drum floggings, horn blowings, and shouts greet it, while even poor Swédé grins from ear to ear. And so to bed, to the music of hyenas, jackals, and a distant lion.

CHAPTER 4

THE Turkwel River, being a mere trickle at this time of year, was easily forded. But in the rains it can be a rushing, roaring torrent. Away down on the plains it becomes lost in sand and runs underground until it finally reaches Lake Rudolf. All the rivers are like that, and it is only here and there that the water is sufficiently near the surface for humans and other animals to reach it. All the natives of those parts sound with their spears, not by shoving the spear down to see if it reaches moisture, as a white man would, but they tell by the sound the spear makes whether water is near or not, the spear butt penetrating hardly any distance at all. A primitive form of what we see hailed as the newly invented Depth Recorder?

Once Turkwel is clear of the foothills round Elgon's base, its banks are covered with a belt of thorn bush on either side. This bush is used, or perhaps I should say was used, by great numbers of elephant and rhino. Without the traffic of these animals it would be impossible to circulate at all in the thorny maze. I intended to make an excursion down river to try for some of the grand old bulls who used Turkwel at this time, leaving the main safari in a secure camp where the northern trail crossed it. Preparations were at once begun on the site we chose for a good strong thorn zeriba to enclose the whole of the tents and donkey boma. Good grazing was within reasonable reach, wood and water were abundant, and the second headman would go to a native settlement high upon Elgon where banana flour could be bought with beads and dried meat. The others who remained in camp would busy themselves with cutting up and preparing antelope hide pack saddles to be ready to receive the shorter tusks as they came in. For this purpose the raw hide is soaked until soft and securely tied round the tusks while wet. When it dries, the hide shrinks and holds the tusks in such a way that the points and sockets do not gall the animal. This requires some art as every tusk has a different curve. The stay-at-homes would very largely provide themselves with meat by trapping francolin and bush partridge. In addition, they had a fine stock of smoked meat.

On the eve of our departure some native Karamojans came in. They seemed glad to see us and brought two calabashes of honey. Immediately I asked them for elephant news, and they said some big fellows were drinking at the river, lower down, each night. This news put everyone into extreme good humor. I must certainly say my boys were always perfectly charming in the way they would search out elephant news among the natives. When tidings were scarce, they would beg to be allowed to search the bush themselves. But usually my standing reward of a yearling heifer for news resulting in the death of five or more bull elephant brought some native hot-foot when any elephant were within fifty miles or so.

The Karamojans said they would sleep in our camp. They were given some flour and a cooking pot; meat they were tired of, as they generally trap and spear a great quantity at this time of year. Of course my boys were much too civilized to invite pagans to eat with them. Were they not clothed!

These small bush excursions of mine were quite simple affairs. No tents were carried in the dry season. A camp bed, cooking gear, a small box of cartridges, and a change of clothing were lightly distributed among fifteen or twenty porters. No women were taken. The whole crowd would be sandal-shod and was required to follow us wherever we might go, to travel in absolute silence on elephant trails, and to stop behind when we came close to game. All we leading files did to enable them to distinquish our path from innumerable game tracks was to break and leave hanging in the direction we were going an occasional branch or bunch of long grass. Every now and again, as we left some well-defined track we had been following for some time, someone would score across it two or three times with a spear butt or drop a branch across it, thus showing that it was closed. Meager as these signs undoubtedly were, it was very seldom that the boys got lost.

Bright and early we said our farewells and strode off behind our guides in a tight little line. I had, besides my .275, a .303 with a ten-shot magazine—an excellent elephant rifle. I was always hoping that sometime somewhere I would have an opportunity of using the whole magazineful on some group of bulls that would be bewitched into standing around while I did so. Needless to say, it only happened when I carried some other rifle.

At about this time I was playing about with the idea of a peep sight instead of an open V back sight, but I found it slow in picking up the object although excellent for deliberate shots at some range. I now know that this was solely because my apertures were too small. If I were doing it all over again, I think I should use only apertures of large diameter. Speed in picking up the object is of the utmost importance if the bag is to grow. The first shot is, of course, quite deliberate, but the succeeding ones are taken at speed in thick stuff as the animals are so quickly swallowed up in the surrounding sea of bush. Thorn bush is generally of such a character that the heart of an elephant is often shrouded but the head fairly clear, so the brain is much more often exposed to a rapid shot than the heart. To this shot I owed very much of my success. There is nothing more satisfying than the complete flop of a running elephant shot in the brain. There is a finality and silence, apart from the report, that no other shot can give. And sometimes others of the fugitive bunch are all brought up standing by seeing their companion stop in his tracks, as it were.

We traveled that day parallel with the river but at some distance from it. Consequently we were outside the dense belt of thorn and our pace was good in the more open park country. Wherever we crossed some great well-worn path heading toward this belt, we knew that there would be found the pits in the sandy river bed where elephant fill their tanks before retiring to their thorny fastnesses. But no path had fresh-enough spoor to delay us. Fair numbers of rhino tracks were seen though, and had we wanted them, no doubt we could have found them.

Toward the heat of the day we arrived at a native encampment where a few women were beating hartebeest hides into shape for laying up into the huge hide ropes used by these people to snare everything from elephant down to dik-dik. They had some goats and sheep, too, denoting that they had recently traded a tusk to some Swahili safari. During our halt the women brought us water and I asked for some tamarind. This, squeezed in water, makes a refreshing drink. Meanwhile our guides consulted a lad who had been left in camp to take us on to where some of the men had elephant under observation. How they ever manage this sort of thing used to beat me. And they could never rightly explain it to a person so dense as a white man. That lad, for instance, proceeded to lead us directly to his fellows miles away in bush which looked to me to be devoid of all distinguishing marks. These men were not fixed on any one spot but were actually following browsing elephant. And yet, after some miles of fast going, we came on the fresh tracks of elephant and very soon thereafter a man appeared quite casually in the bush. There were four, he said, and they were feeding slowly along. In answer to the query as to size, he showed a length on his spear which seemed to me a bit exaggerated.

Leaving the little safari to follow some way behind under the guidance of the lad, my two natives and I took up the trail. Some of the bush had been recently burned; it would be delightful country in which to operate if only we came up with our quarry before they reached the denser stuff ahead. It was quite apparent that they were making for the river, but quite leisurely, as on all sides we saw evidence of their tree-grazing. Every now and then the chewed balls of sansevieria fiber, which they spit out after absorbing the juice, told of thirst. However thirsty, they would not drink in daylight, past experience teaching them that then they might encounter spears thrown from the trees surrounding their drinking place. With luck we might catch them yet.

We rushed along, the natives as eager as myself. Presently they stopped, listening. They turned to me, pointing with their spears. I could see nothing. They heard them but I could not yet do so. I now led on, and presently even I caught the dull sound of an ear flop, then a crash as some tree went down. After a little burst of speed, there they were, wandering so slowly along that one wondered why it had taken so long to come up with them, forgetting that those leisurely strides cover so much ground.

At once an extraordinary tusk stood out from all the rest. It looked of a marvelous length and curvature—more like a mammoth's than an elephant's. As I came to shooting range, I was concentrating more on getting this tusk than on getting the four elephant as I should have been. They were in line-ahead in a perfectly open piece of country, and if I had done the correct thing, I would have had all four most likely. The big tusker was in third position from the leader. Had I shot the leader in the brain, the odds would have been ten to one that the others would have paused and looked around long enough for me to have killed them all. Instead of this I shot the big fellow first. He dropped, but in doing so I think he touched the one ahead. At any rate, the one ahead darted off at a run which alarmed the others. One of these, number four, had to pass the dead elephant, and luckily did so at such an angle as to give me a chance which I successfully took. But the other two got away, and although I followed as hard as I could, they never stopped. I got to within shooting range of their sterns, but not possessing either a weapon capable of sending its bullet right through from the stern nor a burst of speed left in me sufficient to bring me up alongside them, they escaped, leaving me to my fury with myself for having muddled it and to my great disappointment as they carried very nice ivory indeed. We retraced our course while the thought of that pair of magnificent tusks awaiting us calmed me down a bit.

What was my indignation on arrival at the scene to find that the brute carried only one tusk. No doubt about it—one tusk of what would have been a perfect pair. And the other beast had teeth only fit for a donkey load. What a muddle! Never mind, it will soon be forgotten, and meanwhile we certainly had a real "Kilangozi" in the single tusk. What competition there would be for it among the ivory carriers. It ought to weigh 125 pounds anyway. This beast fell with its single tusk upwards, to the confusion of all those near-hunters who so dogmatically state that an elephant always falls heaviest tusk down. As a matter of my experience, any rule applied to these animals is certain to be confounded; they are not governed by rules. And to this uncertainty as to their behavior must be attributed the extraordinary charm of hunting them. Who would ever expect three elephant, remnants of a herd of seven, to turn suddenly while in full flight on a dead-open grass plain and bear straight down upon the rifle? It savors of suicide on their part surely. Similar incidents will crop up as they occurred on the safari.

As it was now drawing in toward sundown, it was decided to sleep by the carcasses, the Karamojans sending back to their camp for women to take charge of the meat and to bring water. For here, of course, there was none nearer than the river. Had the camp been too far, we would have gone there as we could not have depended upon the slain elephant to provide enough for all hands from their interiors, they themselves having been on the way to the river.

All hands turned to stripping the heads for the ax while

my boy smoothed a piece of ground for my camp bed and I cut two forked sticks for my rifles. When the stripping was completed, a great stock of firewood was collected, for it was now dark and the actual cutting-out would have to be done by firelight. My boys and I were devilishly thirsty by this time, and someone tapped one of the carcasses, but it was nearly dry and yielded a very turbid fluid much mixed with a strongish flavor. I could not face it and hung on till the arrival of the villagers. Toward midnight they came, and how sweet the water from their calabashes was. For washing there was none, of course, but sweat can be rubbed off the body in a powder when thoroughly dry and beaten out of clothes also.

When the single tusk came to camp, its proportions were even more striking. It was quite nine feet long with a beautiful curve. Actually, when I measured it with a tape afterwards, it proved to be nine feet, two inches. In a way it was rather a nuisance. One could not ask the natives to carry it home to their camp as it was too heavy for people unused to carrying such weights, and to drag it around with us in the pathless wilderness would slow up everything. So it was decided to leave one porter with it to carry it back, the natives agreeing to guide him to the main camp.

Our little camp was soon a scene of great liveliness. Fires going everywhere, women and men, boys and girls staggering about with loads of meat, their naked bodies glistening in the firelight. Under the more searching rays of the sun it would have rather disenchanted one, I daresay, to discover that much of the glitter was caused by blood, but now by firelight it looked very jolly indeed. They were so happy and so healthy, so carefree and so abandoned to the good things of life. Gone were all community restraints, and, to tell the truth, there were all sorts of high jinks for those whose smell-organization was not too sensitive, needless to say.

On the morrow we were off again, our native guides still eager for the hunt as they had not yet earned their heifer reward. It always seemed to me rather unjust that they should miss it through my faulty maneuvering, as in this case. They had done their part exceedingly well; it was I who had bungled it. However, they never saw it in that light and were full of eagerness to continue the hunt.

For a further eight days we wandered down the Turkwel banks. During that time we gathered in seven more bulls, three of them single fellows of great age and bulk. As is so common in this country, a large proportion of tusks were broken, but in spite of this there was not a tusk under 58 pounds. We were obliged to sleep near watering places on the river, and all our elephant had to be tracked back into the bush after they had filled themselves. This is generally a laborious business as they take in enough water to last them two or three days so they may find the better tree-grazing that lies farthest away from watering places. They will thus wander thirty or forty miles back into the bush, and unless they have drunk late on toward dawn, you have a long stern chase after them. Once, however, we caught five bulls dawdling about the dense strip near the river. Awful stuff it is in spite of being well traversed and knocked about by numerous elephant and rhino.

We heard them at the water holes, and some of the boys said they did not leave until very late. Hoping this would lead to an early contact with them, we were on the trail when it was sufficiently light to distinguish a fresh track from an older one. Fortunately, the day breezes make this possible. By flowing dust, they obliterate the old tracks, and as the breezes do not commence until about ten o'clock, a new track can be distinguished with certainty until that time. After that tracking becomes more and more difficult.

We had scarcely gone two miles, skirting along the edge of the thick belt, when we saw our game ahead of us. Taking the lead, I put on a burst that brought us up to their sterns. It was imperative to get a go at them before they entered the dense bush a hundred yards to their left. But fate was against us. The leading file swung toward it before I could range alongside, and this move compelled us to enter the tangle behind the rearmost animal. To do otherwise than to follow behind is generally to risk alarming them or losing them altogether.

How easily and quietly they slip along through the terrible stuff. No matter how hooked or pointed, the thorns cannot grip their armored hide, and yet it is quite supple. Everything gives way before them as they forge along and closes in behind them with a swish.

It was now a matter of following them until they reached some shady spot where they would probably dispose themselves about to pass the midday heat, fanning themselves and occasionally drawing water from their interiors with their trunks and spraying themselves. The danger was that they might wind us meanwhile. The wisest course might have been to have let them settle and then to have tracked them to where they were, but who could command such patience? Certainly not a young hunter.

As we followed close on their sterns, they suddenly stopped. Trunks could be seen questing about high in the air, testing the wind. As if connected together by rods, they turned and came straight back. What a transformation! From drooping-trousered sterns to high magnificent tusk-shod heads, boring along and foreshortening at a frightful speed. What a chance for the frontal brain shot! In fact, there was no other chance. One could have run, of course, but down that infernal lane what speed could even the fastest man attain, hampered by thorny bush and having often to stoop to avoid heavy branches? Certainly he could not reach any speed adequate to leave elephant behind. The stuff is quite paltry to them and they can do their hundred yards in ten or eleven seconds just as they do in open grass country. The only thing to do is either to throw oneself sideways blindly into the cushion of thorny branches or to stand and kill with the brain shot the foremost animal. Nothing but the brain will do as the shot will be at eight or ten paces or closer. Momentum and the others behind will carry a merely wounded animal right on top of you. I cannot say how I admire those men who tackle elephant in this sort of situation who have no confidence in this shot or who even frankly disbelieve in it altogether. What do they do, I wonder?

At this particular time of my hunting career I was greatly attached to this shot. After some considerable trouble and great pains I had located the spot exactly, and I felt so confident that the turning head-on of these beasts seemed to be the very greatest luck. I killed the leader, and as he crashed down in the tunnel with his legs bent backwards under his body, he uncovered the next whose trunk and tusks must have touched his back. Number two pulled himself up all aback and I got him with a slanting shot behind the eye. Down he went without a sound, once more disclosing a third head moving off into the thorny wall, the head somewhat obstructed by branches. A rather lucky shot got him between eye and ear and down he went with a prodigious sigh. The remaining two had already disappeared into the gray surrounding sea of bush.

After the brain shot it is most essential to see that the legs and body of the shot animal are quivering. If they are quite motionless, at once give him a shot from such an angle as to penetrate the brain—not an easy matter. Otherwise you will never see him again; he is only stunned and will presently recover. This recovery is astounding in its suddenness, and you may be sitting on him when he will swiftly arise and flee. Therefore, noting that all three of our victims showed the welcome signs, we hurried after the survivors. You can never tell what elephant will do. It is always wise to get after them with no delay and to go as hard as you can. They often stop and wait, listening for their companions. You may suddenly come on them. Sometimes they clear out altogether, and in this case you will probably not see them again. If they are still in sight, you can follow with some speed, but if they have to be tracked, it will be a slow business. When they are in sight, tail right onto them. You will get your bare legs torn to ribbons but you won't feel it at the time. Every scar will add to your armor, the scab being thornproof. You will make a lot of noise, but so will they, and they may mistake your noise for that of one of their companions. If they show signs of slowing up, dart in as near to them as you can so as to be ready should they stop to listen. They are nearly sure to turn their heads sometime, just as they did on this occasion, and you will have them.

Guided by the roar of their first panicky rush—about the only time they do make a noise—I was soon behind them in view of the rearmost stern. My boy was cutting off the tails of the earlier casualties. The survivors were now over their fright and going fast but more quietly. Presently they showed signs of wanting to stop to listen. They would halt for a second with the ears shoved out a bit to catch any sound. The halts became more frequent and longer. But there was no turning of the heads yet. Then right ahead a small glimpse of the open country appeared. They reached it and were standing irresolute and listening as I emerged. What a wonderful sight they presented, from toenail to top quite clear of screening bush. And, of course, what easy meat. The best one took a bullet between eye and ear and the other gave a slanting shot as he turned away in flight, bursting one of his tusks from its socket as he fell headlong, chin to ground.

This was one of those days when everything went well. Far otherwise are some. Perhaps the elephant will not pause and give a chance, or they may take alarm and clear out altogether from that part of the country.

Friends have suggested that the advice I give above is somewhat foolhardy. I do not think it is for an experienced hunter who is familiar with and has confidence in the frontal brain shot. For those who are without this confidence there might have been some danger of being run down. The elephant were not charging when they came my way; they were probably alarmed by human taint in the air and were simply fleeing. Often elephant come straight toward the hunter. They look most formidable, of course, and they appear to look straight at one. But they do not connect a motionless khaki-clad figure with that of man. In their experience with that objectionable animal it must be mostly black men that they see. I am sure they go almost entirely by smell or movement. I have repeatedly had elephant hurry up to me on an open plain and shoot off at an angle when they detected my scent, sometimes when almost on top of me and when I would be on the point of shooting them, although they were valueless beasts, cows or young bulls or whatnot. Up to the instant of turning off they had every appearance of coming for one with the greatest determination. Very, very many of the so-called charges are no more than head-on flight. It is lucky that this is so, for a really angry elephant of large size in bush is a terror to all within a hundred yards. It is extremely difficult to shoot him in the brain as his head is constantly in violent agitation. He swirls round as if on a ball-bearing pivot, his ears often obscure the deadly spot as he flogs them about, his head moves up and down, sideways and all ways, and he is a demon to avoid. Sometimes he will rush furiously ahead, thrashing the bush on all sides. As suddenly he will back stern-first, and if you happen to be behind him, look out, for he will suddenly swap ends and there is his ugly wicked-looking head. His trunk seems to reach everywhere. I have gone through all this most unpleasant business, sometimes with cows who have had their little calves trodden underfoot and sometimes with bulls with body wounds. The former are unavoidable, but a mixup with the latter can be avoided by using the brain shot or, if you must use the body shot, by extremely careful shooting. A mortal wound never yet induced rage, at least in my experience.

CHAPTER 5

THE ivory from our five bulls was not exactly massive. At the same time, there were two tusks that would certainly require porters for their transport. The others would go to the donkeys. Meantime it was advisable to return to the main safari at Turkwel Ferry and to push on north. This time I wanted to break fresh trail and new bush up north of Dodinga. I longed to see the far-famed Murua Akipi where elephant were reported in great numbers. From where we were now it lay some two months' journey away, and that only if we did not dwell too long by the wayside.

Our native friends were now satiated with meat and they had earned a heifer. They were therefore quite eager to return. The skulls were soon stripped and the teeth hacked out. Late that night the last of them came in and we were ready to make the long march to base camp the next day. Straight across country they led us, right toward Elgon towering above the bush. Toward evening we made our base and everyone was overjoyed to see us. How very pleasant it is to come home again. The teeth made a nice little show led in by the huge tusk we had previously sent to camp and which its proud carrier enjoyed parading around. I stretched myself along the spotless groundsheet of my tent and had that most blessed cure for fatigue, a thorough massage. I always found this the grandest tonic after a good drink of water.

As this was going on, up came the headman of the donkeys. He wanted his tusks. I showed him which to take. He beckoned and his lads seized them away to the waiting hides they had had soaking a few days. In this dry atmosphere they would be firm by the morning and dry by midday.

After a change of clothing and some excellent food consisting of spitted partridge and banana-flour pudding, I thought of the two natives and how anxious they must be to see their heifer. The herders were just bringing in the animals from the river. How well they looked for their few days' rest. When the cattle were in their boma I told the two natives to take their choice of the assembled heifers. Almost without any examination they picked upon one and proceeded to jostle and push it out of the boma. I said they should leave it in the boma, sleep with us, and leave in the morning. No! They were emphatic and proceeded on their way, the heifer fighting to get back to her companions. Go she had to. Perhaps the boys thought I might change my mind in the night or that something might turn up. How on earth they kept with that heifer all through the bush with no path in the night I leave to them to explain.

While we were away in the bush, Swédé had trapped a score of partridge and had them quite tame. He also had cages for their transport. They are exquisite eating. There were complaints from the headman anent much bickering among the women. As I sat by the roaring camp fire, the culprits were sent for while the headman called to his boy to bring the dispute settlers—a couple of light rhino hide whips. The great beefy wenches appeared in the circle of firelight while an audience quickly gathered. One lady was told to state her case and almost immediately was furiously interrupted by the other. There was pandemonium at once, and it was obvious that nothing but a little bloodletting would settle them. Each was handed a whip and told to go to it. And right heartily they set about each other, swish! swosh!, but turn and turn about. I don't know why but it always was so—each waited for the other to get in a good one. Never did they attempt to avoid a wallop and never have I seen them aim a vicious blow at breast or face. Only at backs or legs were the whips aimed, any particularly curly one receiving roars of applause from the men. Presently one lass would lose her cloth. Shouts of applause! The other one's was slipping down also! More roars! They were both as nature made them! Redoubled cheers, hoots, and noise. At last one of them would burst into tears, throw down her whip, and run off to her tent. It was over and those two would be quiet for a time.

I have tried the same sort of thing with the men by substituting four-ounce gloves for kibokos. It was not a success for it never ended. They pounded each other without ceasing. After an hour or so it became monotonous and no result arrived at. Bare fists were no better. So recourse had to be had to their own method. Each man cuts as many sticks as he cares to. The left forearm is heavily swathed in cloth while the left hand grips the reserve of clubs. The right hand works away at breaking the clubs on the opponent's head or body. They take frightful punishment but never give in. As long as I have ever cared to allow it to continue, not one of them has ever shown any signs of throwing in the sponge.

The headman reported that some Swahili runners had

passed going to Mani-Mani. All the caravan leaders would know now about the approach of our safari. There were now two ways for us to reach our own particular country—Pyjalé's country—where we hoped to leave our ivory, to trade flour, and to pick up some good elephant in the surrounding bush. We knew that Pyjalé's people would have every elephant within sixty miles located as soon as they heard of our approach. One of these routes was the main caravan route with water at just possible distances for a heavily loaded safari, with a good clear trail, plenty of small game for meat, but few elephant. The alternative was to pass west of the Debasien Mountains through the bush with no defined man trail but with plenty of water at convenient distances, abundant game meat, and great herds of cow elephant generally visible to the big telescope from the slopes of Debasie. A bull or two might be picked up. Also, there would be plenty of good pasture and Pyjalé's people would be down with their herds for the early grass along the damp bottom land at the foot of the range, land that is covered with water in the rains. The only drawback to this route was the proximity of the tribe lying to the west. The Karamojan name for these people is Kumamma and they are their hereditary foes. They would not look at the main safari, of course, but they would pick off any straggler with great readiness. As with the Karamojans, the killing of any human, no matter how old or decrepit, in sleep or awake, opened the way to the girls' hearts as nothing else could and entitled the killer to wear the coveted blood red ostrich plumes at the dances and to tattoo his body on the right side for a man and on the left for a woman victim. It was decided to go by this western route and not the one used by the caravans.

At first our way lay through very bad country. Dry bush and stony dry watercourses made conditions possible only for a well-shod safari. The killing of giraffe and the pause in the base camp had afforded the necessary footgear. Our first camp was by the Kilimi River, another of Elgon's perennial streams. Rising somewhere near the sources of Turkwel, Kilimi flows west through vast plains instead of northeast as in the case of Turkwel. In the dry season in such a country a living stream of running water is a great novelty and a great joy to man and beast. Crystal clear, rapid, and cold where she leaves the dark mountain forests, she soon becomes slow, turbid, and warm in her course through the low-lying country, her muddiness caused by the countless game frequenting her. What percentage of her volume she must lose by evaporation and by direct removal of her content by animal life would be hard to compute. With well over a hundred and fifty people to provide for, scarcely a day passed without having to slay a few buck for the meat ration. These had to be provided near the camp or near the route. Carcasses could not be left for an instant as vultures were waiting for every chance. The .256 was seldom idle. All the skins were taken against the day when hundreds would be required for making saddles for the tusks we confidently expected to get.

Great numbers of wild hunting dogs were met with, and very cheeky some of them seemed. They would hardly move off, standing up on their hind legs, cocking their enormous ears at one, and barking, and this at ten or fifteen paces' distance. No wonder there are so many yarns of their ferocity and truculence going about. One of the cattle herders actually speared one with his Masai stabbing spear—an affair much too heavy to throw more

than a few yards. And even after I had shot one or two
with a .22, the others seemed to take no sort of fright.
They merely continued their job, whatever it might be,
disentangling some problem known only to themselves.
Personally, I never saw them attempt to do any of the
terrible things they are accused of. And after meeting
them so often and sometimes in such great numbers, I
find it hard to believe what is said of them. They are in-
quisitive, I think, when they stand around and bark so
threateningly. Natives have it that the lion flees as soon
as he hears them and that even the rhino pays attention
when they cross his path. But when they assert that the
elephant also will stop and alter course because of dogs,
I disbelieve, unless perhaps when old "Ponndalong" is
loath to spoil sport.

As we drew closer to the end of the Debasien Mountains, tracks of elephant became numerous at the river
banks, but so far we had not seen any. As we got into
bush grass country, other game increased and we began
to get eland. They were so fat as to waddle in their gait.
For two cartridges one had the whole safari fed. Blad-
ders of eland fat appeared festooning the camp-gear
donkeys, and in camp the delicious smell of rendering
was wafted about. All hands responded to the good feeding. Cheeks shone and glistened with marrow and would
have appeared rosy, no doubt, had they not been black.
That is one thing I never tired of admiring about the
Wanyamwezi. They reacted almost in an hour to fat
meat. They would half empty a two-gallon bladder of fat
into a cooking pot of gruel and drink it off with palpable
joy, each man absorbing a quart of animal fat. Fruit and
vegetables seemed quite unnecessary to their diet. And
this in a hot—a very hot—climate. Explain it who can!

I knew fat was a necessity at the poles but not on the equator.

When we left our last camp on the Kilimi, we ran through great herds of cow elephant. They were never visible at any great distance from us and yet we suddenly walked into them on quite flat bare plains. I think it was the heat haze plus dust from the herds that caused this poor visibility. But once they came within our view, they rapidly became very clearly set before us from their toe-nails up. Cows, young bulls, and calves filled to bursting point with water from Kilimi stood about like wooden toys from a child's Noah's Ark. In one herd there were certainly several hundred head. But the best I could find in the way of ivory was not good stuff. It looked all right in the distance as it was well washed and gleaming in the sun, but on the scales it figured poorly, being mostly hollow. I killed three in passing, as it were, and with very little disturbance of the herd. Actually, two young elephant continued to play together after I had fired and killed two of the bulls.

I was anxious now to reach the foothills, for in this flat country I could not use my large tripod telescope. This was a fine glass I had got from Dollond; it had a four-inch object glass, a long sunshade, and screw focusing. All it required was an elevation of some sort and it would soon reveal to you many of the secrets of the bush. Anything more fascinating could hardly be imagined than to sit at this glass, slowly sweeping the country and having it all presented like a close-up film. When you suddenly found elephant coming across the field, how exciting to weigh their ivory in imagination! Then you clamped the glass in position and took a look through more normally proportioned eyes and found that the animals must be

eight or ten miles away, knowing too that once you got
down onto the flat it would be extremely difficult to hit
off the spot where you had seen them, even supposing
that they were obliging enough to stay there. Pyjalé was
a perfect expert at this game. He would take a squint
along the outside of the glass to see where it was pointing
and land you there or thereabouts. If you did not pick up
the beasts, you got their tracks.

In one march we reached the foothills. Now we had the
most magnificent going possible—well-used elephant
roads skirting the base of the hills. We spurted along and
soon reached a stream issuing from the old crater. The
safari came in toward sundown. As signs of elephant
were numerous, all unnecessary noise was forbidden and
a quiet and tired safari soon slept by the little brook.

This stream issued from an old crater where I had
had several elephant drives, one of which I have elsewhere described. I hoped to repeat the day when I had
killed eight bulls out of a mixed herd driven out of the
crater by my boys. On that occasion I had occupied a
large ant hill in the middle of the fairway which was
simply littered with these enormous heaps twelve or
fifteen feet high. Also on that occasion I had done some
very bad shooting. Now I thought that much of the bad
shooting was caused by the peculiar movement of the
tangled mass of stampeding animals as they rushed between the gigantic ant hills. I wanted to try to stop the
stampede before it reached the narrow neck of land
which formed the breach in the walls of the crater and allowed the stream to escape to the surrounding plains. I
knew that once the stampeding elephant reached the neck
and were fired at nothing could stop them in their wild
rush for the wide-open places. But if I intercepted them

just before they did so, I thought they might be got into that stupid state they sometimes adopt much to the profit of the hunter. It is something akin to the "ringing" of cattle and is generally due to the absence in their midst of old level-headed beasts of either sex. While I dealt with them thus, my boys were to make their presence known only should the animals try to regain the forest retreats whence they had been driven in the morning. Between us we hoped to bamboozle them completely and make a killing.

All night long there was plenty of encouraging noise of elephant. Much of this was made by cows but there were bound to be bulls here, too. The area contained the only young grass high enough for elephant attention for miles around. Early before sunrise the boys were given various old rifles and a few cartridges. These were the beaters in charge of old Kilassa, himself an elephant hunter of renown. I hoped he would pull out some of the mystery stuff he said he possessed in relation to elephant. I then explained where I was going to be and what I wanted the elephant to do. What he was to do I left entirely to him. They had a long way to go and had to climb the crater slopes so as to reach the other end without disturbing anything on the crater floor. Kilassa was to make a smoke when he commenced the drive.

At sunrise I climbed to a point where most of the floor could be seen and where the big glass would show me whatever it contained. Even with the naked eye it was obvious at once that many elephant were present. The glass showed that most of those still out in the open were cows, but there were two lots of bulls amounting in all to about a dozen. I thought if they could only be moved along my way a few at a time, what a killing there would

be. But how to do it had me beaten. I hoped old Kilassa
would produce the goods. I continued to watch the wonderful scene for perhaps three hours, during which time
the first lot of elephant continued browsing about halfway up the length of the floor. Suddenly my boy said,
"Look!" There was a thin smoke rising from the dark
bush on the right side of the crater about halfway along
and not at the other end as I had expected. I wondered
what this meant and asked the boy. He could not suggest
any explanation. I thought we had better take up position in case Kilassa started anything in our direction.

The grass had looked from our eminence quite short
and nice, but when we got down into it, we found it man-
high and strong. Wherever we looked, there were the
gigantic ant hills showing well above it. Passing rapidly
through the neck, the scene of the former drive, we could
find barely a trace of the slaughter. What was not hidden
by vegetation had been dragged off by hyenas. I suddenly
thought that some of the boys stationed here might be useful in perhaps turning the animals. They would be fairly
safe on the high ant hills. I sent off the boy to bring them
to the spot and told him that he was to stay with them and
to try to turn anything that came their way. Meanwhile
I hastened to find a good high ant hill out in the floor
where I could watch what was going on. I found a beauty
but could not see the elephant we had seen from our
higher perch. There was nothing for it but to wait.

Presently I thought I saw a film of dust rise in the air.
Watching carefully, I could see parts of moving elephant.
They seemed to be heading my way but evidently were
coming quite slowly. Often they stopped and I could not
yet make out whether they were bulls or cows. What was
Kilassa up to, I wondered.

For a longish time nothing happened. Then some heads appeared coming quietly toward me but inclining to my right. Making sure of this bias of the advancing beasts, I ran across to another eminent ant hill where I thought I would be directly in the path of the oncomers. I could now see that the leading files had every appearance of being bulls. I had my .303 with the ten-shot magazine and I quietly drew out the magazine cut-off. What a thrill the sight of the advancing herd gave me. Glancing behind me, I could see some of the boys stretching their necks to see what was happening. Probably they had seen me watching with my glasses and had concluded that something was coming my way.

It was now evident that some very nice bulls indeed were about to offer themselves to me. The question was whether I should open fire as soon as they came within range or whether I should wait until they were right on me and then trust to rapid fire and their surprise to do the trick. At the longer range they might turn back into the crater and alarm the others; then the whole boiling would bear down and pass with the loss of but two or three, just like a pack of grouse over butts. I decided for the shorter range. A rifle report seems harder to locate when very close, and if they hesitated at all, it should mean a few anyway. And if they passed me, the boys in the neck might be able to pause them a bit, giving me another chance provided I was right on their tails.

I let them approach until I stared down into the leader's placid-looking eye. I was on the side of the ant hill about on a level with the very top of their heads. They distinguished nothing. I let fly. Down he went, poleaxed; the others stood, another down! A grand beast strode off sideways. I got him. The others turned and fled up whence they came, I hot on their heels. They stopped, bunched together. I could not get in a shot. They turned in my direction and came like a train. I stopped the first and the others spilled round him at a frightful speed. I was in the eddy of the first beast, as it were. I got in another shot at an angle behind the ear and down he went. Then the rest dissolved in dust toward where my boys were perched. After them again, but as I passed the last beast shot, he seemed too quiet. Giving him one in the ear hole, the welcome signs were produced, and off I raced to where shots and shouts could be heard. What a noise! It ceased and I thought they had broken past. Nothing could stop that headlong flight. I ran up an ant hill and there they were, three of them, bunched together, bewildered, and rather angry.

Darting along, I soon came into range and downed one with my first shot but could do nothing further. The two survivors seemed to be prodding him, roaring and flogging their ears about in a frenzy of fear and anger, with their heads too low for me. I searched for a way to see more of their goings on. As I was trying to get around, I heard a rush coming behind me. Here they came—a whole line of them. Kilassa or our shots had moved the whole place. Their coming made one of the two bulls look too, giving me a chance for a brain shot that I immediately took, but the other was lost as I had to look out for myself now. The whole place seemed alive with elephant and it seemed ages before I found an ant hill. Once there, I could see nothing but fleeing sterns bearing straight for the neck where my boys had been. They were no longer there, but they continued their efforts to turn the stampede from the safety of the higher ground, efforts which resulted only in phenomenal acceleration of the rout. There might be more to come, I thought, and waited on my perch. I felt pretty sure of all the beasts I had shot. Anyhow, I would see any that might have been stunned and left in my haste, for they would be rising now.

For some time all was quiet after this hectic affair. Then I noticed Kilassa's smoke curling up high on the hillside at the end of the flat. Good old fellow, he was going to try to move the woods to me. I wondered if anything would come. If it did, it might be heavy stuff, probably a solitary bull or so. I had better be posted in the neck itself for these. Meanwhile I must have a look at my dead ones.

How I searched for those infernal beasts. The grass was high enough to hide all of them except two that were kneeling. Eventually I found some of them, but two evaded me altogether. I consoled myself with the thought that the boys would find them in the morning, but I did want their tails to add to the others. Finally I could stand it no longer and went straight to the ant hill I had occupied. Search as I would, I could find no empty cartridge cases or signs of human foot. I had lost them! An experienced hunter! I beckoned to the boys sitting on the high ground. My gunbearer came, and in answer to my query as to where the first shooting had taken place, he led me straight there. From this point it was not so difficult to reconstruct the affair and so to find the missing beasts. It was greatly to my relief that I saw them, for until one actually sees them cold, they have a mysterious way of disappearing. Much of this is due to wrong tallying, I think. A head appears over the grass. You fire. The head slithers off sideways from view. Your eye registers a kill on your mind and instantly seeks another target.

That animal may be only partially stunned. You do not
see what the body does. When you seek him, he is not
there.

Returning to our selected post, we laid out the tails.
There were seven. The sun showed three o'clock now,
giving ample time for anything further that might come.
We waited and waited. Something moved away on our
left where the stream passed through fringes of evergreen trees. I caught a glimpse of a low yellow animal,
probably a lion. Then the boy spotted something. He
silently touched my arm and pointed up the hillside. An
enormous elephant was slowly climbing out over the
containing hills. Dirty dog! We felt quite indignant. If
I pursued him, I might miss anything coming along the
flat. But the glasses showed suberb tusks in the old brute's
head, and if I ran out into the open country beyond, got
into the big elephant path, thereby making good time, I
might just intercept him. It required instant decision. Taking a last look up the flat and seeing nothing coming, I
decided to try for the big fellow.

Off we raced, reached the elephant highway, rushed
madly along it, and began to hope we would be in time.
Of course we had nothing to guide us as to where he
would come. As time passed and there was no sign of
him, I began to regret the leaving of the neck. Perhaps at
this very moment elephant were passing through it. Then
we saw him against the sky. What a devastating monster
he looked although yet a good way off. Superb creature,
he was coming straight down toward us. We had but to
wait for him.

How slowly he came though. If we only had him, there
would still be time to regain the neck before dark. Up the
hillside to meet him we went. As we drew near, how won-

derful it seemed to see this mighty six-tonner move quietly and even gracefully down the stony slope, hardly displacing a stone. All the same, he presented a very unusual target as he slithered a bit now and then. His ivory was immense and I hoped he would not damage it in falling on the stones. My eyes by this time were searching out the possible paths to his brain and it seemed that the head-on shot would not do. Sometimes, when he dipped his head, it seemed all right, but it looked risky because he was too much above us. I must get up to his level and deliver the shot from the side. In doing this we dislodged some stones. The suspicious old fellow immediately stopped, up went his head, out went the ears, and up stretched the trunk. What a sight! He was almost sitting down, his two front legs stretched down and out as he braced himself to listen. Slowly his head turned sideways until a little piece of nickel, hot with energy, crashed into his brain. The trunk shot groundwards like a pricked balloon and hung limply swaying. The cocked ears crashed back to a hanging position, flopping feebly about. A great sigh puffed slowly forth, the little eyes continued to blink, and a gigantic shudder filled that massive frame. Otherwise he was exactly as before the shot but now of course stone dead. Thank goodness he had not crashed on his tusks. He might subside yet, but it would be gently, I thought. We could not gather his tail as he was sitting on it, so making certain of the death signs, we left him staring out over the plains he had roamed for perhaps a century.

Descending rapidly to the path, we jogged along as fast as my rather tired legs would allow. As we re-entered the neck we met Kilassa and his band of beaters. They had not seen any big elephant leave the forest and had no knowledge of the one we had just shot. Where he came from remained a mystery. They had quietly moved the bunches of bulls until they joined, and then they had pushed the joint herd in our direction. When I asked the boys how this was done without alarming them, they said Kilassa had made "Dawa" (medicine). That, of course, explained it, to their minds at any rate.

In the forest itself they had heard elephant and seen some big fresh spoor. But they had been much obstructed in their arrangements by vast numbers of buffalo. They had failed to move any of the big fellows from the shelter of the woods. But they had found this!—and one of them produced a piece of ivory broken from a tusk that must have been an astonishing tooth. As it was it weighed, I would guess, about 70 pounds, and it was merely a fragment. It had not weathered much in the fracture and its owner was probably still roaming the forests. I thought that I really must devote a little time to these gloomy fastnesses of the aged and perhaps pick up something out of the ordinary. I had always meant to do this, but the urge to get on toward the unknown had hitherto prevented me.

CHAPTER 6

THE elephant tails were all in. I had tea, a bath, and a sleep. Waking about 11:00 P.M., I had a meal of buck liver and rice and a half bottle of champagne, the last. Another sleep, and dawn found Swédé trying to wake me.

On the way to the forest we passed through the dew-laden grass, luckily much trampled down on the previous day by the various stampedes. But even then one was soon soaked to the skin. The morning air was cold. As the sun topped the hills, we reached the edge of the forest. In the long shadows cast by the trees, the dew still lay thickly. Skirting along the edge, we soon found fresh spoor; it was very evident, appearing dark green where the dew had been brushed off. Most of it was buffalo spoor, but presently we found a fine old bull track leading in the direction we were heading. I had with me this day the ancient Kilassa. Although slow he was a most patient and tireless tracker, much less dashing but far more sure than an ordinary plains native. To assist him in forest work we had a Lumbwa boy, a clever bushman and sharp as a needle. It is remarkable how quick and intelligent Africans are until they reach the age when women call. Then they become stupid and lethargic, in any activity unconnected therewith at any rate.

Kilassa had a prodigious supply of black shag snuff in

a calabash slung round his neck. He stopped now to examine the track and shook out a spoonful of snuff into his hand, proceeding then to cram it up his nose. It never seemed to make him sneeze but it did me at first. When one gets used to it, however, it seemed to me one of the pleasantest ways of taking tobacco. I am always surprised that it has gone out of use with us. Boy Lumbwa wore only a loincloth and was sweet-scented enough, but old Kilassa had on encrusted garments that must have been almost bulletproof. I had often told him that he must wash his clothes, but I never succeeded in getting him to do so. I think he was afraid they would not stand up to a washing; in fact, I doubt very much if he dared to take them off, fearing they would disintegrate before his very eyes. Hence it was not pleasant to follow Kilassa in close stuff.

For some distance the tracks led along the edge of the bush but presently they came to a well-worn path entering the forest. Here there were several more tracks, all leading into the forest and showing the great corrugations of mature bulls. Droppings were cold and oxidized. Probably they had passed in about 2 :00 or 3 :00 A.M. and would now be high up on the mountainside. Once we were well in the bush, paths converged from all angles and tracking appeared to me a nightmare job. The ground was hard and dry and it was rather dark. Yet the two boys held to it somehow through the maze; there was no mistaking the original track when it was occasionally presented deeply imprinted in the softer parts. It was slow work, however, and I began to wonder if I would not have done better spying from the hilltop over the great open country beyond our camp. At the best I would only get one or two of these monsters.

As the sun rose, so did the monkeys and baboons. They had been working the elephant droppings for seeds. From time to time we passed through strong buffalo smell and once or twice we heard them crashing about. It was a continuous climb. At long last Kilassa stopped. Our particular animal had left the path here. Now for really bad going. Slowly we pushed our way through the stuff, bent double most of the time. I glanced at my wart-hog ivory foresight. How white it gleamed. I carried the .275. Through the inextricable tangle we slowly but surely made our way, sometimes losing the track but always finding it again. Boy Lumbwa had the eyes of an owl. There were now signs of His Majesty moving in a more leisurely fashion, and some places were stamped about a good deal. We might hear some sound at any moment now. Of wind there was no apparent sign.

We were all peering at the ground and moving cautiously forward when just in front of Kilassa there was a commotion in the bush. We all stood rooted to the spot, our eyes fixed upon the moving branches. It subsided as suddenly as it arose. Then there reached our ears the wind-breaking of a quiet and unsuspicious elephant. The boys leaned outward to let me pass as I quietly pushed over the safety catch. In a few paces I could make out part of an outline, but what part I could not tell. It was impossible to say where was the head, where the tail. To move to right or left entailed too much noise; to go any nearer than five or six paces was folly. Nothing for it but to watch for some movement that would indicate something.

As I was straining my eyes through a maze of branches, something caught my attention. For a second or two I did not realize that what had moved so queerly was his eye. Once this idea penetrated, I could roughly outline his head. I only waited now to see in what position the head presented itself. Now an ear moved and the root of the movement indicated a half-frontal shot. Therefore I had to place my bullet close to the side of that nasty-looking eye with its mottled brown "white." By leaning a bit, I got a clear path for it and sent it crashing in.

What a deafening noise even a small rifle makes at such a moment and in such surroundings. The next thing I knew was a violent blow from some bough, and as I retreated a step, there emerged the stern of an elephant. Damn! I thought I must have muffed it! The stern came toward me a step or so, and then the whole forepart of its owner swung through the bush toward me, the head low for instant flight through thick stuff, giving me the easiest frontal shot. The forward motion was already so great that as he crashed to earth I had to jump aside to avoid the tusks as they slithered along the ground. Pausing at the ready to see the death quiver, I felt very pleased at getting him so easily after missing him so badly the first time. What nice tusks he had, too.

The boys had wisely retreated some time ago, so now I gave a quiet call for them. I knew they would not be far. Walking round to the stern to get the tail, what should greet me but the head of another recumbent elephant, stone-dead, too. There must have been two, and this was the one I fired at first. His mate had swung round to see him at the shot and had backed nearly into me in doing so. Wasn't old Kilassa pleased? What credit he would get and take for this.

One of the greatest charms of this hunting was the expression of unalloyed joy by all my boys whenever I was successful. In time they came to look upon a killing of five or six in a day as a mere nothing, but now Kilassa's old wrinkled face was one gigantic grin as he saw the two monsters lying quietly there. The tusks were very much discolored with vegetable juices and their colors ranged from black to brown and yellow, only the tips being white.

While we rested and smoked, I wondered how far it would be to the open parts above the forest belt. We must have climbed a long way up in our tracking operations; it could not be very far, we thought, and we might hear or see more elephant. This determined us. For perhaps another hour we climbed, still in forest. We used various game paths just as they suited our direction and came finally to the open country. The forest continued along the stream beds which were now only strips a few yards broad. In a high tree we saw native-made beehives. This was the first sign of humans we came across.

The mountain dwellers on these hills are related to those on Elgon. They are terrified of the Karamojans living around them on the plains, and the Karamojans have an equal dread of penetrating the forest. I had often seen the smoke of their fires showing blue high up the hillside, but I had never come face to face with the actual people. They are said to own a few goats and sheep but no cattle. It is probably owing to this that they can continue to exist so close to the cattle-raiding plainsmen. Kilassa suggested climbing the tree and raiding the honey. This is done by throwing down the hive after cutting the bush ropes holding it in position. Of course, I would not hear of it. Once in my inexperience I had tolerated it, not realizing that the hive would be smashed to bits on the ground. The native owners had never ceased to reproach me for this act every time I

passed through their country, in spite of my having com-
pensated them. It became a sort of standing joke with
them; they would crowd into camp and one would say to
the other, "This is the man who threw his friends' beehives to the ground!" Or some ancient would say, "Have
you crashed any of our honey hives, Longellynyung [red-
man]?"

We were now in grassland. Several hundred feet above
us were precipitous rock walls, remnants of the old crater
walls, I suppose. No sign of the natives could be seen
other than the beehives, but we got a superb view of
Elgon to the south, its base much shrouded in heat haze
but its fourteen thousand-foot crest piercing clearer air.
Away to the west should have appeared the Salisbury
water, but here too the haze was dense. Below us stretched
the crater floor. Judging by the elephant paths, a considerable traffic seemed to have taken place at some time.
I wondered what they got up here. Probably bamboo. We
did not see any, but elephant will go anywhere for the
green shoots. It is to them what asparagus is to us, and
as it is deep-rooted stuff, it taps reserves of moisture that
are not available to more shallowly rooted vegetation.

On our descent through the forest we held to a particularly fine elephant path. Numerous paths converged
upon and joined this one until it was as smooth as a
concrete road and about as hard. It must lead to a salt
lick, we thought.

Much of the charm of this sort of hunting is the constant sense of expectation the white man has. In some
people it becomes a sense of apprehension and must then
be a frightful bore. You may run into anything at any
moment. You may be shot at silently with arrows, poisoned or otherwise. You may fall headlong into a con-

cealed game pit furnished with an upright stake in the bottom. You may run suddenly onto elephant or buffalo. Anything may happen; one feels as if something ought to turn up. But actually nothing happens at all, as a rule. The black man gets no pleasure out of it as he is not expecting any. If he is allowed to, he will carry on a never-ceasing conversation in a normal voice the whole time, causing his white companion agonies of fear that the noise will thereby drive away the monster tusker that the white man's imagination conjures up as lurking round the next bend. I never allowed my boys to talk on these occasions, but the times when this silence led to something turning up could be counted as certainly not more than a score. This was one of them.

The path skirted a break in the ground. Stepping off it, I looked down over a small cliff into a cleared place. In the middle of this space stood a large elephant and by his side there stood a small baby about four feet high. The big one was toying with bits of earth broken from the cliff where many tusk marks showed that this earth contained the much-desired salt. In combination with the earth, salt has the effect of scouring the intestines and removing the thousands of large maggot-like worms infesting them. The large bull appeared to have no ivory on the side presented to us and nothing could be seen of the other one. Kilassa, in answer to my questioning look, whispered, "Mother and calf." This I could not believe. Every characteristic of the bull was there: broad forehead, size, everything indicated bull. We were looking down on them and could not see the genital organs, but I had looked with appraising eye on far too many elephant to mistake cow for bull. Also, I had seen through the telescope once before a large bull with a small calf and no other elephant in sight. Therefore I could not go wrong in shooting this one. Even if he had no ivory, his death might save me from a weary chase on his large footprints some other day, and it would finally settle the question of his sex. It was also an interesting brain shot from an unusual angle: the bullet would have to traverse the hollow between eye and ear and pierce the brain by the shortest route to be found in an elephant's head. I shot and he dropped kneeling. The calf remained by his side, quite unperturbed.

As we gazed down upon the scene, wondering vaguely what to do with the calf, we heard a commotion as of elephant in the surrounding bush. It appeared to be coming in our direction. We awaited events. Presently there appeared to our right a cow elephant's head. Immediately behind this was a throng. The leader stopped as she entered the trampled space; she was very tall and aged, light yellowish gray and wrinkled, and now it appeared she had a very small calf with her. She was not more than ten paces from me and she looked a thoroughly wicked old thing with her ears at the cock and her trunk questing everywhere. She seemed to sense something amiss. The calf that had been with the shot bull now ran to her; she receiving him with lowered head and feeling trunk. Then he moved back to his dead companion. The press behind the cow now filled the space, some of them touching the fallen bull. All showed excitement by throwing their heads about, cocking and shuffling their ears, and squirming about with their trunks. And yet there was not a drop of blood from the wound, so the smell could not have alarmed them. A .275 bullet hole closes up at once in elephant hide and indeed is most difficult to find. It is only to be located by the small ring round it of slightly lighter gray, a circle about the size of a sixpenny piece where the dust has been knocked out. They were obviously not aware of our presence. And yet they were now thoroughly alarmed and roused. They moved uneasily about with short, shrill, trumpet-like shrieks.

I waited to see the much-talked of carrying-away process they are so often credited with, but there was no sign of it. Neither was there any sign of their leaving their dead, so having made sure that there was nothing shootable among them, we quietly withdrew, knowing that in the morning they would all have gone. Shortly after this we reached the open country and arrived in camp without further incident, passing through thousands of gorged vultures digesting the meat of yesterday's bag.

What a scene the camp presented. Everyone was busy drying meat, rendering fat, carrying firewood, or cooking. In a day or two we would reach native settlements where dried meat would be exchangeable for flour and beer. Under a gray pall of smoke the fires looked wondrous home-like in the evening light; the smell, too, to a hungry man, resembled that of some gigantic grill. And there before my large tent were the tusks of yesterday's lot. What beauties! Nothing very big but nothing small. They would all go nicely to the donkey saddles on the morrow while Kilassa got in the ivory from the two beasts up in the forest and I examined the animal Kilassa still maintained would prove to be a cow.

I was rather surprised to find that no natives had come in yet. They should have seen our camp from a great distance. I was anxious to make contact with them for I wanted them to search out elephant for me at the numerous but scattered little watering places frequented by small numbers of large bulls at that time and season.

Before setting out on the morrow, I ran up the nearest hill to a shoulder overlooking the crater floor while a boy brought up the long tripod glass. With naked eye and then with binoculars I searched the country. I did not much expect elephant, but one never knows. There was nothing but buffalo out of the woods. Turning the glass in the other direction, it was another tale. The horizon was almost continuously occupied by elephant. From this height they would be some twenty or twenty-five miles away. Toward midday they would be invisible because of heat haze and, of course, they would be mostly cows and their followers.

Kilassa, some of the tusk gang, and I set off together for the woods. On reaching there we separated, Boy Lumbwa and I to locate the she-bull, and if it proved to have ivory, we were to inform Kilassa of the fact. I was most thankful to have the boy with me. It is always extremely difficult to find dead elephant in woods; at least I found it so. Vultures here do not help, as they cannot be seen. We soon came on the broken bits of branches we had left hanging to indicate our passage, and we came to our game without difficulty. The cow herd had cleared off and with them had gone the calf, I was relieved to see. As we came up to the carcass, there was a short, very curved tusk sticking out that even at a distance proclaimed a bull. Unfortunately the carcass was still in the kneeling position and no part of the sex organs could be seen, so that, unless we could roll the beggar over, Kilassa would still maintain it to be a cow. Although the tusk was undoubtedly that of a bull, it was small, and no one can really be sure unless its size is obviously too large for any cow to carry. Our efforts were ridiculously abortive to move the stiffened mass, so sending the boy to bring the ax gang, I prepared to deflate the now blown-up body by simply puncturing it, hoping that this would make it topple over one way or the other. Nothing sounds easier or is really easier to accomplish than this bursting of a taut belly. But it is not so easy to escape the resulting high-pressure spray of evil-smelling matter. The moment the knife point enters, there is a most alarmingly shrill note combined with a spray of liquid, the smell of which is so awful as to make even a strong man—a white one, at any rate—violently sick. So, having been at this game before, I went gingerly about it.

Cutting a long stick, I lopped off all but one of the branches. This one I left sufficiently long to take the knife handle lashed to it with tough under-bark thong. Then, standing on the far side I tried to pierce the gut low down, jumping for my life as it went home. It takes a prodigious whack to do it and the knife must be keen in the point. Once pierced, it is not long before the pressure escapes, but in this case the body remained as before. I tried a push but nothing budged. Now it was necessary to enlarge the hole so that much of the intestines could escape. By the time this was done, I was in a most unsanitary state and the result as before. However there was still hope that a long lever on one of the legs might shift the body. With great toil I felled a young tree with my knife and tried prizing a forefoot straight. What a hope!

Then appeared the gang, Kilassa smiling when he saw what I had been trying. The tusks they brought were good stuff, one pair looking like 80 pounds apiece or thereabout. Now we tried a combined heave with two of us on the lever and at last succeeded in moving him over, assisted by the slope of the ground. And there for all to behold was the indubitable male sign.

Why this full-grown male should have had a calf with him is a question difficult to answer. What I surmise in the case is that they were brothers, at any rate out of the same mother. At other times I have seen the same strange sight—a massive male with a tiny companion obviously still at the milk stage. Elephant seem to have a well-developed sense of family ties. A cow may often be seen with a following of offspring ranging from a tiny calf up by stages to a full-statured son overtopping mother by a foot or so. I have seen such a one playfully pretend to take a suck at mother's breast without her paying the least attention to the gesture. I imagine therefore that when one meets a large bull with a calf it is a case of two of the boys having a little outing on their own.

CHAPTER 7

MOVING off next day, we struck along the base of the hills through a lovely park-like country—lush grass everywhere with isolated tamarind trees covered with fruit. The ivory began to make a nice little show on the donkeys, but the porters had nothing much to carry so far.

Toward midday we saw the first sign of natives—away in the offing great herds of cattle browsing peacefully with a good number of attendant guards. Soon we came to the temporary grass huts that serve for the dry-season sojourn. The moment the rains came, all this nomadic population would trek back to their permanent habitations in the north. Not a soul came near us nor did they try to avoid us. They appeared quite indifferent to our presence as our long strung-out safari wound slowly along. In their hearts they were longing to come about us, but this is one of their reticences. It is bad form to show curiosity.

Water was obtainable in a dry sandy river bed from shallow holes in the sand, and we pitched our camp round a magnificent tamarind tree whose dense shade would be most welcome. It was only when tents were pitched, donkey boma made, and all was shipshape that a few tall black spearmen strolled casually into camp. There they leaned on their spears surveying the scene with expressionless faces. None of us paid the least attention to them. This little byplay was the invariable custom and any attempt at premature recognition of each other would have been treated with scorn by the participants. At long last the headman of our safari would commence the lengthy greeting customary on these occasions. He would say, "Good day, Bakora!" They would answer, "Good day, strangers!" "Good day, Karamojo!" from the headman. "Good day, travelers!" from the natives. "Good day, cattle!" "Good day, Mani-Mani!" "Good day, the road!" Good day everything and anything!

This having been satisfactorily got through by our headman, who finally ran short of anything more to greet, he would approach with the natives and I would go through a similar performance. Then I would ask for Pyjalé. I would soon see him, they said. Meanwhile quite a crowd had collected round our herd of heifers. These were the most interesting part of the whole show to the native mind, with the ivory a bad second. Presently two or three of the elders approached with girls behind them carrying large pots of beer, a calabash of honey, and gourds of sour milk. The thing to do then was to invite them to drink the beer they had brought. This was a grand idea. It made them very much more genial to think how generous and hospitable they had been to Longellynyung and it did not deprive them of the beer. For me it brought about contact that would otherwise have been more difficult and, of course, it produced a soothing effect on the partakers. Only on my poor thirsty porters had it a somewhat souring effect. They dearly loved beer, and when supplies at all allowed of it, I would share out a pot or two for them.

It is great stuff this beer. The whole grain is in it and

it has the consistency of very rough gruel. When three days gone in fermentation, it is potent stuff and has the advantage that you do not want any food after it for a long time. Also, if you exceed a bit, you stay there for quite a long time. Altogether a most refreshing, wholesome, thirst-quenching, and hunger-satisfying beverage, quite unjustly despised by white men to their own detriment. In its place they take gin, which certainly elevates you a little more quickly perhaps but which most surely lets you down again much more rapidly than the wholegrain stuff. I know that after a long safari my porters would arrive at Mumias tired and thin, and in a week one would not recognize these fat, shiny, laughing fellows for the same men. And nothing but beer would pass their lips.

Presently across the plain I saw approaching a familiar figure, its stature about that of an ordinary man and unusual on that account in this race of tall men. This surely must be Nopak, named so by us for an extremely lucrative foray he had conducted to the country of that name on a former safari when the little man had led me to some truly grand old elephant in a perfect setting of open short-grass plain, greatly to his and to our benefit. What a regular little dandy he appeared as he came swaying along with his tiny feet and hands and the rather lighter color of his naked body all polished up with butter, rendering him conspicuous among his towering black companions.

How beautifully they keep their bodies these people. If they must have something round their windpipes—and even they have not quite escaped this extraordinary human urge to constrict this vitally important part of their anatomy—they have a few rounds of iron ring kept in a highly burnished state. And very well it looks against their dark hides. Moreover, it seems to offer some resistance to a spear thrust.

Nopak had news for us. Elephant were about. Pyjalé too would be here soon. He had married again; so had Nopak. Another child had been born to him. His cattle were well. His wives were well by implication. No one asks that question. If any of them are unwell, it is stated as an extraordinary fact. Nopak had had a dust up with Kumamma. He had a friend over there whom he was in the habit of visiting by night. A lady friend, needless to say. It was only fifty miles to her village, and once you reached it, the precincts of the village were sanctuary. He had often been there before without trouble. But this time the Kumamma bloods had lain for him, patiently waiting for him to leave the village. A friend of his girl's had warned her of their design. She had sneaked him out in the dark. He had got a start before they discovered. But they had chased him hard and were in sight at dawn. There were eight of them. He threw away his sandals and regretted it when he saw some of his own people. They now outnumbered the Kumamma and pursued them. The Karamojans were fresher than the Kumamma. He was not in the fight, as they outstripped him. Two of the enemy were caught and killed. Would he go again? "Yes, Bwana," he said! Why did he not bring his girl away with him, I asked. "She is married!" was the simple answer to that. But would her husband not kill her, I asked. "He may," said Nopak with a careless laugh.

That evening Pyjalé came in. He brought a fat sheep. His eyes were much bloodshot; he had been beer drinking. I took him to look at the cattle; that is what pleases

these people best. I showed him the little heifers that
were to be given as reward for elephant news. I showed
him also the ones I wanted to trade for donkeys and
sheep. I did not particularly want sheep and goats, but
it is seldom possible for one purchaser to produce more
than three donkeys of suitable type for packing, and the
price of fifty goats and sheep is made up on the basis of
ten goats and sheep to one donkey. Hence I would receive
two or three donkeys and twenty or thirty sheep for a
cow. Pyjalé was to tell the natives who wished to trade
to bring along their stock.

What about a little scurry out to Nopak, I asked Pyjalé. He said some lads were already on their way there
to see if any elephant were using the springs at the big
hill. Nopak is an isolated group of hills perhaps a thousand feet high in the midst of vast plains. Its hazy peaks
could be seen from our camp. I had never yet visited it
without getting a few good bulls and I had never seen
a cow elephant there.

There was to be a big dance that night. The moon was
right, food plentiful, safety assured from raids by our
presence, and it would be a great affair. The evenings in
such surroundings always had a touch of poetry. The
garishness of the day gave place to a softer light and the
smoke from many fires hung in filmy clouds in the still
air. Great herds of cattle crawled slowly to their protecting shelters, full, sleek, and satisfied. Masses of cattle
grouped about the encampments while busy women
milked them, calves disputing with them for the precious
stuff. Lines of girls and women swayed gently along from
well to camp, the leather skirts of the married women
swinging in rhythm to their gait, while over the air came
the musical sound of innumerable wooden bells. What a

happy and peaceful scene! One could hardly believe that these same people had quite recently annihilated completely a safari of three hundred guns and eight hundred men and women in the twinkle of an eye.

Pyjalé had taken part in this affair. He was quite open about it, describing it as if it were a very ordinary occurrence. He said they had agreed to crowd about the safari's camp as if on curiosity or trading bent. Every spearman was to wear the spearpoint guards and to mark his man. The traders were quite unsuspicious; unloaded guns were lying about on mats and no guard of any sort was kept. At the signal every Karamojan drew off his spear's shield and plunged the razor-sharp head straight into the nearest trader. In a very few seconds it must have been over without a shot being fired. Then, of course, the boys and women would be run down and speared to death.

These spear-fighters have a highly developed technique. There is no clumsy driving in with great force of the spear, getting it entangled and bent among ribs or blunted on spines. There is merely a lightning-like dart from the elbow and wrist. The weight of the ten foot shaft is ample for penetration; in fact, it enters so easily that almost instantly the pluck-back has to begin. The great art is not so much to get it in—that comes automatically—but to get it out unharmed. It must be remembered that the iron is extremely soft, being smelted from the native ore and undergoing no sort of tempering process. The blades are beaten out quite thin and flat, leaving a small rib down the middle. The neck is quite slender and bends easily into any shape but has the advantage of being easily straightened again.

"But why did you not keep the women?" I asked Pyjalé.

"Oh, well, they smelt so."

"How do you mean, they smelt?"

"Had they not clothes?" Pyjalé queried.

I roared with laughter, pointing to my listening boys who were of course clothed. They looked very sourly at the naked and unabashed Pyjalé, and Suliemani muttered what sounded like "mwanaharam" (child of a bastard begotten in the bush). Pyjalé and his people always had the greatest contempt for clothing. He used to have great arguments with the boys about it. They would maintain that no naked person could be other than a pagan, which of course left Pyjalé quite cold. What did he know or care about religions? He said that people who wore clothes did so to hide something of which they were ashamed. He said his people had nothing to hide. With that he would seize upon and pretend to undress one of the boys who would struggle frantically, just as if he really had something to conceal, while the onlookers laughed heartily.

They certainly are a stoic lot. I offered Pyjalé a sleeping mat and a blanket as the nights were chill. He would have none of it. Scraping a smooth spot with the butt of a spear he would lie down by the camp fire, fix his narrow wooden pillow to his neck, and slumber as a dead man. But touch any part of his naked body, even toward dawn when it is really cold, and you would feel a strong burning heat.

Pyjalé said I ought to go to the dance that night. It started with the moon and would last all night till sunrise. I let it get well under way and then strolled over with Pyjalé.

There were perhaps seven or eight hundred people assembled there on a smooth piece of ground as hard as concrete. They formed a circle, women on one side, men on the other. Into the circle would bound some fellow whose turn it was. He would have on all he was capable of. If he had killed someone in battle or otherwise, he would have a blood red ostrich feather built up three or four feet high stuck in a socket formed by his wig of hair and cow dung mixed with clay. All round this central piece would be stuck other white and black ostrich feathers. This headdress added considerably to the fellow's naturally great stature. His body would be greased and he glinted in the moonlight. His iron collar shone like silver. The iron chain, burnished also, glittered round his middle as he reared high in the air, his spears in one hand, his shield in the other, his arms forming in the air his own private cattlemark, such as one horn up and one down. The horns are broken from the living skull, then tied in the required position with splints and allowed to grow thus.

As he springs up and down he chants his own doings in battle and foray. He cannot overdo this too much as everyone knows exactly what he has done in that line, but as every one of his mates does likewise, his tale becomes a pretty marvelous one in time. After each verse the chorus comes in. Three hundred hefty bucks rear in unison with him and all come flat-footed to earth at exactly the same moment. Six hundred hide sandals hit the deck with one stupendous whack. It is fantastic and can be heard for miles.

Meanwhile, the women waggle modestly away in opposition to the imposing array of masculinity until some girl or even married woman, quite carried away by the bravery and beauty of the chanting male, throws herself with great abandon into the circle and shows in pantomime what favors she would all too readily bestow upon him. With a swoop from the stratosphere, as it were, he meets these coy advances with some decorum, during the first few hours of the dance at any rate. Later on, however, when they are well worked up, the scene is indescribable.

Some of the native customs applied to these dances are rather bizarre. Should any male person be overcome by dance fever and overstep the bounds of strict propriety in a visible and palpable manner, there is at once a terrific outcry from the women and everyone rushes to seize sticks, branches, or lumps of wood. With these they flog and flog the erstwhile joybird until they tire of it and resume the dance. Curiously, the victim does nothing to defend himself nor does he attempt to run away. With stoic patience he takes his medicine.

With the early morning came the natives with donkeys to trade. They would never bring the right number and always brought their worst stock. It was an interminable business. Back they would have to go with their duds and return with others slightly better. This would happen five or six times, so that when a boy came in saying he had found elephant, I was glad to hand the trading over to the headman and prepare for the bush. Our preparations were quite quickly completed as the boys knew the ropes by this time. Off we raced in the hot afternoon air, everyone rather full of beans from the rest in camp and the lashings of milk. At a steady trot we followed our guide while behind came the porters with their light loads at just as steady a gait. There was no path, of course, and everyone had to wear sandals. We headed straight for the blue peaks that looked so far away. We hoped to reach them that night and wade in next morning.

Nightfall found us still a long way from them but

also a long way from home. Now we had to go slower, for which I at any rate was thankful. With the cool night air we kept up a good five miles an hour, the guide and Pyjalé slipping effortlessly along ahead of us. The plains around us sank to amber tints, then to purple, turning soon to silver in the wake of the rising moon. African night life was all about us. Zebra herds charged past with thundering hoofs, invisible to northern eyes except when they crossed the line of silver. Giraffe could sometimes be caught faintly against the light of the horizon. Hyenas howled; a distant lion shook the air. On we pressed, the far-off massif gradually creeping up the sky.

About midnight we reached one of the springs on Nopak. Here we found our guide's two companions. Camp bed was set up, mats unrolled, and a small fire started. Tea was soon made and drunk, forked sticks placed by the bedside for the rifle, and now we would hear what the game watchers had to say.

Just then in came some natives, men and women. This was very annoying. I had told Pyjalé to warn them not to follow until the next day. So they were heartily cursed and told they would be flogged if they made a sound. The two watchers reported that from the top of the hill they had seen eight large bulls in one bunch and three other single bulls. Asked what sort of stuff they carried, they showed on their spears how far out of the head they estimated the ivory projected, about seven feet. It invariably projected that distance and just as invariably shrunk to three or four feet by the time they had been killed. However, things looked good for the morrow, and we all contentedly dozed off.

By dawn we were ready for the hunt. Everyone was

told to remain in camp until sent for, the boy in charge being carefully instructed to keep back the horde of free-meat seekers that would presently come. The two watchers, Pyjalé, and I set off on a well-used elephant path that skirted the hill. We had scarcely gone three miles when we saw a single bull some distance below and ahead of us away down the plain. He was standing in some thin short thorn bush and looked gigantic in the clear morning light. The grass had been burned off and he showed us his full stature from toenails up. Quite motionless, he looked like some massive chunk of rock rolled from the mountaintop. There was as yet no wind as Pyjalé and I strode smartly toward him, thinking to waste no time over the business.

He was a sitter: meat for nothing. At about forty yards I sat down and fired from the knees. It is seldom indeed that one can do this; almost always there is intervening vegetation of some sort. He went down without a sound, never knowing what had struck him. What better death could anyone have? When we reached him, the death quiver satisfied us that there was no necessity for the spear thrust to the heart Pyjalé so enjoyed giving. Cutting off the tail and spanning a tooth with my hands, I mentally calculated it at about 70 pounds. We beat it back to the path where we rejoined the watchers and hurried on.

The path now traversed a neck of flat land running between two of the hills. In the middle of this was a line of dark evergreen trees denoting water underneath. As we came to this line, a lion and lioness struck off toward the hills, their bellies almost touching the ground, their backs bent like bows with the weight of them. We then passed their kill, an eland carcass now infested with vultures. We began to ascend one of the spurs. As we topped the rise, first one elephant then another and another came into view until there were five of them in line-ahead and, joy of joys, advancing along toward us on the very path we stood upon. What a sight! Grass completely burned off. Five of the very largest bull elephant even now within shot! Where now are those miserable men who contend that no elephant yet born scales more than twelve feet in height? Would they go now and apply their piffling scales to those mighty sides? What manner of thing is it to measure them when shrunk in death? I say they looked ten times twelve feet in height. Anyhow, a foot is a paltry thing with which to measure such craft.

Meanwhile, they spread themselves along the top of a gentle rise seventy or eighty yards across a dip in the ground, walking like cats on cushioned feet, looking strangely agile in spite of their bulk. They seemed to fill the landscape. Somehow there was something menacing too in that steady advance. We felt very small and rather lonely, Pyjalé and I, the others by now on tree-shelter bent. There was neither stick nor stone about us. My thoughts flew to the rifle and the deadly little brain piercers it contained. I looked at Pyjalé: complete serenity there.

It would not do to fire when they were still in the hollow ground; they would be lost to view too quickly over the rise behind them should they go that way. I determined to let them advance until they reached the spot where we stood. The leader would, I thought, catch our taint when he reached the spot, stand for an instant, and should then receive my fire. We accordingly removed ourselves along the rise so as to have a broadside view.

All went well except that the leader got our taint while still some considerable distance from where we had stood. He stopped and fell to the shot. The others bunched, but two heads gave fleeting chance shots, one after the other, and both went down. The two survivors then turned tail, one of them receiving but rejecting a hasty oblique shot from behind as he turned. He staggered sideways and I thought I would get another chance, but no, he pulled himself together and set off after his diminishing companion, his stern tucked under and *ventre-a-terre.* Phew! This meant a long chase.

Hastily assuring ourselves of the completeness of our work on the third, we waved up the watching guides and gave them hasty instructions how to deal with the meat cutters. They were to fetch my boys and such natives as had collected at the spring. No one was to cut meat until all the heads had been cleared of skin and flesh to let the axmen get to work. Then Pyjalé and I took up the chase. And what a dance those two brutes led us. Hour after hour in a sweltering heat we followed at a fearful pace. The tracks led us in a westerly direction and filled us with despair, for fifty or sixty miles in that drection lay great sheets of water and swamps with high grass that would still be unburned. Pyjalé kept up a killing pace.

We were now leaving the burned-up country and entering treeless plains of tall grass over which a man could just see. It was dry but not yet dry enough to burn. It had cutting edges and myriads of hair-like spines. These penetrated a civilized hide and irritated its possessor to distraction. How I wished I had not fired that fatal, or rather unfatal, shot. The worst of a chase like this is that, if you follow it diligently, you soon find yourself too far in the soup to turn back. The return journey is always terribly wearisome, but if one has not killed, it becomes a nightmare not to be contemplated. The only thing is to buoy oneself up with the thought of camping by the slain. The sooner the kill the sooner the rest so urgently required by white skins in a country meant for black skins.

When the sun was blazing straight into my face, we entered greener grass. We hoped we were approaching water. By this time my saliva was powder and my sweat dust to be brushed off in a little cloud. Pyjalé was all right except that his eyes were clouded and mottled. He said water was near. We came to it and found that our infernal fugitives had drunk and bathed. Refreshed, they had then continued their flight. But we too were now refreshed and the pace became once more both steady and hot.

The sun was now sinking into the horizon haze, and if we did not soon come up with our quarry, it would be a night out for nothing, always a nasty affair as we carried no food. In this long grass there was slim hope of buck meat. The only possible hope was a water buck, a strongish-smelling brute at the best of times.

Suddenly Pyjalé stopped in his tracks. My heart gave a bound of joy. I thought he saw elephant. It wasn't elephant but the next best thing to it—some white cow-birds circling about in the air. These birds follow elephant for the flies, bugs, and other insects that are disturbed by them in their way through the bush. Of course it might mean buffalo, but much more probably elephant. We could not see as the grass was now become greener and more upstanding. Underfoot the ground was all cut up by elephant tracks made in the rainy season. We fairly flew toward the birds whither our fugitives' tracks led us. On turning a corner of the grassy lane, we came on a sight that effectually cured me of fatigue: a mass of bull elephant in a water hole, splashing, squirting themselves, and generally having a good time, while cowbirds rose or lighted on their ridge-like backs, leaving their mark in streaks of white on the dull gray hides. Not a moment to be lost; we must into them.

One bull stood outside the ring on hard ground. I killed him instantly. At the shot the whole muddied mob came splashing toward him. I shot the largest of three heads in the front of the spray-shrouded melee. Each time I could see a head clearly, I fired; at such a distance one could not miss. Three succeeded in getting away, we close to their heels. Reaching harder ground and shorter grass, they suddenly stopped. I was leading and, I suppose, more intent on my feet than I should have been, for I nearly bumped into a motionless stern. Running a few paces back from them, I saw them turn deliberately toward us, forming into line abreast as they did so. Then they launched themselves straight toward us. So close were they that I had only time to shoot one as they came, one as they passed, and into the third I got an oblique body shot just abaft the end rib. He of course carried on, but feeling pretty sure of him I took a hasty look for the all-important death signs on the other two before pursuing the sole survivor. We soon came up with him and found him unmistakably stricken. With a bullet in his brain he too crashed to earth.

Back now to the mud bath with all haste; some might be still alive. I did not know how many there were down. Reaching it, we stood by the bull I had first shot. There in the water lay four great carcasses quite dead. Some of the ivory looked fine. The teeth of the bull on the bank were really first-rate; they might make porters' loads. Now to gather the tails. I raced off for those in the distance while Pyjalé secured those in the mud hole. Rejoining Pyjalé, we laid out the tally. Eight grand bulls, making with the four of the morning a total for the day of twelve.

By this time a reaction had set in. I was devilishly tired. I could do nothing toward making camp for the night. Pyjalé had to do everything. He sought out a dry place away back from the water with its mosquitoes. He cut grass, got some firewood from somewhere, and finally cut some gland meat from the head of one of the bag. After a little rest I felt better and tried a smoke. I noticed my hands were covered with dry blood; I really must wash them. Taking my rifle, as always, I staggered wearily down to the water hole for a last drink and a wash. I drank and had just commenced to wash when, looking up at some sound heard subconsciously, what should there be but a large bull elephant approaching the water hole. It was now dusk but shooting was still possible. Seizing the rifle, I stood quickly before him and with a single frontal shot brought him suddenly down. Well! I was amazed! Was this day never to end? What stupendous luck!

CHAPTER 8

AFTER a hectic fight with mosquitoes and sleeplessness, neither bothering Pyjalé to any extent, we were on the return trail early the next morning. What a distance it now seemed without the excitement of the hunt. We found a huge camp of natives and all the meat of the three bulls roasting on platforms. The ivory had been taken to camp. Here everything looked very snug and home-like. The ivory had been washed and gladdened the eye. Certainly two of the tusks would require porters.

It now became necessary to dispose of this ivory because of the further lot down in the swamp country. We could either bury it or send it back to the base camp. The latter was decided on. But now there were not sufficient carriers for the rest of the stuff. So it was decided to wait for the return of the boys from the base who were to bring an addition to our strength. We had not yet worked out this country and might possibly get more. Meanwhile there had gathered a mob of natives numbering three or four hundred who were still meatless. We would now go with them and have the carcasses in the swamp prepared for the axmen.

After rest and refreshment we set off. The ivory had long since gone to the base. As we were sufficiently numerous to make a well-defined path, the returning porters would easily find us. By the evening we were once more on the scene. How different it now seemed with a decent camp and, above all, with a mosquito net.

It must be understood that none of the native women who accompanied us had ever penetrated so far into the dangerous no-man's land where we now were. It was the common stamping ground of the Karamojans and their enemies, the Kumamma. The whole mob of girls, boys, young women, and men kept close to our heels the whole time as we were their only safety. At night some people might have found their proximity embarrassing. They crowded close around my tent, the smoke of their fires, the reek of the roasting meat, to say nothing of their strong body smells, combining to render sleep almost impossible.

The reader will be rather tired of this endless killing, no doubt, and will welcome the news that only outstanding incidents in the doings of the safari during its fourteen months in the bush will henceforward be recorded. In pursuance of this merciful resolve I will only say that we enjoyed remarkable hunting in the country round Nopak. It lasted twenty days and the total bag of elephant reached twenty-seven head, all good stuff. Of one outstanding day I feel I must write.

We had been joined by Longellynyung, my blood brother. He came with his usual enormous retinue. No less than three of his youngest wives were along to look after his comforts. He was a sort of Father Christmas, producing eggs, chickens, beer in quantities, of course, and the little white millet so much prized in that country. With him too he had his usual platoon of sons. These he scattered to the four winds in search of elephant while he and I remained at our ease in camp where we had a grass shelter built for our comfort. It was a most intriguing party for, according to native custom, if the old boy died I would succeed to his wealth, including his wives. This made these young ladies extremely coy and attentive and the old boy seemed to make a point of keeping them against the collar.

With such a number of searchers it was not long before elephant were found. "Brother" kept assuring me that he and I would show them, meaning that he, as my guide and friend, would far outdo any other searcher for elephant. The moment news came in, we left the camp's delights and followed our new guides. In answer to my questions the old boy kept telling me that I need not worry, that he had the matter in hand, and that all would be well. But everything was not all right, at first anyhow. For no sooner had we arrived upon the scene than the little herd of seven bull elephant betook itself to instant flight without any apparent cause. Hour after hour they showed us nothing but their sterns, and had anyone said that before evening I would have killed them all I would simply have laughed at him. Go as I would I could not do better than preserve station four hundred yards behind them. Never once did they stop or turn out of their straight course. They gave no chance whatever, and I began to think that Longellynyung's medicine was not going to act after all.

Finally the old boy, who seemed as fresh as a daisy, halted me with upraised arm. Rapidly he spoke to the following. Off they sprang right and left into the tall grass, almost immediately being lost to sight but for a glimpse now and then of a streaking black head. The old boy and I continued the stern chase. By this time our quarry was almost hull down in the sea of grass, only the tops of their backs showing slightly. Longellynyung now strode ahead of me, his spindly shanks bearing him along at a surprising speed, his knubbly feet and strong ankles spurning the pathway of forward sloping grass, while his huge peruke swung from side to side. What a little lion he was! The boys had now totally disappeared. Suddenly the fugitives stopped. Trunks reared up, testing the wind. Longellynyung stood aside and we both spurted toward the elephant. The boys were holding them up in front. How I wished I was within shot of them.

Then it began! The whole team was rushing down on us at a rate that bore them up against the sky as they rapidly foreshortened. Soon they were within shot and got it. This new attack paused them. Down they went! Spears were now flying from behind and from the flanks. Longellynyung closed and let fly a spear that caught one in the trunk, sticking there as I downed him. By this time everyone was shouting, blood was at fever heat, and I don't think I have many times shot so badly. One bullet caught a tusk during the mix-up and it was lucky that no one got shot. Boys were drunk with fight and appeared right in among the terrified animals. Longellynyung too was there prodding away with his spear. Never have I seen bull elephant so completely bewildered. In one determined effort the sole upstanding brute rushed headlong past me with a mob of infuriated natives at his stern. He too fell to a well-placed shot in the brain, his stern resembling a gigantic pincushion.

Longellynyung came shouting toward me. He was tremendously worked up, the sweat pouring over his bloodshot eyes, his lips drawn taut over his glistening teeth, a horribly bent and bloody spear in his hand. Then he threw himself into his particular dance attitude and began to chant, leaping in the air. All his numerous progeny joined in. Obviously this was all in my honor and it rather embarrassed me. White men are so inadequate on these occasions. I was just wondering what to do about it when one of the recumbent bulls commenced to rear himself aloft, having been only stunned by a bullet passing close to the brain. This broke up the happy party as I had to attend to the patient. Two of the others also were suspiciously quiet so I stood by them while Longellynyung straightened his spear and then gave each a lightning stroke to the heart. Seven great fellows lay within the space of a tennis lawn.

Longellynyung was extremely proud of this day. He was, I think, a little jealous of Pyjalé's constant association with me. Pyjalé knew this and had not come with us. When I wished to reward Longellynyung with a cow, he would not take it. "Are not all your cows mine and are not all mine yours?" he asked. "When I want cows and when you want cows I will ask and you will ask!" Only he was much more loquacious than that, being in beer at the moment. His list of things we might require of each other was alarmingly extensive, ranging from cows and rifles, the greatest of possessions, to chickens and wives, the least. Longellynyung and I hunted together thereafter with varying success, and I became very much attached to the old man as indeed I think he did to me. Thank goodness he never asked me for a rifle.

This old man had such a reputation for prowess in fighting that his word was law. In this he was quite alone among leading Karamojans. But, unlike other Africans, supreme power had not changed his simple kindly nature. When sober he was quite modest—one would almost say shy—and even when in his cups he was merely boisterous.

A quite lovable man was Longellynyung. Like everything else, we shared the same name. After the brotherhood ceremony I had taken his, but as I was quite incapable of pronouncing it, let alone of spelling it, he and I continued to use the comparatively easily negotiated Longellynyung. As the country was now pretty well worked out and due for a rest, it was decided to head for the permanent villages of Bukora, sending a runner to fetch the main safari to meet us there. Under the orders of Longellynyung the natives agreed to assist in the carrying of the ivory to their villages, a task they do not relish and would not have tackled unless told to do so by him. They considered that porterage was women's work and most of our tusks finally did arrive woman-borne, although they set out from camp on the heads or shoulders of men. And very much better porters did the women prove to be. In fact, in almost any trial of stamina or hard work the women were streets ahead of the men. In this race of decidedly tall men the women were rather squat and broad.

Working gradually north, nothing much of moment occurred. By this time we were on extremely friendly terms with the natives. Our stock roamed the countryside unmolested. People had ceased to bathe in our drinking pools since the beatings had finally convinced them that we really did not like it. Whilst in Bukora, Pyjalé and I had a discussion on women. I pointed out to him a certain damsel, remarking that she was certainly a good-looking girl. He did not think so. I asked him to point out one that he liked. There was not one there that satisfied his taste, but he said if I would go with him he would show me a real beauty. We went to a village some miles from camp where he asked for someone to bring us a drink.

Presently there came to us a maid bearing a calabash of water on her head and carrying a half-gourd drinking cup in her hand. She stopped in front of where we sat on native stools, sank onto her knees, and gave us a drink. When she had gone, Pyjalé looked at me for comment. I could not believe that this podgy, squat, coarse-hipped girl was his beauty and said, "That is not the girl?" But it was. What a blessing it is that tastes so differ.

Of course these fellows are not looking for charm and allure, delicacy and grace. What they want is a bearer of strong children, a worker—and docility. From Pyjalé's point of view this girl may have represented these virtues far more strongly than the lighter-colored, finely shaped creature whom I had thought so good-looking. With his intimate knowledge of his people's histories and family records I have no doubt that his choice was much the wiser of the two from his point of view.

Seeing some boys with very fresh-looking red ostrich feathers mounted on their heads and new tattoo marks still festering on their bodies, I asked Pyjalé what had happened. He said they had raided and killed some Kumamma girls. Now I had already tried to stop this disgusting practice, but I resolved to have one more go at the problem although I felt it was pretty hopeless. I asked Pyjalé to call a gathering of the old men as I wished to talk to them before I left their country for the north, and I asked him to arrange with his women for a good supply of beer. Beer requires three days for its preparation, and on the fourth day a long string of women came wending their way to our camp. By midday a black mass of humanity had gathered in the shade of a huge fig tree in camp.

The elders were invited onto a large groundsheet.

Tobacco and beer were served. For some time conversation was general. Then one distinguished-looking old fellow with a small bald head and a prodigious peruke hanging from the back of it got upon his feet and made a long speech: the usual flowery stuff about their being my children, how I would beat them if they were naughty, how I would feed them if they were hungry, and so on. He was followed by others much on the same lines; the beer and 'baccy were doing their work.

Finally I got Longellynyung to tell them what I wanted to say. And he put some right good stuff into it, shouting in his gruffest voice from deep within his mighty chest. How he glared at them and what a great deep chorus of assent he got whenever he stopped to be prompted. He was perfectly willing to say anything, and he said it as if he associated it with himself, as no doubt he did. The gist of what I told them was that I was delighted with my visit to their country. Their elephant were good, their women fair, their beer excellent, but—here I paused and so did Longellynyung, glaring more ferociously than ever at the now silent throng—there was one thing wrong: the killing of women. That really must cease. There followed a long, involved lecture on the habits of white men and their horror of killing women. Did they not see that even cow elephant were sacred to the white man? If they spotted the difference in ivory borne by the two sexes, they did not let on. I ended on a note of threat as to what would happen to anyone killing a woman, leaving it vague and mysterious. Longellynyung ended by saying that he was with me in all I said, unblushingly presenting to his audience the tattoo marks for women-murder occupying every available inch of his extensive torso.

But, they replied, if we do not kill the enemy's women,

they, the enemy, will increase and overwhelm us. Would I also stop the Kumamma from killing their women was another awkward question. What could I answer?

We were off on the morrow to the Jiwé country and hoped that on our return we should not hear of any more killing. The meeting broke up in great good feeling, but as to stopping woman-murder I had my doubts. I really think the only way to have done so would have been to hang a few of the killers to conspicuous trees. That would have aroused a strong feeling of injustice but it might have prevailed. Certainly it would have done so had it been equally applied to the Kumamma.

Between Bukora and Jiwé there is a stretch of country that is quite waterless in the dry season. In order to make the traverse as easy as possible it would be necessary to load up the waterbags and to set off in the afternoon. First of all, however, it would be essential to leave the ivory in a safe place. Now in dealing with natives there is only one way in which to insure the safety of any form of wealth and that is to leave it in their charge. If one strives to hide it away secretly, they will surely discover it and purloin it. If one leaves one's own people in charge of it, they will try to outwit the guardians; if these are inadequate, they will even attack them. But if it is publicly put in charge of a village, it is safe. Therefore all our tusks were cut from their hide saddles and carried to Nopak's village. Here a large pit was dug in the floor of one of his huts. Into this each tusk was neatly stowed, a short piece of stick being handed to Nopak for each tusk entered, this being their sort of bookkeeping. Finally the earth was trampled solid and the superfluous earth carried forth. Then the women watered the fresh earth, smeared it with cow dung, and smoothed it all over.

Barring a successful raid by an enemy tribe, the "mal" was now as safe as in a bank, perhaps safer.

Now disembarrassed of our nicely growing load of ivory, there were plenty of vacant saddles for water carrying. That evening presented a busy scene, boys preparing the bags and filling them while I attended personally to the sewing-in of the bottlenecks of some that were broken. As each bag was filled, two porters staggered back to camp with it slung on a pole. The losses from these bags is considerable of course. The canvas I used was ordinary heavy, green, rotproof groundsheet. The green copper treating of it seemed to have little or no effect on our hardy stomachs. Personally, I avoided water from the very new ones, but I never saw any hesitation on the part of the other members of the safari to partake thereof. All that night the bags would stand in camp full to the brim, thus affording an opportunity to spot the badly leaking ones. Then just before saddling-up time the boys would finally top them all up.

Leaving the Bukora country about 3 :00 P.M., we were soon in the no-man's zone between Bukora and Jiwé. My "brother," Longellynyung, accompanied us for part of the way. He had arrived at the last moment with a beer-laden bevy and had tried to persuade me to stay another day to drink the beer. I stood over the row of pots and called up a boy from each tent group, motioning him to take away one pot. In a twinkling all were gone, and in another twinkling all were back, empty. The headman blew his whistle. With a rush and a roar every man seized his load and formed in line as the safari song broke forth. We were off.

Longellynyung was supremely lit up and exuding beer at every pore. I tried to dissuade him from going with us, thinking the old man might come to harm in the fighting zone on his return. But on my hinting at this, he sprang to his feet, seized his spears, and gave us a little exhibition of spear fighting with the utmost fury and spirit. The vigor he put into it was astonishing, but had his reputation not been what it was, it might have appeared just a little bit ridiculous; apart though from such nasty white-man thoughts, it was quite easy to imagine the impression his unique appearance would make upon anyone against whom these berserk caperings might be directed. His bloodshot eyes glowed even in the strong afternoon sunlight, the corrugations of his sweat-covered skin reflected a thousand pinpoint lights, his spindly knock-kneed shanks blurred with the rapidity of their movement, while the most terrifying sounds from that prodigious and grotesque torso tore the air. His mere appearance would clear any arena of opposition or, as they so aptly describe it themselves, turn the enemy bones to water. Longellynyung returned to us with rather a sheepish little smile, as if to say, "Pardon this show of feeling." He was much relieved by it nevertheless. Then we took up the trail.

Our way led us past a rock massif. On our reaching about halfway along it, evening was drawing in. This massif was much frequented by lion and great numbers of hyenas. They found protection from the sun in its rocky caves and holes, therefrom issuing in all directions to the surrounding game-infested plains. Of water at this season there was none within forty miles. Unless they traversed that distance, they had to satisfy their thirst upon the blood of their victims, a sure incentive to keen hunting. As we reached an embrasure in the rocky range upon the flat bottom of which we proposed to camp, a lion

appeared crossing our front, trotting briskly away toward
the darkening plains. Our line of advance threatened to
cut his so he broke into an empty-belly lope, so different
from a full-belly slouch. I was carrying the .256 game-
getter, and giving him a fair lead, I sped a bullet upon its
way. My timing in those days was of an automatic ac-
curacy. The conscious section of mind allowed the rifle a
certain amount of lead, but the instant the projectile was
started upon its way the unconscious section took charge,
corrected the rifle, almost invariably in a forward direction, and a clean and thrilling kill would result. This applied to fast-traveling elephant and to fast-flying birds.
It was only when the subconscious aimer was not functioning that a miss would result. So in this case my lion
broke together, turned one somersault, and lay prone.

Suddenly on my left there was a growl. Here a lioness
found herself obliged to alter course and seemed dis-
satisfied about it. Beyond her there appeared other
furtive forms on the move but now almost indistinguish-
able from the background in the fast-gathering gloom. I
settled the lady's troubles and ran rapidly back to try to
intercept some of the others. It was rather treeless country and there would be difficulty in making a decent thorn
boma for the cattle. Since we did not want a stampede
in dry country, it was imperative to shoot up as many of
these carnivora as possible. They had, however, crossed
our path heading for the far places, and I caught but a
fleeting glimpse of a disappearing stern. I succeeded in
introducing a nicely judged bullet which, but for the
above-mentioned subconscious aimer, would have passed
harmlessly beneath the bounding rascal. The correction in
this case was high, with the result that he was caught on

the spine just abaft the shoulders while on the rise. I judged that the others would not trouble us that night, and so it proved.

On these occasions and in the dry season no tents would be pitched. They were quite unnecessary as our start would be early, somewhere around 2 :00 A.M. in order to cover as much ground as possible before the sun came overhead. Just enough of a boma would be formed to keep the cattle together and then firewood would be collected. Then the water bags would be unloaded while a shallow pit was dug. Over this a good groundsheet would be placed and the bags emptied into the resulting bath. Now the headman would measure out to each person sufficient water for drinking and cooking. I personally would have enough for a wash-down. The cows in milk also would have a good drink, but of course the poor donkeys, bearers of the water, got nothing. Each of them could have emptied a whole bag. It was never found practicable to carry enough for all hands. Still, the human element was thus kept in splendid health and fitness. Upon these two essentials—health and fitness—happiness and content follow hard, in Africa at any rate, and that is the secret of success in Safari-land.

Longellynyung had left us long before we reached camp, and now my only permanent native attendant was Pyjalé. While still in Bukora, his native country, I had debated with myself whether to let him choose his reward—cattle—and to let him have them at the beginning of the safari instead of at the end, thereby saving the beasts from their wearisome trudgings through the northern bushlands. But I had decided that it would be trying a primitive man rather too much to call thus upon a sense of long-sustained loyalty more reasonably to be expected from a more highly developed race, and I had not mentioned the matter to him. But finding him rather wistfully gazing at a very nice-looking cherry-roan heifer, I asked him if he would like to mark it for himself. Taking no chances, he rapidly and deftly squeezed her teats, looked in her mouth, and then answered, "Yes, Baba!" Confound him, he always called me Baba. I always consoled myself with the thought that he was merely trying to say Bwana.

These safaris, lasting the better part of a year away from his home, must have been very trying for Pyjalé. He was a young man with nice wives of his own, cattle and sheep and goats. His home life must have been extremely pleasant. His life with us, on the other hand, must have appeared to him little short of penance. He did not form friendships or adopt any of our customs such as the wearing of clothes. Nor did he fraternize with any of the tribes through which we passed although they spoke a common language generally. There he remained in our midst, a perfectly serene, self-contained, and most efficient human unit devotedly serving a most alien and, to his way of thinking, outrageous if not ridiculous personage of strange habits, stranger appearance, and strangest demeanor for a period of time that to his reckoning must have appeared interminable. He showed at all times a great physical self-control, as when he once spent seventy-two hours without water in his search for elephant. He also showed great mental quality in dealing with ten or eleven months of supreme boredom. He could only acquire cattle by this service whereas the other boys were under money-spell and could look forward to a prospect of delights to be attained by money-power. Pyjalé at the best might acquire yet another wife.

On the morrow we should enter another country: that of the Jiwé, a small but very compact, rich, and independent tribe speaking the Karamojo dialect but the deadly enemy of all its neighbors.

CHAPTER 9

ON OUR way into Jiwé next morning we met some
Jiwans running down zebra. They had speared several and had captured a foal which they brought along for
sale. I told them to bring it to camp and I would pay for
it then. I regretted this afterwards as it never arrived.
They had tired of the task, I suspect, and had speared it.
They said it had escaped.

They were always a rather overbearing lot these
Jiwans. They were truculent and proud, conceited and
rich. I often thought that it might come to a showdown
with them. Should it do so, I meant to rush one of their
stockaded villages when full of cattle and give them a
good dusting from that stronghold. I could easily have
made a large part of their quite open country untenable
to them. There was not a vestige of cover anywhere.

The cause of their swelled heads was a recent stunning
victory over a neighboring tribe. This tribe had acquired
a large number of trade guns in exchange for ivory from
traders on the Nile some three hundred and fifty miles
west of this. Trusting more to the reputation given to
these new weapons by the vendors thereof than to any
prowess in their use they themselves had acquired, this
tribe foolishly attacked a hard-bitten lot of doughty
Jiwan cattle raiders with the result that not one of them
lived to tell the tale. After the first discharge of their

muzzle-loading pieces, which made, it is true, a devastating noise but little else, they found themselves helpless before the horde of spearmen who soon settled the business. Thereafter the Jiwans thought that firearms merely made a big noise and a nasty smell, and their remarks about them were to that effect. Besides being the possessors of all these captured guns, they had brought off some finely executed raids on their softer Nile-valley dwelling neighbors, thereby adding still more to their armament and wealth. But it was chiefly at their dances that they used this alien armament, and then only to produce noise. It was amusing to see them at it. At first the powder charges would be very small, then they would grow larger and larger as the dance fever mounted. Each gunner would outrival the other to see who could produce the greatest noise, smoke, and fire, each discharge being greeted with a yell of consternation and applause from the girls and children. As each man discharged his piece into the air, he shoved it bodily away from him, thus trying to escape the heavy recoil of the overloaded weapon. Finally the competition would end in some frightful burst, a hand blown off or eyes blinded, and the dance would once more resume its more usual course. It will thus be seen that they were in a very nasty state of ignorance of the potentialities of the modern firearm, and I felt that it might save much trouble and possibly bloodshed if I demonstrated to them in some way they could understand the deadly power we carried with us in such small and innocent-looking brass cases.

With this worthy object in view I waited until such time as a goodly audience had collected. It was evening and everyone was awake but idle. The herds were slowly trailing toward the milking places where smudge fires lent long lazy smoke streaks to the peaceful scene. I strolled leisurely over to our cattle herd with a long slim .22 Colt concealed at my waist. As I came within certain range of one of our bullocks, I deliberately but swiftly shot him in the brain and swiftly concealed the weapon again. The bullock fell together at the shot. Every eye was on the affair amidst a deep silence. Hardly had the report been heard. At once a Mussulman donkey man rushed up and cut the animal's throat. I continued my stroll. Coming to where my Masai cattle herders stood leaning on their spears, I told them to start up a game we had often played, only warning them to make it easy. The game consisted of their throwing up lime fruit one after the other as fast as they could while the rifle or pistol tried to catch each one at the top of its rise. When hit, the fruit sends out a fine cloud of spray, and it is surprising how easy it is. Now, of course, there were only pebbles instead of limes. These also are quite good, flying into bits if solidly hit or whirring away into space when only grazed. From a distance it is surprising how effective such a show can be. To be really impressive it must be carried through with speed.

So now the two boys began collecting pebbles of a suitable size. At a signal they began throwing up a succession of absurdly easy ones. I now produced from under my armpit a Mauser pistol already loaded with butt attached, and in my left hand I held a spare clip of ten cartridges. The boys kept up a continuous stream of pebbles and I kept up as continuous a stream of bullets, and many from the two streams intercepted each other. As the little affair progressed, I moved round so that the broken pieces zinged about the camp and the heads of the audience. What with the whines and crashes and vicious reports and flashes, it was quite an impressive little show, I thought. Of course it produced no outward or visible impression on the Jiwans, but I rather gathered from Pyjalé's grin that the oracle was working. I thought too that their swagger and bounce were rather less than usual after this episode.

That evening there was another little demonstration, this time of the pain-killing effect of native beer. One of the tusk carriers had thought himself invited by some Jiwans to drink beer in their village. In return for a piece of giraffe hide they had filled him to the brim. Then he became quite masterful and determined to stay where he found himself. They could not void him from the village and came to camp with a tale of his doings. Indeed, we could hear him, now that our attention was drawn to it. He was supremely drunk and singing lustily. I am no great disciplinarian either for myself or for others, much preferring the softer road of *laissez faire*. But there was one thing to be avoided in our contact with these wild unruly tribes: no man of mine should be caught in intrigue with native women. There lies the sure road to bloodshed. Once started, there was no telling where it would stop. Therefore there was one rule governing our safari life that might not be broken: no man should enter a native village or hut even when invited to do so by the owners.

Obviously this boy had broken the law and must pay for it publicly. The headman hurried off with a posse to retrieve the criminal. He arrived, carried bodily by the posse, and still singing. Before all beholders he laid himself flat upon the ground and took a fearful beating without a quiver in his song. He seemed not to feel anything and had to be told when the beating was over.

Then he sprang lightly up, charged with bare legs and feet straight into the mass of wicked-looking thorn bush forming the cattle boma, and proceeded to dance up and down on the myriad-pointed fence. In order to save the latter from complete obliteration, he had to be forcibly removed and lashed to a tree where he continued to bawl throughout the night except for short but welcome breaks when he was being soused with water by the camp guards to assist nature in the sobering-up process. It may, and does, take a lot of beer to make black men drunk, but it also takes a lot of time to make them sober again. Their extraordinary powers of retention lead them to heights of intoxication unknown to our less efficient organisms. It is to this capacity for absorbing such colossal amounts of alcohol that the remarkable runnings-amuck one hears of must be due. All the ordinary emotions such as fear of pain or death are completely in abeyance. This explains much of the death-defying valiance shown by black men during the war in East Africa, where repeated charges on their part withered away to machine-gun fire, leaving swaths of corpses both of the human and of the "Pangani Whisky" variety.

This country of Jiwé lay high among abrupt outcrops of rock. At night it was cold and windy. There were no mosquitoes, but there were myriads of flies as might be expected with such numbers of cattle about. I was sitting close to the roaring camp fire that evening when Pyjalé came and squatted down. He had been out to friends for the evening, milk-taking, and had got news of some interesting elephant country away toward the west. His informant had promised to come in the morning. I was glad to hear this news. I had never had a really good hunt in this part. Previous hunts had hitherto resulted in contact with cow-herd stuff, young bulls, and the like. At the same time it was pretty obvious that good dry-season territory must lie away off toward the Nile valley. The grass I knew to be big, but daily now one could see the smoke of distant fires.

Pyjalé's friend turned up in the morning and it was soon arranged for a raid into the big grass and swamp country. They all said I should not take my milk cows with me as there were bad flies down there. Instead I took a Dutch cheese which had shrunk to the size of a cricket ball and the consistency of superfine concrete during its racking voyage of many months in a chop box. Indeed, in the dividing of it I regretted I had no hacksaw in my otherwise fairly extensive tool outfit. It certainly was sustaining and contained within its cast-iron walls more nutriment to the cubic centimeter than any other form of nourishment known to me. How arises it that none of the nomadic tribes, living almost exclusively on their cattle as they do, have lit upon this excellent device for keeping their fluid victuals not only in a sanitary state but also in a most transportable one? Not even among the Arabs is it known, and I have been told that there is not even a name for it in that language.

Leaving everything in charge of the headman and under the responsibility of the elders of the village where lay our camp, we took to the bush and had soon left behind us all trace of Jiwé and its independent tribesmen, not without, I confess, a little anxiety for the safari. I still had the .303 ten-shot rifle and wondered if I should require it this time. It is always exciting breaking new ground, but on this occasion my hopes had not been raised by native accounts of great numbers of elephant. Indeed, the Jiwans generally show an indifference to, and a detachment from, the subject of elephant not found among the poorer and less war-like tribes such as the Bukora, Dodinga, and Dabossa. And here it may be remarked that tribal interest in hunting methods for acquiring wealth varies in inverse ratio to fighting abilities. The pleasures of the chase that appeal so strongly to the waning powers of the more advanced races find but scant space in the make-up of primitive man.

Much of the country still remained unburned. Wherever this was so we came in contact with that obnoxious growth, spear grass. And now it was at its most poisonous stage. Fully ripe, every seed was armed and prepared to penetrate whatever might touch it. In the case of smooth hairless hide, such as that of these unclothed Africans, it could not prevail and was perforce obliged to tumble harmlessly to the ground. But in my and my clothed boy's case it surely fulfilled its destiny of overcoming all opposition and penetrating to unusual places, in the process exasperating its host to a pitch of frenzy. The seeds would thereby be transported to some spot beyond the reach of more normal wind-borne traffic. How such stuff can ever be digested seems beyond the ambition of even the ostrich. And yet elephant may sometimes be seen forging slowly through it sweeping great trunkfuls into their mouths just as if they wielded gigantic scythes.

Small animals seemed exceeding scarce in this spear grass country, for which I could not blame them. They would surely have found an area of young herbage somewhere else. What we did see were great numbers of marabou storks fishing for the last of the water-living creatures in the rapidly shrinking pools still left in the hollows.

All that day we continued our march to the west. It was now much hotter, and as we looked backward from the top of a rise, the distant Jiwé country presented itself as quite a high plateau. The hills we had seen from camp began now to approach us, and the columns of smoke were all about us. So far we had seen no actual elephant although their tracks were about. On this foray we had no following of natives as we had had in Bukora. They knew, I suppose, that we were bound for a far land; anyhow, the Jiwans were so rich in cattle and sheep as to be indifferent to other sources of meat supply. This in a way made it easier to deal with the inhabitants of the country whose presence was evidenced by the numerous fires around us. During a halt I asked Pyjalé if he knew the people and country we were entering. He said he was without knowledge of them, only he had always heard that their country held great elephant renowned for heavy ivory. I then asked about our guide. He, Pyjalé said, was not a real Jiwan at all but had been taken on a raid while still small. He had been well treated by his captors and had been used often as intermediary in their periodical palavers.

That night we camped at the foot of a rocky hill jutting abruptly from the surrounding plain. We were now in the land of visible standing water instead of the sand-buried wells of the uplands. Consequently, we had a strong infestation of mosquitoes to plague us. Near by lay a small and poor village with a scanty herd of goats its only evidence of wealth. On our arrival our guide had gone straight to it and he presently brought some of the villagers to camp. They looked a bit scared, I thought, so it was briefly explained that we were come to hunt elephant and that, if they showed us their whereabouts, they would profit. I thereupon gave out various and sundry beads and iron chain and asked for a guide to show the way up the hill at the foot of which our camp lay. We could easily have found our way up it ourselves, of course, but we were all still strangers to each other, and natives utilize holes and caves in rocks not only to hide in themselves but also to hide away their secret stores of honey grain and so forth, and I thought it might alarm the women to see strangers about their treasures.

There was still daylight left and I was anxious to get up there with the big telescope to have a look around. The natives reported elephant everywhere and I might spot something. Hurrying up a very narrow path, we soon reached the summit and were rewarded with a splendid view of the surrounding country. More and larger sheets of free water lay westwards like silver reflecting the sky. But the atmosphere was so charged with smoke from the grass fires as to make the telescope quite useless. In the early morning it would be clearer and I felt confident we should see something.

During our descent I was halted by a cry from one of the boys in camp. All I could make out clearly was the word "chui" (leopard). The boy was pointing toward a spot beneath me so I gathered that one of those village-haunting leopard was about somewhere below. These animals are completely familiar with the presence of human beings and take heavy toll of the goat and sheep flocks, occasionally even attacking old people and children. Moving cautiously downwards, which I came afterwards to regard as a mistake, I failed to see or hear anything. Had I moved along clattering over the stones as before, I would not have aroused the suspicions of the cunning rascal as undoubtedly I did. For the sight of a pale-colored creature snooping around in a stealthy way might have aroused the attention, if not the apprehensions, of a much less guilty conscience than that of a goat-eating leopard. Be that as it may, the fact remains that I never caught a glimpse of the brute that evening. Moreover, I had an intense sensation of being under quite close inspection while waiting in a small clearing where I thought I might catch a glimpse of my opponent. Conviction of this came when I met a woman carrying water to the village. She pointed silently to the path that lay before us, and darting along it, I actually heard a cheeky cough between me and the village, and only a few yards ahead of me. Try as I would, however, he or she came off victor in this game of hide and seek.

On inquiring of our guide, I was told the villagers quite often saw the beast and that it drank openly at the pool. In answer to a query as to why the men of the village did not destroy the beast he gravely said he did not know. This meant that superstition imbued the animal with the possession of someone's departed spirit. I resolved that, if I stayed on the following day, I would have another try at making contact with the ghostly rascal. That night arrangements were made to visit the reputed haunts of elephant in the neighborhood while runners were sent to warn the king of this tribe of our arrival.

Early next morning we were astir and sunup found all our little packs ready for the bush. While waiting the arrival of our guides, I suddenly remembered the leopard. Raising the glasses I always carried slung around me, I began to search the rocky face. It was in deep shadow with the sunrise beyond and I could make nothing out except a mighty lot of dust on the glass. On the point of taking them down to clean them, who should walk into the center of the field but my opponent of the previous evening. He was crossing the very skyline away from us. I looked at the boys' faces around me. No one had spotted anything and I began to wonder if I had not imagined it. Quickly I asked which way our course lay and was relieved to hear that we would circle the hill on our way to, I suspected, the sheets of swamp water I had seen from the hilltop on the previous evening. Thus there would be a chance of viewing the other side of the hill under the brilliant light of the rising sun.

Pushing along as smartly as possible, we soon came in view of the opposite hillside. Giving it a rapid glance, nothing was revealed, but on a more intense scrutiny a yellowish gray line was discovered crowning a slanting slab of rock just under the skyline. At one end of this line there appeared a small round protuberance that could be nothing but the leopard's raised head intently regarding the halted line of humans below. That yellow line of body was scarcely three inches above the almost intersecting edge of the slab. What chance for a bullet? The slightest fault in elevation and a clean miss was bound to result. The head gave the only chance, so the head it must be. To delay longer would be certain to arouse a conviction in his mind that he had been spotted. Looking with the naked eye over the intervening air space between him and me and imagining the curve the bullet would be required to make—an invaluable aid to marksmanship—I reluctantly came to the conclusion that nothing but a hair-raising fluke could bring it off. However, I was prepared for this and was about to press off one very hot shot from the long Gibbs .256 when my target kindly stood up broadside-on and took it just right, drooping together and plunging over the edge of the slab out of sight.

Now it was quite impossible to measure the air line of this shot and almost impossible to measure the distance over the ground, so broken was it once the rocky hillside was reached. But judging by the fact that the flat measured two hundred paces to the rocks and comparing the sight of this stretch with the sight of what remained uphill, that bullet must have traversed at the least three hundred yards on its way to the vital spot which was at most the area of a saucer. The elevation line indicated by the preliminary sight over the barrel had an indication factor corresponding to that used in shooting a giraffe in the heart at five hundred yards' range. One can dimly imagine the effect on the native mind hitherto unacquainted with the potentialities of modern firearms. I now rushed up the hillside to make sure of the end of the affair. I also told the boy with the large telescope to follow. On reaching the spot, there he lay, a large old dog leopard with dirty teeth and very long claws betokening a long life. The shot had got him exactly upon the vital spot, blowing out his tiny heart in a spray of blood and tissue. Wisdom ever prevails with gathering years and I do not say now that it was not a fluke.

It soon was evident that we stood in the presence of elephant. The large glass showed a wonderful display of ivory. There were tusks there of such portly proportions as only dreams reveal to overheated imaginations. There must have been several tons of ivory standing around that landscape. Hurriedly counting eighteen bull elephant within reachable distance and hoping we would not be stopped by the considerable sheets of water shown by our aerial view, we rapidly descended to our waiting safari, dragging our bag with us. Reaching the plain once more, all hands fell to skinning, a job tedious enough at the best of times. Leaving instructions and a guide with the skinners, off we set hard in the direction of the swamps.

Looking down from the distant hilltop upon the land surrounding our game, it had had the appearance of a well-kept lawn. But now as we approached, it was evident that things were not to be quite so easy as one might have thought. The lawns turned out to be anything but well kept and, in fact, to possess no points of resemblance whatsoever. Possibly lawns that had undergone a continuous series of full-power earthquakes might have borne a faint resemblance to the tangled and chaotic devastation that now met the eye. Everywhere uprooted trees and stripped stark stumps littered the landscape. Wherever water had lain, it had been churned into a maze of pot holes filled with liquid mud incapable of further settlement. Huge piles of dung lent their sweet aroma to a sweltering atmosphere oscillating with the buzz of myriads of gigantic elephant flies. Solitarily pathetic, there stood about tattered bunches and mud-bedaubed remnants of what had once been a standing field of tall grass.

From the foregoing description the reader will perhaps surmise that here something out of the ordinary had taken place. It had. All the elephant in creation not only must have passed by here but must have paused fully determined that their presence should leave its mark. Never in all my wanderings had I seen such desecration of a countryside. And it was all made by big stuff. Not an immature track could be seen.

CHAPTER 10

NOW the going became perfectly damnable. On we hurried, stumbling into pot holes up to the waist in mud, our feet slithering about as if on glassy ice. Soon we were covered from head to heel with the stuff. One simply could not keep it from the rifle. Luckily these military-type bolt actions take a lot to make them jam. I could not help smiling as I thought of the large caliber double-barreled ordnance affected by some hunters and the nice state it would soon have reached in these conditions. One smear from a blade of grass on those so-accurately fitting action-faces and either the monstrous thing would not close or if it closed would not open. I congratulated myself on having climbed that fence some good while back.

I carried the .275 and had the .303 in reserve. I thought that, if chance should show me a large bunch of bulls together, I would use the .303. But the .303 as turned out by the factory is not a smooth-working action in conditions such as these. There is not the polished finish on the rubbing faces that there is on the Mauser or the Mannlicher-Schönauer, and I had not the supreme confidence in it that I had in the Mauser in spite of having spent hours trying to smooth out the tool marks on the action body. I therefore decided to stick to the old stand-by. It was the .275's day out.

Once I fell headlong into a mudbath. Everything was soused. Really, the poor little rifle must have some attention. The barrel passed no light through the bore. There was nothing for it but to wash it out with a further supply of liquid mud. Finally I got a pull-through to traverse it and on we went. As the cartridges in my belt dried in the sun, I kept shaking the belt to work away the mud. Presently we came to a sort of lagoon sixty or seventy yards broad and running away on either hand out of sight. All the tracks seemed to cross it. Our guide plunged in, the water coming higher and higher until he was swimming. We followed and presently all assembled on the opposite bank. Pyjalé produced his knife and, bending down, began to insert the blade flatways between the leeches and my skin. We were covered with them.

The grass was still green here and fire could not have prevailed. In parts where the grass had escaped the trampling hordes, it stood quite high. Judging by the numbers of leeches in the deeper water, we ought to find our game at least on terra firma. The leeches get into the elephant's trunk and, according to native tales, the sufferer beats his trunk against a tree until it is so bruised and swollen that the end closes up and he suffocates. I can hardly believe this as I don't see why the elephant should not breathe through his mouth.

At last we sighted a bull and made straight for him. I was disappointed. I could not see any others. Pyjalé and I walked straight up to him and halted about thirty yards from him while I gave a last glance at the rifle. As I opened the action to look at the bore, there was a great splash on our right, and very close, too, followed by unmistakable elephant noises. With a glance and a grin at Pyjalé we stole rapidly toward a line of tall grass, pushed through it, and discovered a very pretty party indeed: one, two, four, six, eight large and jolly fellows all wallowing in the soup below us, some great mud-covered tusks among them, too.

Obviously the fellow on the bank had the first call on our services and he seemed well content with what he got. At any rate, he made no protest. At the shot the whole tureen hove itself up bodily, torrents of liquid mud cascading between the gigantic bodies. As if rigidly held together fore and aft, the phalanx moved solidly in the direction of their fallen comrade, rising like some monstrous creation of pre-history or Hollywood as it reached the edge of the bath.

We met them and we downed five of them just as fast as one could fire. They were sitters of a sort rare even in those days. Three got away simply because I had to reload. If I had only had the ten-shot rifle, I believe I would have had the lot. Pyjalé darted his spear into two of them who seemed inclined to protest while I rushed after the dripping sterns now fast diminishing as they careered headlong from the horrid scene.

How these beggars did travel! They were so gun-shy I felt that surely gunners in the Nile country must have been pumping wisdom from trade guns into them. A killing pace even on good solid ground, it was simply murderous here. I was soon done in and had to slacken speed. Pyjalé spurted away as if on a tar track with superb long easy strides, barefooted now as sandals are a washout when wet. How I envied him as I came panting along, eyes blinded with sweat-borne mud, cursing myself for a short-winded fool of a white man, vowing to myself that I would stain this pale hide of mine to the color of theirs. Blue, crimson, and yellow would do it. Then I came on Pyjalé gazing intently ahead as he leaned easily on his spear. Without a word or gesture from him I too looked ahead. What a sight!

Our three fugitives had been swallowed up in a concourse that looked like no other sight I had hitherto seen. They literally dwarfed the landscape. I had not the time to count them but I should say there were about two hundred. At first glance I thought they were cows. But no! Every animal of that vast herd was bull, and moreover good bull. The value of that display was almost incalculable. How on earth should we set about them was the question of the moment. They were slightly alarmed by the hurried arrival of our fugitives and were drawn together in a solid mass ready for the slightest signal to start a movement that might soon develop into a stampede. It would seem so inadequate to kill only one or two out of that vast array. Yet I felt that they were on their toes, ready at the slightest sound to pivot unanimously and present a united backside view to us. It was exasperating, for had they been scattered all over the country we could have dealt with them in piecemeal fashion.

"When in doubt, barge in" is never bad advice, so I motioned rapidly to Pyjalé to go round one way and I would go the other, and he grasped the idea without further palaver. I chose what I thought would be their line of flight by the direction in which the majority seemed to point and made a detour sufficiently wide to remain invisible to them. Reaching a point where I thought they might pass, I began rapidly to close in on them. I could not see Pyjalé, but he must have seen me, for when I signaled with my arm "let 'em come," he startled the rearmost with a jab in the backside that hurled the foremost ranks right upon me. My eyes and whole attention became fixed upon only those animals in the dense rank that bore straight toward me. My life depended on killing those particular animals. They were not wicked brutes seeking to destroy me; they were simply enormous animals in rapid, panic-stricken flight. If I failed to kill the opposite number, I was in danger of being run down and trodden underfoot. The others that my eyes were obscurely aware of passed harmlessly by; they could not stop or turn even if they wished to because of the press from behind, so the whole thing resolved itself into shooting a gap in the line for myself. Of course, if I had run away, I really would have been in danger. I have seen boys killed that way, caught up and passed over in a twinkling, and yet a black can run like a streak at such times.

I don't know what possessed these elephants. They should not have been so nervous away out here. But they came in a frenzied hurry that gave me but three chances in front and two behind, the two latter being raking lung shots through the short rib. Of the three in front two were dead, and Pyjalé tackled the other while I pursued the herd. There was no hope of catching them, of course, but my two wounded were off with them. A frightful bellow arrested me and brought me back as hard as I could go. Visions of Pyjalé spitted on a tusk or torn in two gave speed to my legs. Soon the sight of an extremely angry elephant loomed up. But where was Pyjalé? Then he joined me from the side with that funny little shy grin he had. "Where's your spear?" I asked, still hurrying toward the roars and bellows. He pointed to the angry bull. I saw what remained of Pyjalé's spear sticking in his trunk which he was thrashing about in an alarming way while blood and foam fell in showers all around. I immediately soothed the poor fellow and asked Pyjalé why the devil he had only one spear with him. Usually he carried two. I could not catch what he said as he began to dig his precious piece of ironmongery out of the trunk in which it seemed to be tied in several knots.

While this disentangling went on, I had a smoke, consoling myself with the thought that if those two fugitives had their bullets right they would be our meat anyhow, and if they had not, then nothing I could now do would help them. When Pyjalé had retrieved his spearhead, for of course the wooden shaft had gone long ago, he proceeded to bend it straight over his knee. I swear no iron known to us would have come through the process without breaking. Then we took up the trail of the retreat at an orderly pace.

Although the country was flat, one could not see far, and yet the grass appeared to be trodden almost flat in all directions. In spite of this we abruptly came on two elephant standing motionless forty paces or so to one side of the track of the retreating herd. One of these was obviously stricken, with drooping trunk and ears and motionless tail. But the other looked quite fresh and perky, listening with cocked ears and searching trunk. Without making any mistake I sent him hurtling earthwards with a bullet to the brain. At the report there was hardly a move from the wounded one. He, too, fell poleaxed to the ground. But where was the other wounded one? I could swear that fresh-looking customer had never felt a bullet. He must be further on.

It was now getting late so we did not stop to take the tails but hurried on. Pyjalé seemed to think but little of it and pursued his way with his usual placidity. Nothing happened and we finally gave it up. On the way back, however, I felt strongly that the wounded beast was about. As we passed a small thin tree that might possibly just bear Pyjalé's weight, I motioned him up it. As he peered around, I had the never-failing thrill of watching his face. No emotion ever showed itself on his graven mask; only a dwelling on one point of the horizon indicated his having seen something. Down he came without a word and led off through the grass, to present to my satisfied eyes a fallen bull stone-dead.

Rapidly cutting off his tail and glancing at his tusks, we beat it back to collect the other tails on our way to camp, wherever that might be, fairly well satisfied with twelve head of good stuff and yet wondering if by some different method we might not have done better. Certainly with the ten-shot .303 I think I would have had the whole of the bathing lot, but in that case we might not have found the big lot.

That driving onto the rifle of panicky elephant? That does not seem to bring very satisfactory results. They come too fast or the rifle is too slow. Something is wrong. Fifty head come and forty-five go! Poor scheme that! With such thoughts to help pass the now weary miles to camp we strode along, one of us at any rate dog-tired. As night closed in on us, we arrived at the place of the drive and were gratified to see the three corpses still there. When one has not the time to verify brain-shot elephant, one always imagines that some of them may have been only grazed and that nothing but a mark upon the ground where they had fallen would be found. When this did happen, it never failed to infuriate me. It seemed a low-down trick to play.

Our tally of tails was now six. We felt pretty certain

of the six at the bath. It was there we hoped to find camp. So off we set in the dark, Pyjalé of course leading the way. In traveling by night through unfamiliar country, it is a tremendous relief to have a native to break trail. The only drawback is their speed. I do not think that they see any better by night than do we, but they feel the ground with their naked feet. This applies to a totally dark night when there is no moon. A shod man cannot do this and is either stepping on air or meeting the ground too soon and stubbing his toe.

After what seemed an interminable time, we were overjoyed to see the lights of camp reflected on clouds of smoke. Instead of our modest little camp of three or four fires it soon became evident that a great assembly had gathered. And so it proved. What in the distance we had thought to be our camp was a meat-roasting by the natives. Incredibly diligent on such occasions, they already had every carcass stripped, heads severed, stripped, and detusked, and all the mass of meat cheerily simmering on great platforms over the fire. Away from the reek and noise we found our little camp looking snug and home-like in the firelight. A very large fat native wearing a felt hat and a coat of sorts sat smoking on a stool with a few attendants about him. He had brought beer and I had one magnificent pull at the stuff. It was maize beer and pretty potent on a very empty stomach. Swédé told me he was the king of the country. I was much too tired to attend to him then. Later on, however, I sent for him. He came with numerous presents and had great tales to tell of the doings on the Nile. He said he frequently visited it to sell ivory to the Greek traders. He said that they paid twenty "ginea"—Egyptian pounds or guineas—for one hundred pounds of good ivory, and that with the "gineas" he could buy powder, percussion caps, lead, cloth, and the usual trade goods.

A girl belonging to his retinue wore a remarkably fine ornament. I asked if I might see it. As the stone was threaded into her hair, she knelt down so that I might the better see it. It was oblong and about an inch and a half long. One third at each end was of a rich chocolate brown and a pure white porcelain band ran across the middle. It appeared to be made from one stone and was beautifully polished and very hard. Nothing so genuine or enduring could be found among trade articles that I knew of so I asked where it came from. The king told me they were very ancient Nubi ornaments, but where they were made he knew not. How much more beautiful was this lovely stone than the meretricious Venetian glass trade-stuff; yet, when I offered the girl a handful of the latter in exchange for it, she was quite willing. But I had not the heart to rob her and gladdened her with a gift of the beads.

The king was very anxious that I should join forces with him and raid the Jiwé. It was his tribe that had had such a severe doing before, but he was quite confident that if we combined we should lick them. I said I did not desire cattle. "Well," he said, "I will take the cattle and you can have the women!" I explained that all I wanted was elephant and that if he would show me great numbers of them I would give him something really good. This remark was rather unfortunate as it conjured up in his mind visions of powder, caps, and maybe a rifle. However I did not know this until afterwards. He said there was one place he knew of where no man dared go, so strong was the infestation of elephant at this time of year. "But they will be cow herds," I said.

"No, no, all bulls, huge tusks!" he said.

"Lead me to it," I said.

We arranged that all the ivory was to be carried to his village to await our return. Late that night the last of the tusks came in under Pyjalé's guidance. What a day he had had, yet he showed no sign of fatigue. The next morning the king and some of his people led us off across country. We seemed to be going in the same direction as that taken by the fleeing elephant. I asked if we would reach the promised land that day. They said no, but that we would sleep near it. Knowing what they called a day's travel, forty to fifty miles, I said it would be on the Nile. They laughed at this and said no, the big river was five days away.

All that day we rushed along through dry, partly burned ridges alternating with swampy bottoms. Strangely enough we saw no elephant but there was no lack of tracks. When I wanted to follow up some of these, the king said no and pointed on. He would show me so many on the morrow that I would be frightened to fire at them. As he was well lit up with native beer, I did not believe too much in anything he said.

Small game seemed very scarce. It was probably concentrated somewhere enjoying the young grass. Once we disturbed some buffalo and the king begged me to shoot one or two for him, but fearing his people might drop out of the search for elephant, I would not. That night we slept about four hundred yards away from a marshy lagoon, trying to get away from the mosquitoes, but this was soon proved to be the wrong thing to do. Pyjalé, hearing elephant down at the water, woke me and we went off to have a look. There was a fairly good moon, and as we approached the water, we could hear them splashing and belching all over the place. I thought that if they were hippo they would most certainly have made their characteristic noise by this time. Anyhow Pyjalé would not be likely to be mistaken and there had been no mention of hippo by the natives.

The moment we reached the water the air became much cooler and there was a thin layer of mist filling the hollow which was well lighted by the quarter-zone moon. The mosquitoes were absent in this cool air but simply swarmed in camp. Some of the splashing seemed quite close and yet we could see nothing. We went along the shallow valley for some distance and came very close to some elephant bathing. We could not, however, make them out sufficiently well to shoot so we returned to camp without disturbing them, thinking to deal with them on the morrow. As we neared camp, we entered the warmer air on the ridge and became once more the unwilling hosts of mosquitoes innumerable.

What it is to be young! The morning found us up and about, fresh and eager for the hunt. This time I carried the .303 ten-shot rifle and hope ran high. Scarcely had we gone a couple of miles when we ran into elephant. Contrary to our usual custom we had a considerable number of natives with us, including the king, and, as usual, they would persist in talking. The native man has a very resonant voice which booms away for an immense distance. The country seemed much more open than it really was, and as elephant blend extraordinarily well with most landscapes, considering their size, the upshot was that we suddenly saw some rapidly disappearing sterns ahead of us. We had stampeded some elephant we should have got. A bad start.

Cursing the noisy gang soundly, we shed them off with

orders to remain where they were until fetched. Then we continued on our way. I thought we ought to follow the animals we had disturbed, but the old native who now took charge said no. Without explaining why, he led off across country once more. It began to annoy me to leave elephant behind us. I could see no sense in it. It seemed ridiculous until, on topping a rise in the ground, I saw at once why he had been blind to any other attraction. The old guide stood aside, relaxed, watching me as if to say, "There you are! What are you going to do about it?" And indeed it was a problem. There below us lay a large elongated flat of verdant green simply smothered with elephant. Quickly getting the glasses onto them, I soon discovered that they were herds of cows, calves, half-growns, and young herd bulls. Nowhere could I see any really old bull stuff. I regretted now having passed good elephant on the way here. I cursed the king for bringing me to cow stuff, but I could see that he simply thought I did not care to tackle so many beasts. There was nothing for it therefore but to demonstrate.

The cow herds are quite easy to deal with but the ivory from the young bulls is poor weighing stuff. It looks nice and white and long but it is a snare. Actually it is very hollow and tapers from the base to the tip, whereas old ivory holds its diameter throughout a great part of its length and the hollow closes up with age. Then to get at the bulls you have to thread your way between groups of cows. Those with small calves become excited and make noisy demonstrations. They often cover the bulls and prevent one from getting in a shot. Altogether they are a nuisance. At the same time, by working persistently at them, good bags may be made. I have several times taken fifteen head of bulls right from the midst of cows.

But the weights of ivory from fifteen such would barely equal that from half the number of big bachelor fellows.

We soon came to realize that the grass the herds were so intent on was already grown uncomfortably high. It was now about six feet and much resembled a dense crop of green maize. It would be no picnic working out bulls in this stuff. Coming upon the first group, it was evident that at least two of them were bulls. I could not see their tusks as the grass hid them, but one gets to tell maturity pretty well by the hollows of the temples and the general lack of fleshiness about the head. There is a roundness about the forehead of an immature bull not to be found on the fully adult. And then, of course, stature is useful when there are others with which to compare it.

Getting a clear slant at one of the bulls, I fired and dropped him. There was immediately a great to-do. The best thing to do after killing in long stuff is to run as quickly as you can and mount the carcass. This will add five feet to your stature if he should be lying and six feet should he have fallen kneeling. This often leads to further chances. Cow herds do not as a rule stampede. Whether it is they are fearful of losing their young or whether it is mere cussedness, it would be hard to prove. But hang around they very often did and could not be got on the run, much to the profit of the hunter, of course. On this particular occasion they hugged the fallen bull. They were terribly excited, ringing round the body with lowered heads and cocked ears. I thought they might be going to carry him off as so many writers would have it they do. But I was once more disappointed; they made no effort whatever to touch him. Meanwhile I was impatient to reach the stance because the other bull I had seen had disappeared. We therefore started making our queer noises. The effect of these noises was invariably either instant flight or a precipitate charge in the direction of the noise. This is what happened now, and I had to paste an old cow who insisted upon too close a view. The shot caused a halt; every head went up with an air of hurt surprise as if to say, "Hullo, you low-down cuss, it's you again, after all." Now they began to move off and I reached the dead bull.

From the eminence of his arching ribs I could see numerous groups about, none of them much alarmed apparently. There was a bull standing up rather conspicuously from a large herd about three hundred yards away. Although the actual heart was covered, it seemed a feasible shot. Waiting until an intervening cow moved a bit, I let him have it. He got it all right, as his cringing twist indicated, but what a commotion as, with a bellow, he started off, taking the whole show with him. That is the difference between the heart and the brain shot. Now I had to look for the brute. And the moment you left your perch you could see nothing. Had he been shot in the brain, one would have run swiftly and mounted him. But in this case the distance was too great for the brain shot.

While Pyjalé and I were questing around for him, I felt a light unhurried touch on my arm. I looked back and saw a bunch of fleeing elephant coming along the grassy lane we were in. Stepping aside, they swiftly passed us as I wondered how often that sort of thing has been described as a charge.

Just as we had resumed our search for the wounded bull and with my mind rather filled with complacency over the foregoing event and our dealing with it, we sustained a real and genuine charge. A single and very tall gaunt cow arrived on top of us like a tornado from the blue. We removed ourselves somewhat reluctantly from her way, but this only infuriated her. I still could not believe she meant business. Every time we moved she spotted us, so we stood stock-still. At us she came, bristling with vice. She certainly looked as wicked an apparition as could be imagined. She came so close and with such determination that I raised my rifle to settle her when she suddenly stopped with stern down and upraised prow. With a piercing scream she brought her two enormous ears together in front of her head with a clash and then stood absolutely motionless, staring straight into our faces. Finding us as still as she was herself, she suddenly pivoted round and rushed off about thirty paces. Then she swung round again and faced us. The instant we began to move off, she was on us again. I began to wonder what it was all about, this unusual fuss. So when she came rampaging along again, I shot her. On inspection we found her newly born calf trampled to death.

Mounting the dead cow, I found nothing could be seen. I vowed never to use the body shot again, which was silly because it is a most useful shot in its proper place and time. But now we had to find our bull somehow. If he had fallen, it would be a matter of mere luck should we run across him. But if he had not, our only chance of seeing him would be from the back of another elephant. So we pursued the herds. When we came upon them, all the scattered herds had collected into one great gathering. When they do this, nothing a hunter can do to them will move them from high grass into open country. He may shoot bulls from the group until the supply or the hunter is exhausted. And so we did, only the supply on this occasion gave out when I had killed seven. We saw no sign of the wounded bull so guessed he must have fallen. Natives found him the next day very near the place where he was shot.

CHAPTER 11

THIS Nile country being now thoroughly disturbed and meat-stricken, it was decided to collect all the ivory and to trek back to the main safari in Jiwé. In order to carry all the tusks it was necessary to obtain carriers from the king. And now the difficulty about his present cropped up. It appeared that he hoped for a rifle. But this of course was quite impossible. Finally after much palaver I succeeded in inducing him to come to Jiwé with me. I had to promise safe-conduct for him and his people when they left on their return journey.

All went according to plan, and when the king had recovered from his disappointment at not getting even powder and caps let alone a rifle, he seemed quite pleased with the presents we gave him. Under the escort of two of our askaris he and his people returned to their own country.

We did not cache our ivory with the Jiwé people as there was a mutual feeling of distrust between us. Instead we carried it with us into the neighboring country of Dodinga. Here we made a permanent camp, buried our ivory, culled out the sick donkeys, and left the headman in charge. From this camp we wandered in all directions, gathering in some very nice teeth. It was here I met and slew an elephant carrying teeth of 148 and 145 pounds.

I think this animal was not constitutionally a carrier

of heavy teeth. Their weight was due to their abnormally small hollow ends rather than to their dimensions. They were indeed almost closed up. This fact coupled with the mossy appearance of his head pointed to great age. As he stood motionless before me, he gave me the impression of retaining only a very feeble and deeply seated vital spark. The only sign of life was in his eye. When he was cut open by the boys, seven perfectly round smooth balls were found in the intestines, ranging in size between that of a toy football to that of a billiard ball. On cutting into these balls, they appeared to consist of a substance resembling compressed curry powder. I took it to be dried bile, more especially as his liver contained large sacks of a similar substance. Many of the old elephant killed in this country were similarly afflicted.

In no part of Africa, except on the highlands of the Ubangi watershed, have I been so impressed with the ferocity and wildness of nature as in the Dodinga country. She there goes in for grotesque and savage-looking rock formations, their summits generally occupied by swarms of gigantic baboons and jutting abruptly and nakedly from rugged vegetation as scarred and worn as the hills themselves. Even its denizens had something of the same character. The elephant were hoary and massive, the buffalo numerous and contemptuous of man, while down below the escarpment rhino were swarming and aggressive. Everywhere were great elephant roads worn deep into rock or clay. Great bathing pools showed where the massive beasts took their pleasure in the rainy season. Almost oppressive evidence of bush devastation met the eye on all sides. Scarcely one tree or bush could be found that did not bear upon it the signs of having been violated by the tree-browsing pachyderms. Only the euphorbias with their poisonous juice stood unharmed in the desolate landscape.

Impressive as "Nabwa" was in the dry season, in the time of thunderstorms it transcended itself. Instead of bright sunlight there was a greenish purple gloom overhead. Sudden winds of hurricane force sprang up, dying away in torrential cloudbursts. Lightning flashes supplied the chief illumination. Thunderclaps of the most appalling intensity shook an earth still quivering from the preceding discharge, while the miserable hunters, pale, cold, and depressed, cowered dithering under the shelter of an elephant ear cut from their latest victim. After a night of acute misery the sun would burst upon the soaked, torn, and horrible scene and transform it into one of surpassing beauty. Lilies that had pushed up through the moist earth in the night burst forth into glorious color, projecting into the now gentle atmosphere their heavy sweet perfume. Graceful tiny dik-dik played daintily about while that most beautiful of African antelope, the lesser kudu, lent contrast to the more massive forms of animal life as the hunters hurried away once more upon their blood trail. The effect on my boys of this peculiar country was to reduce them to silence; they spoke in whispers. Such was "Nabwa," the native name for this primordial wilderness.

From Dodinga we wandered away into the blue hazy mountains and plains of the north, hunting with the Dabossans and penetrating to the centuries-old stamping grounds of the abundant elephant of that region, experiencing the ups and downs of the hunter's life. Sometimes a month would pass without the sight of an elephant and then in a few days we would be almost immobilized by the weight and number of our tusks. But ever we would manage somehow to stagger onwards, caching ivory here and there until such time as the retreat would be signalized. Then all hands would become bearers of ivory. Every man and boy, whether askari or body servant, would be pressed into bearing a tusk. Every donkey would be loaded to capacity and the safari would wend slowly but joyfully homeward, making up for lack of speed by lengthening out the hours of travel. And what a welcome it would receive when it neared the base camp. Long before our arrival a runner would be sent through to warn the camp of our approach. The women would then have time to wind up any little intrigues they might have embarked upon during their husbands' absence in the bush and would appear fresh and loving for their further bedevilment. Food would be prepared and beer made. Then on the actual day of entry all would flock out on the trail in their brightest and best-washed clothes to meet the sun-blackened and bush-weary file of tusk bearers while the boys and children beat drums or blew their water-buck horns and the wives seized upon the camp paraphernalia to bear it along as, of course, no one would give up his tusk, however heavy.

Now a pause would be made to ensaddle as much of the ivory as could be borne by the donkeys. The much-needed rest was welcome to all except to myself. One day would suffice, and I remember being struck by the fact that this day was the first I had had in ten months. Such is the attraction of the hunter's life.

It was during this pause in our retreat that the following incident occurred. While the preparations were going on for the retreat, I thought I would take a stroll into the bush that ran right up to the base of the Dodosi rock. Possibly I might get a dik-dik for the pot. I carried the .275. The cool of the evening made it most enjoyable and there was the quiet rustle of African life as it busied itself after the heat of the day. Suddenly I became aware of the presence of something. It is a curious fact that whenever in the proximity of large game, there comes over one a sort of expectancy. I do not know what causes this. I had seen no sign of anything yet. I have often thought that it must be caused by the last remainder of some olfactory sense that we have lost.

Proceeding cautiously on my way, my reason argued that there could be no big animals so near to our camp and the native villages. Every day this bush must be traversed by natives—women getting firewood, men cutting ax handles, and so forth. Guinea fowl were about in great numbers and dik-dik stood about or sprinted across the openings. I might have bagged several had I not been warned and strung up.

Suddenly there dashed away with a crash some large animal through the thicket, almost immediately bursting into view in the shape of a large bull elephant. Without any conscious aiming of the rifle, I saw him fall flat to the shot, disclosing another just beyond him. Notwithstanding that he presented an almost stern view, he too fell to a bullet directed toward the center of his cranium through the neck, a clear case of subconscious aiming.

When they fell they were traversing fairly high stuff. This now hid them from my sight. As I hurried toward them, I wondered if I had been dreaming. I was quite relieved to find they were realities. The first one had fallen with such force as to have burst the bone sockets, and I could draw out the tusks without more ado than to cut away the gristle around the lips. His four legs all lay straight under him pointing backward. Hurrying to the second one, I found that he, too, was dead, but his tusks were still fast in their sockets.

Now, I thought, I will astonish the boys in camp. Cutting off the tails, I shouldered one of the tusks and started off for camp. What a devil of a weight I found it! I guessed it to weigh about 70 or 80 pounds and I had only half a mile to go. How, I wondered, do they carry tusks weighing 150 pounds day after day—and a rifle, too.

The moment I left the cover of the bush I was spotted, and as I staggered up the slope to camp, quite a crowd of natives and all the camp people turned out to see this strange sight. As I approached them, I tried to assume an air of ease, not so easy with that infernal tooth. There was deep silence as I entered camp and threw down my load with the fresh blood on it. This was "medicine." They had not heard a shot!

CHAPTER 12

THERE joined our staff at this time a gigantic lad with a quite unpronounceable name, so we called him Haram. He was six feet six inches high, weighed about one hundred and eighty-five pounds, of clean high-tensile muscle, and had the brain of an immature ostrich. He was remarkable, too, for having a very short body and very long legs. Regarded merely as a specimen of physical perfection, he was superb. He was, however, a poor specimen of Homo sapiens, for he was of all men the most stupid. Luckily for the rest of us, no doubt. Had he combined brain with brawn, little could have stood against him. As it was, I once saw little Nopak give him as good as he got in an hour's fight with sticks. He was a thoroughly nasty, quarrelsome beast, disliked by every male in his tribe for his extraordinary success with the women. Apparently he had everything they wanted, and it was after one of Nopak's girls had shown her interest in Haram's attractions that little Nopak called out the giant.

Of course the challenge was accepted with avidity, and as I watched the reddening of the Goliath's tiny pig-like eyes, I began to feel apprehension for our little friend. In my ignorance I made Pyjalé park their spears by my tent. I say in my ignorance because, when I asked Pyjalé whether they were not liable to resort to spear fighting, he laughed and said, "Oh, no. That would cost too much." Had either been killed, the survivor would have had to pay in cattle and sheep.

So off to the bush they went to cut sticks. Already brain outsmarted brawn, for Nopak borrowed a "panga" —a long bush-cutting knife of good Sheffield steel we carried—while Haram contented himself with a soft iron native knife with which to cut his stuff. In these native encounters each contestant cuts as many and as large sticks as he can conveniently use. One at a time they are employed in the right hand in belaboring the opponent. When one is destroyed, another is taken from the reserve in the left hand, which acts as a shield also.

Presently Nopak appeared with some prodigious bludgeons of hard tough African bush and then Haram came in with a bunch of rather slim-looking withies. I detected a grin of confidence on Nopak's face, but if the armaments had been reversed and Haram had got hold of what Nopak intended for him, there is little doubt that one whack from one of those clubs powered by Haram's muscles would have cut poor Nopak in two. As it was, Nopak toward the end of the encounter began to tire through the sheer weight of his armament. At any rate it so appeared to my anxious eye.

I only wish I could have secured a film of that fight. How feeble beside it appear our glove encounters. Here there were no rounds of three minutes each. Bang! Whack! Swosh! For an hour on end. And at a speed! I can only liken it to a mix-up of two overheated stallions. And the result? Nil, I should say. Neither conquered the other. I think nothing but death would have settled it conclusively. There comes a limit to what even African bush can stand, and the two combatants were finally reduced to whanging away at each other with nothing but a short bundle of white fibers resembling fly switches in their impotent hands while the ground all around lay strewn with the broken pieces. Eventually, of course, they had to throw away these ridiculous stumps. Nopak came smiling toward us quite unharmed and hardly out of breath while the giant strode over with sulky mien to get his spears and then away on his own ploy.

After witnessing such a scene, one cannot help wondering whence these Africans derive their prodigious strength and energy. Their food is such that the white man would die on it in a month. It consists almost entirely of raw, coarsely ground millet flour once in the twenty-four hours with a little sour milk, occasionally a little meat, and seasonally some honey. After a good harvest some beer. Add a little blood from their horned cattle from time to time and long periods of semi-starvation eked out with what meager roots and wild plant life they can garner at the expense of much traveling and digging. This reminds me that there is an excellent wild root to be gathered in very scant quantities in the bush that is quite worthy of domestication. Its outward sign is a very long, thin, and wiry sort of vine or creeper with very small leaves. If you dig down this leader for a couple of feet in the hard-baked soil, you reach some knubbly-looking tubers bigger than a walnut but smaller than a large potato. Then you have most excellent scouse, to a hungry man at any rate.

After thus reviewing the food intake of these natives, a white man naturally wants to know why they do not kill some of the apparently abundant herds of horned cattle, goats, and sheep that meet the eye on all sides. It is not easy to give a satisfactory answer to this question.

To do so shortly is impossible. The fact remains that they do not do so. One is inclined to say that this is only another sign of stupidity. But it is not so at all. Their insurmountable aversion to killing any stock that is healthy can be likened to the miserly feeling that overcomes one on attaining a certain stage of bank-worthiness. It seems a pity to destroy the beauty or symmetry of a holding, either of horned stock or of the banker's kind, when it has reached a respectable size.

Behind all these fast-held customs lie the teachings of centuries of experience. Take a visitation of the dreaded rinderpest, when perhaps one per cent or even less of all cloven hoof victims survive. The greedy man might have eaten the very one that might have survived. Then again, cattle on the hoof mean women. Women mean beer and food, huts, beds, milk, butter, mats, fires, cooking pots, and babies; someone who can love you and whom you can beat up when you feel that way. Pyjalé often told me that when a young man got a two-year-old heifer as a reward for elephant news from us, he would be a rich man with plenty of women in fifteen years; that by that time, if he survived the constant wars with neighbors, smallpox, raids, or rinderpest, he would then be able to make himself a wooden sleeping pillow large enough to contain in comfort, when used as a seat, his waxing buttocks. His life would then consist in tallowing his iron neck collar and burnishing his iron chain bellyband, buttering his body, drinking his beer, and beating his wives. Little wonder they searched so diligently for the retiring elephant.

Our science books tell us that energy is heat. Conversely, heat is energy. Why then does a hot sun cause a white man to wilt and a black man to feel good? Science says the sun's rays contain harmful elements as well as beneficial ones. Moreover, these harmful ones must be guarded against as in extreme cases they may be lethal. Therefore one is told to cover the head, neck, and spine with such clumsy abominations as solar topees and spine pads. But where stands the naked African when these death-dealing rays are about? It is no answer to say that they are only savages. The facts must be faced. They are our superiors in sun-resisting. Through centuries of evolution and exposure to the sun nature has caused such a heavy pigmentation of the skin that the sun's harmful rays are filtered and rendered harmless. What is more, the sun's heat—which you remember is energy—appears in the form of a capacity to give off work without recourse to any other form of energizing the body such as eating. This free-for-nothing energy is what enables our native Haram to clear in his stride a stream that I must swim across—to my profound disgust and annoyance, I may tell you.

I could give many instances of this—to us—strange capacity to draw energy from the surrounding atmosphere. There was the native who ran and walked, he must have run most of the way, the incredible distance of three hundred miles on bush trails to fulfill a task the reward for which was a heifer. I saw this boy leave on his mission and I saw him when he returned. Unfortunately I did not weigh him before and after, but it was quite evident that he had not drawn all his requirements from food. At the end of his journey he was, if not emaciated, at least pretty finely drawn. He had traveled a good part of the time by night—a most tiring business as anyone who has done much of it will agree.

If then the sun can be beneficial, as the evidence would

tend to show, how comes it that there is no attempt on the part of the white man to produce artificially a medium designed to filter out the harmful rays while allowing the beneficial ones to do their stuff? In short, why don't we stain ourselves the proper color for the job? I cannot believe that we are so lamentably stupid as to allow any consideration of "color bar" to influence our feelings in this connection. And yet it seems strange that after all our colonial experience in tropical lands we cannot yet pop into the first chemist's and for sixpence reappear a lovely sun-resisting mahogany color. Probably our scientists would try to persuade us that a livid purple would be a more suitable color for the purpose. I personally would not hesitate an instant to color myself purple, blue, red, or black if I could thereby draw energy from the sun. As I would be unable to see myself, the effect of my appearance on my beholders would leave me quite unmoved, while in pursuit of elephant at any rate. I can imagine, of course, occasions when a simple suit of Boots' anti-sun stain might not be the most appropriate garment.

Here I am suddenly appalled by the thought that it is almost certain that the scientists would insist that their chemicals would only act efficaciously when exposed undraped to the sun. Heaven forbid! Think only of your neighbors in that connection. One or two here and there of course would pass muster and even give pleasure. But think of the awful monstrosities and protuberances, now so straitly controlled, suddenly unleashed before your shuddering eyes. And the lackings, too! What about them? How, I ask you, is a flat-behind or buttock-less person going to strike the eye even when clothed in the most celestial blue? Yet drastic as it would be, it appears that nothing short of the complete disrobing of the so-called civilized races could have any chance of recalling them to the proper care of and pride in their bodies.

I do not think that the period of regeneration would necessarily be of long duration. After all, a baby is mostly all right. It would appear that they begin to go wrong when they acquire an interest in clothes.

Man in his upright state was intended to have good, muscular, outstanding buttocks. From the hips all important functions start. Without good buttocks the hips are like a hammer without a head. I make so bold as to suggest that the much-despised buttock is the one sure and infallible sign of the virility and fertility of a race. There is no one particular form of buttock about which one might say that and that one only is the model to be encouraged. For example, there is the wide, flat, badger-like stern of the strong, hard-working European peasant. In this instance we see the result of the struggle between the insistence of evolution that a muscular stern is necessary and the deleterious effect of hiding from view what should be regarded as an object of beauty. The makings of a suitable stern are still there, but they have been sadly neglected.

While in Karamojo we sometimes had a casual visit from a certain native man. Although a big, strong, upstanding fellow when facing you, he had a most unfortunate back aspect. He was deadly poor and in consequence suitably humble. He was rather a pathetic person in some unexplained way——the sort of man about whom one makes the remark, "Poor devil." For a long time I could not understand what it was about him that produced this effect. But when Pyjalé advised me to reward this "poor devil" with a bullock when he had palpably earned a heifer, I made a more pressing inquiry——after I had given him his well-earned heifer, of course. Latomé was his name and that means elephant man. The reason why he was called that was not that he carried unusually large teeth or teeth more prominent than usual. No, it was because his back view resembled that of an elephant. In short, he was what is so common amongst us but so rare out there, a buttock-less man.

Once the allusion had been explained to me, I saw it at once and I confess I could not help laughing, for the stern of an elephant is one of nature's biggest jokes. It is only when his front end is opposed to one that the laugh transfers itself. Now while this conversation with Pyjalé was gong on, Latomé was standing over there in camp with his back to us. When I guffawed, he turned toward us. And would you believe it, he knew we were laughing at him. I felt sorry for hurting his feelings, but he soon made it evident that such was far from his thoughts by laughing heartily, the while smacking his behind. Of course Pyjalé had perhaps embellished his tale with subtle references to the fact that the sight of fleeing elephant sterns is often accompanied by a certain looseness of the bowels, not unknown as a symptom of fear among man also. At any rate, Pyjalé made it clear that a man without a decent stern was regarded among Karamojans as on a par with a eunuch. Poor Latomé! Victim of such degradation, no woman would marry him. Solitary must be his existence. At the dances, having no convenient coattails to hide his affliction, he was the butt of all and sundry.

It was curious to see how many civilized types were represented among these people. As I sat in the shade of our great spreading wild fig tree during one of our rests for buying flour, I would have ample opportunity to watch the lively scene. Indeed, I at first had to act as a sort of policeman. All these savages were armed to the teeth. All carried spears and even their fingers were garnished with iron rings, having either a sharp blade mounted on them or a long iron hook. Pyjalé suggested that these knuckle-dusters were useful when dealing with the coy maidens.

It was customary to issue trade-good rations to the whole safari whenever the food situation allowed of it. Venetian glass beads, brass and iron wire, black leaf tobacco, and fine iron chain were the chief media of barter. Besides these articles, smoked bush meat such as elephant, giraffe, or buck found a ready market, as did the hides of such animals cut to sandal sizes. Hence each safari tent formed a little market of its own.

In the beer season——that is, just after a decent harvest had been secured——there would be much drunkenness among the natives. Any trouble we experienced was almost always due to beer. Three-day-old beer is extraordinarily exhilarating stuff when converted by native digestions. And how lasting is its effect!

The sort of fracas that would arise might start like this. A magnificent-looking six-foot four-inch slab of glistening ebony would decide to accompany one of his daughters to oversee her trading. His belly distended with enough beer to send a brewer's dray, horses, and all reeling, he would rub up his iron neck collar with mutton fat, smear his greasy hands over his victims-killed marks so as to make each facet of the corrugations glisten in the sun, give his knuckle-duster a polish with a handful of sand, don his sandals, bawl out for his shield, seize his two stabbing spears, and come to camp, daughter with tiny calabash of flour perched on saucy head.

How often have I watched with apprehension the approach of these troublesome gentlemen. In that country with every vestige of vegetation close cropped by stock and all remnants of bush long since gone by goat-cropping, you can see them glistening in the sun a mile away. They do not reel in their gait like common drunks and they do not walk painfully straight. But they exude a very nasty aggressive demeanor. You know how a perfectly motionless bull can convey what he thinks about you without doing much about it; that was it.

At first he surveys with scornful air the bustling scene around him. Then he advances to a closer inspection of the display of goods laid out on mats. Round and round he goes with his daughter on his shadow. By this time my eye is on him. But what does he care about that? Were he sober he would be somewhat cowed by my handling what they all knew and dreaded—the Bom Bom, they called it—a Mauser pistol. Never had I occasion to use it seriously, but I had taken every opportunity to acquaint them with its lethal properties. But against a full head of high-pressure native beer all caution flees. His bloodshot eyes might glimpse some trinket that his fuddled brain desired. Completely forgetting that he had with him the wherewithal to buy what he coveted, he would stoop suddenly, seize a handful of whatever had caught his fancy, withdraw the leather guards on his spearpoints by grasping the buttons between his toes, and swagger off quite slowly with his booty. Of course the owner of the goods would set up an outcry that would pale our air-raid sirens. With one swoop and bound the camp askaris would arrive on the scene and so would I, while the whole market concourse stood up and watched in a death-like silence.

Our drunk had now awakened to the fact that something was amiss, a fairly obvious fact as he was being closely bayed at by some twenty husky Mnyamwezi porters just awaiting the signal to give him the works. Meanwhile he would prevent a too close investigation of his person by stabbing his gleaming spears around.

The camp askaris carried each a bag of nice stones and often this supply of missiles would be augmented by others lying about. Everyone would have something to help in the good work. Billets of firewood and even copper cooking pots—until the damage caused them by contact with drunks became too serious—were pressed into service. And with a will! At a signal the barrage would be laid on as from one arm. Nothing could withstand it. One saw some splendid shield work, and it is safe to say that most of the frontal attack was killed by clever shield work or dodged. But the four-pounder on the spine or kidneys, followed by a deluge of husky porters, would soon pull our friend down in spite of lusty thrusts from his darting spears and some hefty daisy-cutters from his shark-hook knuckle-dusters. Even now it would be by no means over. Prostrate and battered, he would continue the battle with undiminished fury. What strength in that hot, greasy, wiry body. With perhaps half a ton of porter brawn on them, I have seen them rise from the ground spilling heavy men right and left as if they were feathers. But finally, of course, weight and eagerness would prevail and our sublime drunk would be pushed, hauled, dragged, and prodded back into camp. His shield and spears would be impounded at my tent while he himself would be expertly tied up and laid out under guard until such time as some of his excess of alcohol would dissipate itself and he could be given a good hiding and sent packing. This sobering-up process was a lengthy business, however, and we had recourse to dowsing with buckets of cold water periodically throughout the night. Generally the drunk continued to bawl out songs at the top of his voice even under a deluge of cold water.

I must say that they took all this in very good part. In fact they treated the whole business so lightheartedly as to destroy much of its effect. The comic sight of some Croesus being stretched out and whipped like any small boy thoroughly tickled his friends and neighbors. Even the victim himself would nearly always return with a chicken or a calabash of honey as a peace offering. Of course he would receive a gift in return, and I was astounded one day by a former flogee offering to take another beating if thereby he could earn some iron chain that he desired.

Just as with us, it was the well-established wealthy men of middle age who were the loudest-mouthed. Only they had access, through their many wives, to the copious sources of joy, native beer pots. By that time of life sex-adventure had ceased to attract. They had reached the saturation point in that line. As for the visible effects of self-indulgence, the difference between them and civilized man was very marked. You never—and I mean never—saw a potbelly among adults. You would search in vain for a bowler hat. True, the women had honorable ones when at the drop. But when one regarded the heads of the rich men, one could not help laughing. Here were all the signs: polished egg-like skulls reflecting sunlight, their huge perukes clinging precariously to the last remaining fringe. The stiff attitude of the head caused by the excessively high burnished iron collar reminded one so of our own people in high, boiled collars. But as far as their bodies were concerned, there was nothing that was not admirable. Firm, flat, muscular stomachs. No deposits of fat anywhere, and yet all well covered and a. fine healthy bloom on the skin. Sex organs well developed but without signs of excess. They are extraordinarily continent, these people, when one regards their opportunities. How often have I heard men grumble most audibly at having to return once more to sleep with a certain wife. With them the act of copulation is not undertaken for pleasure only. It is solid business, and if results are not achieved at a reasonable expenditure, the world soon knows about it. And from all accounts it is a pretty grim affair, for the ladies at any rate. I remember asking Pyjalé what was the matter with some women who were lying on mats outside a hut. They were as pale as their color would allow, drawn and exhausted-looking, and I quite seriously thought they must be ill. P. said that their men had returned the day before from a week's foray in no-man's land and that the girls had been put through it during the night. Think of that!

I have seen the bucks setting off on those forays, and as a field training they are no joke. It is the real thing all right. They are out for blood. Should two parties of about equal strength meet, it is war to the death with a lot of spear work of the deadliest sort. Even if one side is outnumbered, the retreat entails twenty or thirty miles of running at extreme speed and, of course, every conceivable stratagem is brought into play. Their commissariat arrangements for eight or ten days were simplicity itself: three or four handfuls of raw millet in a calabash and a little water—nothing else. For the rest, a lion might be robbed of his meal, an ostrich might be found partially blinded by the swelling of ticks clustering round the eyes, a buck might be run down when mud-bound after rain on black earth, or a beehive found.

The sex relations of these people differ largely from our own when it is a question of choosing a wife. I remember remarking on an extremely attractive woman of perhaps twenty-two or twenty-three years of age still in girl's dress, which is nothing but a tiny ornamented fringe slung on a string round the waist. It astonished me that such an outstandingly beautiful creature should be still unmarried, more especially as she appeared to be as full of sex appeal as a Scotch bun is of currents. I asked P. about her, and he seemed equally astonished to think that I should think of anyone marrying such a woman. "Why, she is a ——," said P. This might be translated very mildly as "winking eye"—only it wasn't eye. Now that my attention was drawn to the point, the damsel did indeed seem to have a roving eye. But in spite of P.'s criticism I still had it at the back of my mind that these people had a different estimate of beauty from ours. So again I tackled him. "Apart from being a ——, don't you consider her a beauty?" I asked.

"Certainly she is," said P. "She wouldn't go far as a —— unless she were."

"Well then," said I, "why does no one fall in love with her?"

"Everybody does," retorted P., "and that is why nobody will marry her. Not only does everybody love her [that is, sleep with her in P.'s language], but she loves everybody. So there you are."

There was a goodly number of unmarried girls about the camp at the time. There was a flour market on, and I asked P. to point out what he would call a good one to marry. Now this was in P.'s own country of Bukora and he probably knew most of them in the most intimate way. These people are not buyers of pigs in pokes. He knew also their characters, dispositions, and capacities for work, as well as their bed-worthiness. So that when he indicated a modest, quiet-seeming little maid with no more pretentions to good looks than those bestowed by kindly nature on any of her obedient children, I guessed that much more lay behind his judgment than met the eye. I then made my choice, and this threw P. into convulsions of laughter. I inquired the reason for this excessive mirth. But P. adopted his paternal air, as if these finer details were best concealed from infants. That it was a good joke was quite evident when I saw P. telling some of his friends about it. Nettled by this, I asked cook Suliemani what the joke was all about, but he, in his clothed superiority and ignorance, I suspect, could only rejoin resentfully that they were all, including Pyjalé, bush bastards anyway.

At this time our relations with these natives were of the friendliest nature. Our great herds of donkeys, cattle, and sheep roamed the countryside in perfect security, and any petty pilfering in camp ceased as it only resulted in the thief's wives, cattle, and sheep being seized by the natives themselves and brought into camp to be held as hostages by us until such time as the thief came to redeem them. He would then be tried, and if found guilty, he would be fined ten times the value of the stolen article. Whereupon two or three of his fattest sheep would be chosen from his flock and killed. Soon a fine feast would be ready and everyone, including his neighbors, would partake of it, to the great satisfaction of all concerned. For the unsheathing of a spear in our camp, the penalty was ten goats or sheep, and the free feast would include the whole crowd.

At the beginning of our contact, however, things had been far otherwise. Then the natives were extremely truculent and hostile. Many were the anxious moments when every attempt at imposing some sort of discipline on these wild scallywags had been instantly greeted with the rushing off of every warrior in every direction, followed by the issue of that weird Wah! Wah! Wah! from the women of every stockaded village as they rushed the shields to their men. Then the assembling of warriors, the howling of the old men, and the roars that greeted their speeches; the to-ing and fro-ing as the gatherings grew; the herds stampeding to safety; the withdrawal of the young women, all toward the horizon: all these signs of imminent violence scared the life out of my boys.

With some twenty-five Sniders and a very limited stock of ammunition, together with my half dozen personal rifles, we would have had no chance whatever if we had been resolutely attacked. The natives could have mustered two thousand spearmen and have rushed us easily. Young and inexperienced as I was, it still seemed to me to be fatal in the circumstances to have shown any sign of fear or even of precaution. So when my headman came with advice to build a strong zeriba of thorn bush round the camp, I simply laughed. He said we were about to be attacked. The whole safari sided with him. They were scared stiff and so was I, but I did not show it. Instead I seized my ten-shot .303 and a lot of ammunition, and with two or three stout boys with Sniders we marched with as resolute an air as we could muster toward a dense black throng gathered under a tree whence issued the biggest noise. I must confess that I had no very clear idea

of what I was going to do. Nor had the natives. I just
felt that our only hope lay in tackling the affair boldly.
And sure enough, such an unexpected move on our part
began to pay visible dividends long before we neared the
concourse. First the bawlings began to diminish. The
roarings now had a note of hesitation in them. Droppers-
off sneaked away more and more. Finally a sullen silence
fell upon the mass of glowering spearmen.

What would have happened will never be known, for
by a strange act of destiny a great mob of zebra came
rip-snorting right across our front. I say strange act because we were right in the midst of thickly built-up country. Immense stockaded villages squatted dourly all
around us and normally no game would be seen anywhere
in the neighborhood. But the unusual commotion among
the natives had trapped this herd of zebra and the aforesaid to-ing and fro-ing had somehow confused them,
with the result that they came barging, squealing, and
kicking right across our front just when I was fully prepared for some bloodshed. Here was a heaven-sent opportunity to demonstrate before an attentive audience the
power and scope of a modern rifle. I went out to meet it
in no uncertain manner. In a few seconds the line of the
stampede was accurately spaced with dead or dying zebra.
As the herd passed directly between us and the enemy, an
extraordinary motion became evident, partly excitement
at the strange spectacle, partly fear of the vicious reports of the rifle, and largely helped by the zing of one
or two misses I made in the terrific excitement of the
moment. Even when the herd was stern-on and had
reached a distance beyond fair dealing, I continued to
pump in solids. Finally my last shot caught one fairly in
the stern at what viewed sideways appeared an immense

distance, foundering it instantly. The war that never began was finished. Over they came in twos and threes, shamefacedly and placatory, "Camarade! Camarade!" They had been converted.

So obvious was their *volte-face* that I felt we could now bullyrag them. We made them skin the zebra, cut up the meat, and carry everything to our camp. If anyone tried to make off with any tidbit, I would seize a native club and knock him about. So that they could the better work, we gathered their spears into bundles—they didn't like this at first—and carried them to camp. Finally we had a pile of meat of a fantastic height. A mob of the bloodiest but most submissive natives assembled and we took the opportunity to tell them that we were always only too anxious to find an excuse to fight them, but that really after man-killing, elephant-killing was what we liked best. We never had any serious trouble after that. And what was better still, our reputation spread to far-off tribes, thereby saving us much trouble.

CHAPTER 13

I T WAS our intention to hunt the dry low-lying country to the north of us, and so now it became necessary to establish a base camp in Dodosi and to lay in a large stock of flour as there would be no opportunity to buy any further supply for many months. We intended to stick to the wilderness entirely, drifting from one water hole to the next, being guided thereto mainly by elephant.

As it was now the dry season, this trek meant that sometimes one, two, or three days might pass without our reaching water. Such being the case, all women and children would be left at the base camp together with any footsore, weary, or sick there might be. The first headman would be in charge. In the preparation of this base camp native custom was followed; that is, the donkey and cattle boma was completely surrounded by grass huts, the whole being enclosed in a stout thorn fence fifteen feet high by ten feet thick. It was never considered necessary to make latrines as the numerous vultures looked after everything, and what they left, the kites, jackals, and hyenas took. A suitable site was found away from the villages somewhat with plenty of bush for firewood, water, shade, and grazing. As Swédé was to remain, he was careful to bear in mind country good for partridge-snaring in choosing the camp site. He was tremendously adept at this game and kept himself and his wives and their followers in meat always. Whenever I returned to the base camp, I would find a pen stocked with thirty to fifty of these delightful little birds, fed plump by Swédé. They are exactly the shape and size of bantams, but darker in color, and lend themselves very readily to domestic wont. I have little doubt that they— or their Asiatic cousins—are the original stock from which came our domestic bantams.

Before leaving this considerable body of people in the camp, it would be necessary to kill a good stock of meat for smoking down into biltong, not only for rations while we were away but also as a trade medium for flour-buying. Therefore while building operations went on in camp, Pyjalé and I took to the bush with a good company of boys to do the necessary converting of flesh on the hoof to flesh in the load. Anything would do, of course, for trade purposes, but as many of the boys were Mussulmen who did not eat elephant meat, it would be necessary to kill some buffalo or giraffe, eland or other antelope. And it would be essential to have with one all the time some follower of Mohammed to cut the animal's throat.

As luck would have it, we ran into a large herd of buffalo not more than three hours from camp. They were feeding slowly along in park-like country and looked sleek and fat. Experience had taught me that if you want to make a killing of these animals, the best way to go about it is to mortally wound one or two of them in the lungs. Before death supervenes, they barge about bellowing and blowing frothy blood about in great quantities. This has the effect of infuriating their companions to such an extent that they concentrate only on goring the stricken beasts, making the while such a tremendous din themselves that the hunter can get in his fell work without their paying the least attention to him. Only you must not have any crazy spearmen with you, for the sight that drives the buffalo mad has very much the same effect on natives, and they go berserk into the melee, spearing right and left, holding onto tails, dancing in front of charging buffalo with the horns of the furious beasts crashing on their shields. It all looks fine but the net result in slain buffalo is generally meager. Very seldom a boy is hurt.

So now I hit a large fat cow through the lungs with a solid .303. Although buffalo can be easily killed with soft-nosed bullets planted in the soft parts behind the shoulder—indeed, I have killed in recent times many buffalo with the .22 high-velocity soft-nosed bullets—by far the best bullets for all-round shots at buffalo are the solid variety. For all end-on raking shots the solid is very effective; for these shots the expanding variety do not carry on far enough, breaking up too much on encountering bone. And for broadside shots solids are sufficiently good if properly placed. The neck shot with a solid is the most effective of all.

The stricken cow started up a tremendous pandemonium. All the animals in her immediate vicinity turned toward her, heads up, gazing in astonishment at her antics. The rifle was not idle, naturally. More and more of these little groups were formed. The outlying buffalo began to converge toward the scene. Pawing up the ground and bellowing hoarsely, some advanced upon the froth-blowers. More and more pressed on behind. Soon their blood was up and goring started. The bellowing could have been heard for miles. I was now shooting to kill outright. Neck shots, chest shots, all sorts of shots presented themselves. I daresay we might have killed every buffalo in that herd. As it was, when about twenty were down, I stopped. Gradually, as the stricken animals became silent, the remainder cooled off somewhat. More and more they began to move off, and finally they broke into a lumbering trot, disappearing in a dust cloud as they gathered speed.

Pyjalé and I descended from our ant heap and approached the field. Eighteen large fat beefs lay upon the ground. I thought I had one or two more and we searched around a bit. I felt pretty certain that there were no wounded, but to make sure I told P. to follow the herd a little way. He had not gone fifty yards when he called, pointing to beyond a large tamarind tree. I sprinted to him and saw a black form in the undergrowth about the stem of the large tree. It was quite motionless, but we approached cautiously as it appeared to be standing up. When quite close, I motioned P. to chuck a spear into it. He did so and there was no move. So we knew he was dead. He lay over one of those heaps so often found at the foot of tamarinds. He was a large old bull, quite dead.

We were extremely lucky to get so much meat that everyone, Moslem and pagan, could eat so near to the base camp, and a runner was sent forthwith to bring the women. In Africa it seems quite normal for men to send for the women whenever faced with a job of work. There is no doubt that they are much better at these jobs than the more delicate males. There was soon a merry meat-making in the bush that night.

Two days after this we struck out for "Nabwa," as they call the bush or wilderness. It was one march from the base to the last water hole on the trail to Dabossa where we would leave this trail and take to the game paths of "Nabwa." We were some forty strong with twenty picked donkeys, two milk cows, Pyjalé, myself, and a Bukora youth P. was anxious to train up. His native name was so unpronounceable that we called him Boy Dodinga for short. He was said to know a lot about the country we were going into.

When we arrived at the top of the escarpment overlooking the vast extent of country that would be our hunting ground for the next few months—until the rains came indeed—I halted and called for the big telescope. Before us lay a checkerboard of bush and open glade with abrupt volcanic massifs breaking the valley bed. Very far away to the east could be dimly seen hills that must neighbor Lake Rudolph, while far to the west could dimly be made out the outline of ranges in the Nile country. We were, I should think, some two thousand feet above the general floor below us. Only heat haze prevented our seeing the hills of Abyssinia to the north. Boy Dodinga pointed out in the far distance a water hole which he said never dried out. But we had found it bone dry on a former safari. Indeed, it was there that Pyjalé had gone three days without water, and I had nearly killed him by giving him milk instead of water, the milk turning to powder in his mouth.

Far across the sea of bush a massif stood out, the solitary eminence for forty or fifty miles. We had used a water hole up in the rocks of this range and had not liked it very much, it being much troubled by baboons with their filth. Boy Dodinga said he knew of a much better one. It looked as if he were going to be useful to us.

Up here on the top of the escarpment the days were cooled by pleasant breezes, but down there below we knew of the heat in store for us, where the sun seems to bore right down through you, making even the native skull ache and the urine to become scarce and heavily pigmented; where sweat blows off in powder, drying as it issues from the pores; where rifle barrels can scarcely be touched and ivory becomes so hot as to blister the carrier's shoulders; where even the game stands panting in the meager shade of the prevailing thorn bush. And yet this country is undoubtedly healthy. There are no mosquitoes in the dry season, and although numerous in the rains, they are not infected. There are no tsetse flies, but every other sort of fly is well represented.

Camping at the bottom of the escarpment, all available water bags were filled overnight to be topped up next morning before the trek. There was a delicious spring, crystal clear, at this camp, and it never ceased to delight me. Yet the natives said it was not good. When I first heard this, I tasted it more critically. Still finding it excellent, I thought they said this because they are not used to spring water. The only thing that I could see wrong with it was that it was very hard. And yet tea made with it was very dark, so there may have been some sort of salt mixed with it.

It is curious to reflect that however much we progress in the art of communicating over vast distances with each other, we still completely fail to establish any connection with our so-called dumb friends, however intimate we may be with them. We can speak to a man on the other side of the world but we cannot warn a donkey in our camp that he had better take a good drink as it will be his last chance for some time. When cows exasperate us by refusing to drink merely because it is too early in the morning, we stand dumb before the task of telling them a long waterless march lies ahead of them and that it would be well to drink deeply before setting out in spite of the early hour. Hence it was that only one or two of the animals availed themselves of the opportunity when they were driven down to the hole below the spring in the early morning. None of the water bags showed any great loss during the night and at sunup we were off. Henceforth we would have no man-made trail to guide us during the dark hours so our movements would be confined to daylight and moonlight.

We were soon in a sea of gray, lifeless-looking thorn bush. During the grip of the dry season this withered look would be general. The dry season in Africa corresponds to our winter and has much the same effect. Sap stops flowing and leaves fall to the ground. Very little game was seen in spite of the proximity of the spring we had just left behind us. It was too much haunted by man and by leopard living in the rocky recesses of the escarpment. Always as we traversed the bush in the dry season, the same old thought would arise: where do the animals go in the dry season? The answer is partly that they are still about but that their tracks do not show on the hard-baked ground and that all tracks are soon obliterated by the midday breezes blowing dust about. But reason as one may, it still remains a mystery. An occasional lesser kudu was all we saw.

It was too long a march to reach the first water hole in one day so we camped toward four o'clock. This allowed the donkeys to have a dust bath and to get a little grazing, such as it was; it looked so dried up as only to aggravate their thirst. The water bags were brought up, a depression dug in the ground, a canvas sheet spread over it, and the bags emptied into it. Then the headman seized a saucepan and measured out to each camp its ration of water. Meanwhile the poor donkeys scented it and came running upwind only to be denied and driven off. Enough for all hands and the milk cows was as much as we ever managed to carry. It is not so great a hardship to the donkeys as it sounds, as all over this dry country it is usual to water the ordinary stock every second day when the dry season is so far advanced as to necessitate digging deep in the sandy river beds. When the water has to be hove out in calabashes, the watering of large herds becomes a tremendous task. Moreover, it was a man task at which it was not customary for the women to join in. The women could look after themselves but the horned cattle must be guarded against a raiding enemy.

Soon the welcome dusk crept over the camp, but although the sun was down, heat still rose from the ground. Notwithstanding this, it soon became pleasant to sit by the roaring camp fire where one had to beware the scorpions dislodged from their haunts in the dead wood. I asked Pyjalé about some magnificent herds of cattle we had passed on our last trek before leaving Dodosi. One of these had consisted entirely of black heifers. Pyjalé said they were all of one age. They would number perhaps six hundred head. Another herd was made up of about four hundred head of all red bullocks, likewise of one age. One point I remarked on was their peculiar horn formation. All had one horn pointing straight down while the other one pointed straight up. Pyjalé said all these cattle belonged to one man and that, besides these herds that we had seen, there were other herds of six-year-old bullocks, of red heifers, of cows in milk, of cows in calf, of yearlings, and of calves. Some five hundred people were directly supported by these herds, drinking their blood and milk. So much had these people come to look upon these cattle as their own property that whenever the owner wished to detach a few head of cattle for the purpose of buying another wife, they raised as much uproar as if they themselves were the rightful owners.

I wondered how this multi-cattle-millionaire had come to acquire so much wealth. It seemed strange how one man could do so under a system where only personal fighting qualities counted for anything. And Pyjalé told me how it came about.

It appeared that long ago, when the millionaire was young and as poor as anyone else, he and his brother bloods arranged a little raid on their good neighbors, the Dabossans. Their luck was in. They surprised a rich encampment where most of the spearmen were beer-drinking elsewhere. Whereas most of his brother bucks could not resist the charms of the Dabossan maidens and started to flog their reluctant victims through the sixty miles of bush that lay between them and home, the would-be millionaire stuck grimly to a bunch of horned heifers, bringing them along at the gallop so fast that they outstripped his less farseeing companions who were presently caught up with and killed by the infuriated beer-drinkers. Our friend just squeezed home by a short head and was set up for life, there being no others to claim a share of the spoil. In such simple beginnings are such great events grounded, for throughout the Karamojan world this man's fortune was a byword and he was considered to be the richest man in the world.

I asked if he lived differently from other people. Had he a better house, better food, or anything of that sort? No. Apparently he lived exactly as anyone else. His beer-drinking might be a little more frequent than that of more normally "wived" men for, of course, he had more wives than normal people. But he slept on the same sort of bed, ate the same food, no more no less than any-one else, and shared with all and sundry the milk, blood, and grain that constitute their diet.

And so to bed under the star-strewn purple dome, to a sleep untroubled by the mosquitoes or tornadoes of the wet season.

HAD there been a moon, we would have left camp after a rest of a few hours and have trekked on to the water hole. As it was, we could only travel by daylight. The safari was put in charge of Boy Dodinga whose job it was to guide it to the water hole. P. and I and a boy I was trying out as a new gunbearer—Manyema having stayed at the base camp with worn feet—would be free to follow any tracks we might meet with.

The cows being milked, we set off at the first of the dawn. It is a grand sensation to know that your safari is in competent hands, that you are free as air, and that the chances are distinctly good of your finding your home all ready for you at the end of your day's hunt. For many miles we traversed the same gray thorn scrub interspersed with open glades. Hunting dogs crossed our path once and we saw a few lesser kudu. Some elephant spoor of indefinite age was examined and rejected. We were now not more than about fifteen miles from our water hole and we should be crossing the spoor of elephant using it. A fresh rhino track bore confirmation that water still existed in the hole. No matter how informed and convinced one may be in Africa that water does exist at a certain place, it is always a great relief actually to see the stuff and better still to feel it. We presently began to meet with sand grouse—another sign that water exists within twenty miles or so.

The sun being well up now and the heat beginning, the daily breezes were getting up and obliterating spoor, making it difficult to know just how old were some tracks we met. Following them a little way, however, put the matter beyond doubt. An elephant had ejected balls of sansevieria fiber not very long ago, and when we came to his droppings, we knew we were on. There seemed to be only one animal, but the chances were he would join up with others in the noon siesta area.

The tracking-down of the game devolved chiefly on Pyjalé. I think blue eyes are at a disadvantage when dealing with sun glare. At any rate, I could never keep on at it for any length of time. And yet blue is the color of the north where ice-blink during the centuries would have dealt selectively with eye colors, one would think. Perhaps blue is the color of the temperate zones, and black, or rather purple, the color of the equator and sub-polar regions. Anyhow P. could puzzle away entangling tracks for hours on end without any sign of eyestrain, and this in spite of a complete absence of the shade of either hat brim or eyebrow. The African eye is not deeply placed, nor does the African indulge in bushy eyebrows. His eye is small but not at all well shaded.

After about three hours of difficult going we were close up to our quarry judging by his dawdlings and the frequency of the droppings. The first indication that there were more than one elephant was when we noticed some trodden dung. The liquid squeezed from the aromatic pancake by the loaded pad still discolored the scorching soil with its moisture, and there were even tiny bubbles still puffing out along the edge of the wetted ground. It was pretty certain that we were close to our game.

I got halfway up an accommodating thorn tree; maybe my eye would be twelve feet from the ground. Away over there were the topsides of two elephant. No need to speculate on their sex. Bull was written all over them. As I watched, one of them started to spray himself with water. Up would come his trunk from under the surface of the sea of bush, round it would swivel, directing a sun-gleaming jet of water to his sizzling flanks. P. came up to have a look. The elephant continued his shower bath so copiously and so lavishly that I said to P., "He must have water there," although I knew there could not be a drop anywhere within miles, so convincing did it look. P. merely grinned and said, "No!" So strongly are we given to believing the evidence of our eyes that I searched everywhere for evidence of a pool of water as we approached our game. Of course there was nothing of that sort to be seen. Indeed, on coming to the place where he had been bathing, there was not even a sign of moisture. The spillage from his hide must have gone up instantly in invisible steam, if indeed it ever reached the ground.

The breeze was constant and it was easy to get to a suitable range of twenty paces, the favorable character of the bush making a shot at that distance a certainty. But the other fellow was not in sight. Therefore it would be necessary to mount quickly after the shot onto the dead animal so as to be able to get a view and a shot at the second one. In pursuit of this logical scheme I approached to eight or nine paces, sent a .275 crashing into his brain box, dropping him instantly in a kneeling position.

Using his crumpled-up forefoot as a step and his swinging ear as a handrail, I was up on his roof-like back almost before the report of the rifle had died away. His whole carcass throbbed with the mighty beats of his still pulsating heart. In the brain shot the heart goes on beating for some time after the nerve paralysis, the eye rolls, the eyelid winks, urine is passed sometimes, and often there is a discharge of spermatozoa from the penis. The only other sign is the quivering of the whole body. From the considerable elevation of his back—some six feet—I could see his companion about fifty yards away. Unfortunately he was standing stern-on to me, but as he was questing with his ears and trunk for his mate who so recently was in full view and sound of him, it was almost certain that he would give a chance before long. Although the range was rather far for a brain shot and the stance not too good, I did not mind giving him a heart shot as there were no others in sight. I decided to wait for a chance at a vital spot, heart or brain. As it happened on this occasion, that was the wrong thing to do. Without turning sufficiently to give a chance, he strode off into the thorny ocean. This meant an instant pursuit.

Pyjalé had cut the dead elephant's tail off, so away we went at the run. We ran because, if we did not close sufficiently with him to sight him, we would be compelled to return to the slow and laborious tracking. It is extraordinary how difficult it is to keep direction for even a few hundred yards with the sun overhead, no landmark in sight, and a fluky wind. Only a native-born African can do it. On this occasion we were lucky to come up with the animal himself and not merely with the tracks. P., who was loping ahead, drew up in one stride, almost making me collide with him. There was no need to indicate the elephant; he seemed at once to fill the landscape.

He was still stern-on and listening. The slightest noise

and he might either flee or he might turn toward the sound. This is where the charming unexpectedness of elephant hunting comes in. You could think up a dozen things he might do and then he would do something quite unexpected. We arrived at a position some nine or ten paces astern of him and I paused, waiting for a move on his part. A tense moment! Slowly he voided, plop, plop! Solid dollops of aromatic dung. He was not alarmed apparently. His head swung slowly sideways until I was staring at his slowly winking eye. Surely he must either see my red face or the black one of Pyjalé, both staring intently at him. If his head swung another inch, a tiny .275 would crash into his brain. But it did not.

He moved on, we following as if connected solidly to him by steel rods. Again he stopped. How I longed for a real man of a rifle that would send a bullet right up his anus into his heart cavity through that mass of vegetation in his stomach. But that would not be a very sporting thing, and perhaps it is better as it is.

He seemed very undecided in his going; he was hesitating and unsure of where his companion had gone, I daresay. One more advantage of the brain shot: it left the others wondering. He suddenly stopped as if he had just remembered something. I was rather close to his stern and backed away. An elephant's feet are all bunched up close together and his ends overhang a lot, especially the head end, so that if you are very close to the stern and he suddenly whips round, as they can do, you are likely to find yourself uncomfortably close to the eight-foot-long trunk. In this case he came round sedately enough and gave me an easy shot to the brain pan; all I had to do was wait until "imagined" brain came in line with my rifle sights. He dropped poleaxed. I turned to grin at P.

and over his shoulder saw the new gunbearer just returning with a very apologetic look on his face. The
swing round of that fearful head with the gleaming tusks
had been too much for him. This little hunt was very satisfactory. Everything encountered had been overcome.
No remnants had fled to instill less experienced companions with panic some other day. There had been no unnecessary noise or fuss. The ivory was satisfactory.

It was now hellishly hot and I personally was pretty
parched. "Where's that water hole now?" I asked P.
with a smile. I knew that is what P. would have asked
me. He understood instantly that I acknowledged his being right about it. However, I patted the flank of the dead
elephant and P. took the guard off one of his spears,
gave a tentative prod or two, the while measuring by
eye the correct spot, then drove the spear head in. Out
gushed a stream of pure water, quite clear after the first
gush had carried off the blood from the incision. The
boy filled our calabash, then drank with his head to the
stream. P. followed suit while I waited to let the calabash cool a bit as the blood-heat of the water used sometimes to make me vomit. What quantities of water they
carry, these pad-footed perambulating tanks. I suppose it
to be a provision of nature that there is no bulkhead between chest cavity and belly, thereby allowing a greatly
increased grazing area when water is scarce. One can
imagine that such voracious tree-grazers would soon consume the most abundant pasturage if they were restricted by water shortage to a few square miles of bush.
What a life is that of an elephant! During the dry season
he must tramp twenty-four hours a day, pouring in stuff
as succulent as can be got at one end and pouring it out
of the other. Hardly time to sleep at all. But in the rains

it is another story. The earth bursts into tender foliage and grass and water are everywhere; that fathomless stomach can be filled in a mere eighteen hours or so and a snooze can be taken for two hours, lying down on a gentle slope to facilitate getting up. And don't they snore! On a still night they can be heard for miles. And those nasty Africans, listening in, draw to the spot and spear them with broad-headed spears, then run away leaving the keen-edged iron working fearful damage.

Toward evening we came to our camp by the water hole, the quiet countenances of the donkey herds first indicating that all was well and water present. Our camp of course was well back from the actual water hole so as not to disturb it unduly. That night I discussed with P. and Boy Dodinga a project I had long had in mind.

When elephant are persecuted at one water hole, they soon wander off to another, however far away it may be. Then when they are caught there, off they go back to the first one or to some other one. Now I had these camp guards whom I had taught to shoot with a .22, natural-born hunters and doing nothing. What about leaving four of them with decent rifles at this water hole? Even if they did not kill many, they would at least prevent refugees from our front from settling down in an area inaccessible to us. The boys thought well of the scheme, and when I asked if any wandering Turkana or Dabossans would try any fancy games, P. was quite emphatic in his negative. So we called up the four most experienced of our askaris—as they loved to call themselves—and made the proposition to them.

Like the good sportsmen they were, they jumped at the chance. I explained that I would not be returning until the rains—some two and one half months off—that I would leave enough flour for that time, but that two of them could go to the base camp if they got short. For meat they were to endeavor to rely solely on elephant for their supply, but I gave them permission to shoot a rhino should elephant utterly fail them. They were moreover to make themselves a strong thorn boma well back from the water hole among some large rocks where a particularly large one would form part of their rampart and a lookout at the same time. Any ivory they might get was to be buried. The headman was now given orders to put aside enough flour and a few goats and sheep for them while I went through my ammunition stock to see what could best be spared.

In my search for the ideal weapon for my purpose I had accumulated a number of quite good rifles. I had a double .400 by Fraser of Edinburgh, a beautiful weapon but delicate. Then there was a .303 from the Army and Navy, a splendid gun with which I had killed over two hundred elephant. The rifling was a bit worn from the cleaning it had had, but it was still all right. I had another .303. Then there was a single-shot falling block .303, quite a good shooting weapon if somewhat of a slug at reloading, and one of those grand old game-getters, a Martini-Henry .450, the rifle that in the hands of the Boers exterminated South Africa's fabulous fauna. Finally I decided on the three .303's and the Martini-Henry; the .400 was too fragile I thought to be depended on, but they could have it as a stand-by as I did not want it anyhow.

On looking through the large stocks of ammunition, I was much tempted to leave a lot of it behind. But always the thought of getting into a do with Abyssinians or others restrained me from doing so; a few hundred rounds would soon go if it ever came to serious hostilities. As far as the quantity required for the actual hunting was concerned, there was no anxiety. The average number of solids expended on game was at this time barely two rounds per head of elephant killed. But as this method of counting the solid ball ammunition at the beginning of the safari and again at the end took no account of rounds that might be used on buffalo, giraffe, lion, or buck, the figure is necessarily inaccurate as regards expenditure on elephant alone. On the other hand, it was not often that one cared to fire a shot when elephant were about. When I wanted meat, I usually preferred to go out from camp expressly for that purpose, accompanied by a Mussulman to bleed the animals so that all might partake of the meat. Then I would carry the Gibbs .256.

In spite of the fact that we expected to be away about two months only, we all took a most affecting farewell of our four stalwarts and their two boys. Their camp was as neat a little affair as one could desire and quite invisible in its setting of thorn bush. Nothing but the low tunnel through the dense thorn zeriba and a thin curl of blue smoke indicated human occupation, while the ever waiting vultures might have indicated anything. We renamed the place Camp Kilassa after old Kilassa who was in charge, and we cached the ivory there as well as other superfluous gear.

Our route now lay due north along the slopes of a high rocky range. Everything was dried up and parched and game was scarce. The odds were against meeting with elephant until we had passed the end of the hills and had reached some swamps situated amid great arid plains, almost dried up now, but in the rains forming considerable sheets of water, the overflow making quite a respectable stream. Here we were as certain to find elephant at this time of year as anything connected with elephant can be certain. But to reach that region would require some very strenuous marching.

Boy Dodinga thought there would still be water high up the mountainside above the Baboon Pool. We all hoped he would prove to be right, for last time we drank there, it had seemed to us to resemble baboon urine rather than water. It was simply a huge hole in rock with a small surface exposed to evaporation. Its approaches were such as to allow only man or monkey to drink therefrom.

While traversing the pass that divides this range in two, we reached the place of a former kill, effected on a previous safari. What a difference! Then the whole country had been covered with green and flowering vegetation, the air moist and heavily scented, the ground cut up in all directions by game of every sort. Now there was not a blade of grass, every bush looked gray and withered to death, the ground reflected a brassy glare, while no sign of life brought relief to the monotony except the dipping flight of the small hornbill as it flew from patch to patch. I was curious to see what remained of the skulls and large bones of the former kill.

For some time we could find nothing, not even a skull. I began to think we had mistaken the place. But no. P. had been with us and he was not likely to go wrong. It was only two years since we had taken the ivory from eleven skulls there. There must be something left. At last someone found a piece of skull about the size of a football but so weathered and old-looking that one could hardly believe it to have been alive only two years ago. Presently other remnants were found, and it was borne in on us that everything of that boneyard had practically gone, weathered away, gnawed down, dragged off, burned, disintegrated. So much for the fables of elephant cemeteries, I thought.

When we reached Baboon Pool, we were glad to see that water still remained. Even if it was concealed under a filthy scum, the donks and cows would fill their bellies. Boy Dodinga, P., and I climbed the mountainside to look for better stuff. In surroundings without the slightest sign of the presence of the all-precious fluid we presently came on a tiny ring of fresh verdure, in its midst a soup-plate-sized ring of yellow scum. Parting this curtain disclosed a bright blue, crystal-clear fluid—a natron spring. How delicious it looked but how damnable it tasted. We partook of it as there was nothing better offering, but even through strong curry one could taste it. P. and the cowherd and I were the only ones who drank decent stuff that night; we had milk.

Our way led us along the bank of a dry river bed for miles. At one spot water was sometimes found near enough the surface of the sand for elephant and man to reach it by digging. We were not counting on this questionable supply, but should there prove to be water available, we would of course stop at it. Otherwise the safari would continue for another ten hours' march.

It was about 2:00 A.M. when we started out from camp. An enormous African moon shone overhead, lighting everything with an arc-light effect. We plodded along, each on his own carpet of purple shadow. Presently we saw a dark mass ahead of us; the large deep-rooted evergreens denoted a subterranean reservoir of water. The silver ribbon converging with our path from the right was the dry river bed filled everywhere with glaring bright sand. Just ahead of us, at the intersection with our course, it made a bend away again, and in this reach we would find water or not as the case might be.

As we approached, a large dark object drew my attention. It looked very like a rhino. Sure enough, it moved off in that characteristic manner of the rhino—as if tacking—so that he may see behind him without turning round. His presence here made it almost certain that we should find water.

On turning the bend and opening up the reach of glistening sand between the banks of dark trees, it was at once evident that elephant were present. Away in the distance were some shapes well out in the stream bed that could be nothing else. This was fine as it meant almost certainly that there was water. It was a lovely camp with abundant shade, and filtered water from the sand was such a god-sent drink in the dry season. Everyone loved that camp; it lay amongst some wonderful game country when—and only when—it provided water. Now for some moonlight shooting, I thought, as we halted to scheme things out a bit.

Although we traveled much faster than the safari, the latter had a wonderful way of speeding along in the cold of morning. Hence it was just possible it might happen along before we had done with our job and so scare off our prospective victims. Therefore Boy Dodinga was told to go back on the trail a mile or so to halt the safari until we sent for him. Then P. and I got down into the river bed and strode along in the already long shadow of one bank.

Out in the middle of the river bed—here about seventy yards broad—there were two objects that began to assume the shape of elephant as we rapidly approached them. They were motionless and I wondered whether to attempt the brain shot at the first—always a risky shot in moonlight—on the chance that the second one would delay long enough for my eyes to recover from the sudden contraction of the pupils caused by the muzzle blast of the first shot to enable me to give him one in the ribs before he reached safety on either bank. These speculations were abruptly terminated by a large object appearing suddenly in the sky in front of us.

The bank was here about ten or twelve feet high, and this object soon revealed itself as the head and forepart of an elephant coming down the bank. He was not more than fifteen paces from where we stood spellbound. What a monster he looked as he slithered to the bottom, but his tusks did not look impressive. In the still air he might not get our taint, so I let him go in the hope of something better among the other two. He was on his way to join them anyhow, and we escorted him in the shadow as he silently flitted along the brilliantly lighted strand.

We could now distinctly see the other two. They were drinking leisurely at separate water holes. Many heaps of sand dotted about indicated a high level of water in the river bed. We got within twenty yards of one of the drinking beasts without any difficulty, and from this range his tusks showed up fairly well, being dark and stained. Although they were nothing abnormal, they would probably weigh well judging by the massive proportions of their wearer.

On trying my sights on him, I could see nothing of the others. The moon was not sufficiently behind us to show them up. If I moved round to get it over my shoulder, I would have to leave the shadow of the bank, and I could not believe that they would allow me to move about in that glare of light although I had often before walked about among elephant at night as if they had been wooden ones stuck to the landscape. However there was no alternative to the brain shot except a risky heart shot, and this meant that the others would almost certainly escape. Then the thought suddenly struck me that if I left the black, and therefore familiar-looking, Pyjalé behind in the shadow, I in my washed khaki would not alarm them. Acting on this, I motioned P. to stay and move along the bank while I boldly moved out into the full blaze.

In a few paces I passed safely through the zone of greatest danger, which I took to be the emergence of my figure from the shadows. But all was well and I passed safely behind the creature. Once on the other side, the rifle sights showed up fine, and I was now almost between the enemy. The other one appeared to be smaller, and as he was busy with his digging operations, I could not make anything of his ivory.

At this instant the one we had met first was advancing straight toward me, it seemed. I felt rather shaky, I must confess. I was surrounded on three sides and I had lost confidence in my shooting with the loss of daylight. I remembered vividly firing at a rhino in moonlight once and my bullet striking sparks from a stone twenty feet to one side of him. But I could not very well retreat with P.'s steady eye on me, so I took as good an aim as the circumstances allowed of and fired. What a flash even a .275 makes when pupils are wide open. Blinded for an instant, I turned to face what had been the oncoming elephant, the rifle almost at the firing position. Instead of oncoming, he had changed to along-going—to my relief—and was now broadside-on but in rapid motion. I became aware that the one I had fired at was down, so I gave the fleeing one a bullet in the ribs, hoping for the best as I could not see the sights. On he went and up the bank, to be swallowed up immediately in the bush. The third one that had not been fired at had somehow disappeared from the scene. The first one seemed very motionless so I gave him a settler, and it was just as well I did so, for it threw him into the death throes, showing thereby that he had only been stunned. Up came P., very well pleased.

So much for the brain shot by moonlight. I never attempted it again, needless to say. In fact, I doubt very much if it pays to shoot elephant at night under such conditions. If these three had been unmolested, they would probably not have gone back so very far into the bush surrounding this watering place, and very likely we would have come up with them in daylight and dealt properly by them. As it was, we had one down, one wounded that we might or might not get when daylight came, and one fugitive who might take a number of others away with him. And, not least, we had effectually fouled the watering place for some time to come. Against these considerations must be set the difficulties pertaining to the daylight method: tracking in dry bush, the terrific mileage to be covered, the sweat and toil of bringing the ivory in from a distance.

Dawn was at hand so P. sprinted off to bring in the safari while I went over to the camp site to smoke and think over the entrancing night and to gloat over the beauties that surrounded me. A lovely camp, sweet water, good game lands, a good rifle, faithful followers, no contact whatsoever with the outside world, and not even a native African village within one hundred miles. What other paradise could a hunter ask for?

Soon the scene was transformed. Smoke quickly curled up from numerous fires, boys rushed off with cooking pots

to fill at the sand holes, the headman got his loads piled
while a gang set about building the donkey boma. Incredibly soon a meal was before me and soon downed, too.
There is nothing like night marching to give one a hunger
and to make one sleepy, too. But, alas, we had to follow
that infernal body-shot bull. He might be quite close or
he might be any distance away.

I was pretty weary, I know, when P. and I took up the
trail. He looked all right, blast him, I thought, but that
was because of his color, I consoled myself. Then commenced a devilish job. We had to carry our fellow's track
through a perfect maze of other tracks on the hardest of
hardpan soil. It was terribly laborious and our speed perhaps one mile per hour. Luckily the bush was fairly open,
being pretty well worn off by traffic and rubbing and grazing, and I saw away through it what might have been
anything but luckily proved to be our quarry, stone-dead.
What a relief! Even P. must have been delighted. The
tusks were only moderately good, but what did that matter when we could return to camp and have that good
long sleep in the shade that seemed so inviting?

The carcass by the water holes looked pretty flat when
I turned out in the afternoon after a heavy sleep. What
a liver it gives one, sleeping in daylight after a heavy
meal of meat. There are no people anywhere who can
consume more elephant meat and fat than Mnyamwezi,
and I had with me the very elite of them. But in spite of
their efforts, there was still a pretty nasty mess and I
decided it would be as well to move on. From here we
should reach the big swamp, so orders were given for the
morrow. Meanwhile I thought there might be a good infestation of hyenas and jackals come to the carcass that

night—maybe a lion. I determined to take a look when the moon rose.

Hardly had the sun set than up she came, magnified enormously by the laden air, but it would be some time before the slanting rays reached the carcass. Already there were chucklings and scufflings for what the vultures had left, while from the mountainside there echoed the howls of hyenas. While waiting by the camp fire for the moon to rise, I thought it would be best to take the .256 in case there might be a lion at the carcass or water hole. It would be best, I thought, with its soft-nosed bullets. Unfortunately the fore sight was very small and would be invisible in even the brightest moonlight, and the homely piece of wart hog tush that slipped over the fore-sight of the .271 did not fit the Gibbs. It would have to be the .275, although I always rather begrudged using the elephant-getter on less worthy stuff.

Presently I strolled down to the bank and looked over it. The following scene disclosed itself: a heaving gray mass marked the site of the carcass, a loose ring of dots surrounded it at a little distance, while a chattering snarling movement slid slowly across toward the far bank. Just as it reached the edge of the sand it dissolved. With extraordinary suddenness a figure appeared; it could only be a lion. Motionless it stood for an instant; then with a vibrating growl it advanced like a gray streak toward the carcass. As suddenly the group round the carcass dissolved in all directions with snarling protest. His Majesty had arrived. Without more ado he laid into it, encircled at a safe distance by his indignant and protesting audience.

He seemed to be lying down to it and gave but a poor target. After only a few seconds—during which I was trying my sights on him—he left the carcass and walked over to one of the water holes. The moment he turned his back there was a rush by the hungry mob. Three big brutes—probably striped hyenas—got hold of a long piece of intestine, dragging it right under where I lay on the bank above, fighting and snarling and stinking like fury as they ate their way along the savory stuff. The lion returned to his feed, causing another stampede, and as I prepared to shoot him, I perceived there were two of them now. How the other had arrived without my spotting him I put down to the vagaries of moonlight.

I could not make out any difference in size between the now recumbent figures as they tore away at the carcass, and I was about to take the easiest shot when on the opposite bank there appeared a gray movement against the background of dark bush. Hullo, I thought to myself, better wait and see what we have here. I thanked my stars I had the .275. It might be elephant, but more likely rhino; and yet, it seemed too high for rhino.

Whatever it was, it kept coming on and would soon reach the river bed where recognition would be certain. By gosh, it was an elephant! For a while he stood motionless on the opposite bank, doubtless sniffing the horribly tainted air. Then down he came quite silently to the glittering floor beneath me, advancing steadily toward the water holes. I must say he looked the monarch of the forest all right. Everything gave way before him, if without panic yet without hesitation. What an emblem for any country to emulate. Sagacity, love of peace, and goodwill embodied in irresistible strength and armor. I was curious to see what the lions would do when he came to them; they appeared to pay as little attention to him as he to them. A case of complete confidence apparently. He passed by them maybe fifteen paces distant.

The reek from the already somewhat ripe offal and the abundant man-smell all about seemed not to ruffle his serenity one little bit. What did upset it though was a .275 between the ribs. With a squirm and a bellow of rage that split the welkin he tucked his stern under him and began diminishing in size in the weirdest way. Simultaneously with the roar something flashed by me with a whimper of fear. Every animal in that gathering had experienced vicariously a full-dress rehearsal of being blown to hell by dynamite. The scene lay still and lifeless beneath me in the cold silver light of the gigantic moon. My anxious ears waited for the hoped-for crash of the mighty beast. Certainly he had gone off in that headlong death rush that betokened a mortal body shot—and that squirm and bellow, surely they could not be mistaken? At last! Over the still air there came the single crash of a heavy body.

This was fine luck, getting this elephant so easily. It meant another day here unless I turned the boys out now. But perhaps I would not be able to find him; he might have fallen in bush. Better wait another day. What did a day matter anyhow? With these thoughts I turned me in to sleep the sleep of the just.

The dead bull lay about where I expected, and while the cutting-out gang worked on him, I went off to the mountain with the big telescope, traversing some dense bush where rhino were numerous. Indeed, we were chased into some uncomfortably sharp-pointed sansevieria by two of them who showed a strong desire to investigate us. If I had not thought we might find elephant about, I would not have hesitated to settle them, the nasty pugnacious brutes.

We climbed a few hundred feet up the mountainside and set up the glass. On all sides the great plain stretched away, open plains alternating with patches of bush. In the clear morning air bands of oryx, giraffe, topi, and gazelle could be seen everywhere. Away to the north Murua Akipi loomed up, while to the west the great plain was rimmed by faint blue rocky peaks. The swamp that formed our next destination lay concealed by the gray patches of bush, but the few dark mimosas marking the wet-season outflow could just be distinguished through the powerful glass. Not a sign of human occupation could be seen anywhere, though there were doubtless bands of roving Dabossans somewhere about on those immense plains.

As it was certain that we should return by this route, it was considered wise to cache the few tusks we had, so they were cut from the saddles and buried in the donkey boma. All traces of the operation were destroyed by running the donkeys in for half an hour before saddling-up time. Late in the afternoon we set off with all water bags full. At sundown the safari halted, water was shared out, and temporary camp made. One hour after moonrise we were under way again, arriving in the morning at Swamp Camp. Here we had a site cut out of the solid thorn bush some way back from the swamp so as not to alarm anything coming to it. A path just wide enough led into this camp on a curve so that the camp itself was quite invisible from the outside. The only drawback was the scanty shade given by the thorn bush.

At this time of the year the swamp was simply a dry plain of dark soil, tremendously poached up by game tracks. In the rains, however, the whole great pan is covered with water and twelve-foot grass. Patches of the old grass still remained, but some of it had been burned off and much of it eaten off or trampled down by elephant. Now the young green shoots were coming up for all the world like young maize without the heads. It would almost certainly be frequented by elephant and most probably by bull stuff only. Just why this should be so always puzzled me. Not once in my twenty-five years of hunting have I found cow elephant on these isolated patches of swamp grass. Always bulls and bulls only—sometimes in great numbers and of all sorts and sizes except the young herd bulls. These latter are seldom found detached from mamma's apron strings.

As soon as we were refreshed, P. and I set off for the swamp. It would not do to take chances. However silently my well-disciplined safari might conduct itself, there was always the chance that some incoming or outgoing elephant might wind our camp and alarm set in. Snooping rapidly along the tree-fringed outflow course, we soon reached the swamp. There was an ancient tree broken off high up but with the trunk still attached so that it presented a sort of gangway up which one could just walk. We had used it before and were relieved to see it still there. Its upper part just afforded a view over the swamp sufficiently high to provide detection of any gray backs protruding from the sea of grass.

Pyjalé was up first with his naked feet while I watched his face. His grin was enough; up I went beside him. There they were—not a great many. We counted a dozen, very scattered, probably some good stuff among them, the grass being just high enough to prevent an examination of their ivory.

CHAPTER 15

O N A CAREFUL count there were fourteen gray backs on show. With the exception of three in a group all were scattered hither and thither. This meant that if they were to prove gun-shy—as was not unlikely with the Abyssinian Plateau only some sixty miles to the north—it would be advisable to go for the group first and secure that at any rate. Had a glimpse of the ivory been obtained showing any outstanding teeth among the scattered ones, no doubt I would have tried first for them.

The morning breeze was now blowing strongly, and with a little luck the others might not connect the ping of the .275 with any particular danger. With hope mounting high, we plunged into the grassy crop with the wind strong in our faces. At once it became apparent that there had been tremendous work going on among the succulent stuff, work that could only have been accomplished by far greater numbers than were now on show. Speculations as to the present whereabouts of the absentees filled our heads as we strode along the countless tracks. Naturally our thoughts turned to the flats beyond Murua Akipi where the grass would be even more succulent than here and where it was almost certain that numbers of bulls would have gathered. Devoutly we hoped it might be so.

It was not until we were within about two hundred yards of them that we caught the first sight of our quarry.

First one high ridged back, then two more showed up. Still no sight of ivory though, for elephant when feeding carry their heads quite low. Luckily for the hunter they raise their heads on hearing or smelling anything strange.

Broadly speaking, one could not go far wrong in shooting anything bearing the unmistakable signs of age, such as a sharp ridge bone, strong folds and corrugations of the skin, and size of course. Therefore we were more concerned with opening our onslaught in such a way as to secure the greatest number in the shortest time with the minimum of noise and fuss. The best way to do this is to approach as nearly to thirty yards from each member of the group as is possible and then to take the one farthest out first with the brain shot. If the group is feeding it will probably be scattered and it may be impossible to attain anything like the thirty yards. This may well become one hundred yards. It should not be more than this because one then risks ruining the whole scheme by a miss at the brain. One must remember that all this elephant shooting is done standing, without any sort of rest.

On this occasion there were only three animals to deal with and the problem was presented in its simplest form. Two were together broadside-on, the nearer partially covering the other, while the third member of the party was out some sixty yards away. All were feeding. Heads were clear of grass from the tusk sockets up. Changes in position were constant but slow. Of course we were downwind. The disposition to be waited for was that the sixty-yarder should present his head in such a way as to make a kill as certain as possible. At the moment of arrival at suitable range he gave only a slanting shot at the brain from behind the ear—too risky for the first shot. We must wait until he came round a bit, hoping meanwhile that the two on our right might continue as they were, browsing along toward the single one.

As they advanced, so did we. Once the farthest one's head came round almost enough for a certain shot, only to swing away again. Perhaps for two minutes this sort of thing continued. Then the chance came. His head came round enough, the .275 caught him correctly, and down he went. Instantly the rifle covered the nearer of the two as his head came round until he was facing directly toward us. He too dropped kneeling to the frontal brain shot, uncovering the one behind him who was staring at number one whose ribs only showed above the grass. This was an easy broadside shot and he too bit the dust. Seven or eight seconds would cover the whole encounter.

The thing now was whether the shots had disturbed the others. Racing to the kneeling one, I soon had a view over the whole scene while P. cut off the tails. There they were! Not a move! The strong wind had deadened the sound. There was not much more to do now than to work the remainder one by one against the wind.

After a glance at each of our beauties—all of whom carried two teeth of from 50 to 80 pounds each—off we set downwind to approach the single fellow intended for our next victim. This was accomplished with ridiculous ease by another frontal shot. Again the rush to mount the prostrate giant. One could feel his great heart still pounding strongly through the soles of one's feet. Mounting by the trunk and over the forehead, one could feel that the head was held free of the ground by the enormously strong elastic sinews of the neck, sinews that constantly bear the weight of the massive head, trunk, and perhaps three hundredweight of ivory. Two lovely tusks revealed themselves during the short journey to him.

Would the others be off was the question. It was soon answered: they were! Watching for a moment while P. secured the tail, it was apparent that they were all drawing toward the northern end of the swamp. But they were not really alarmed yet and might still settle down again without leaving for distant ground.

The only thing to do now was to get out of the grass onto the burnt dry ground and try to cut off their retreat should they be determined on flight. If they once left the swamp, it meant that they would not stop short of the Murua Akipi flats, some forty or fifty miles away, with nothing but burnt-up plains and patches of arid thorn bush without shade or water as an inducement to stop.

At one time it looked as if we might have managed it. Once we reached the edge of the swamp, the going was better except that we had to make many detours to avoid belts of dense wait-a-bit thorn. We were a few feet above the level of the swamp and could see our quarry every now and then. These glimpses were not reassuring. With their uncanny sense of communicating the common purpose, they were bearing down on one point of exit. Their various courses converged toward it while we raced, panted, and sweated to reach it first, knowing as we did that to be late at the spot meant a grilling, roasting stern chase at a killing pace for many miles with the great probability of a fruitless and terribly boring return to camp.

Sure enough they won. We were only in time to join the tail end of the procession. What a sight they presented as they formed up in line-ahead, their great long legs now visible from toenail up as they strode along in that seven- or eight-mile-per-hour gait they have for such journeys. It was now about midday, the wind had dropped, and the heat and glare were terrific. No chance of running these

hard, athletic, racy, thin-legged, dry-country elephant to
a walking pace as may be done in other parts of Africa
by a man on foot. There remained but one possible way
in which a shot might be got. One of them might stop or
slow down to void. If the hunter should be close up behind and should he be capable of a last burst of speed, he
might get a chance. There would be no turning toward
him, thus helping him. No, he would have to range off at
an angle and thus get in a raking shot. It is this chance
that draws the hunter into the most appalling chases time
after time and leads to most grueling waste of energy.

In this case the chances of such a slowing down seemed
good enough. They were full to the back teeth with lush
grass, all of which they would void in the first few miles.
They had not been sufficiently frightened to have reached
the diarrhea stage. We just followed them.

Looked at from afar, they seemed to be traveling
along sedately enough; it was only when trying to keep
up with them that one realized their speed. It is the
length of the stride that does it, not the number of strides
per minute. The whole procession was setting a true and
direct course for Murua Akipi, whose summit could occasionally be seen above the shimmering bush. Our path
was slithery with flattened patches of very moist dung,
and the strong fresh aroma almost choked us as the gray-
trousered sterns flitted ceaselessly away from us. There
was still too much of the dense thorn bush—through
which even an African cannot circulate at speed—for P.
to try a diversion by racing ahead and pausing them,
thereby affording the laboring rifleman a chance, however
fleeting. But he was on the lookout for such a lay.

After some two hours of this wearisome chase, during

which we kept pretty close to the last of the line, I was beginning to entertain ideas of what I found it easy to call wisdom: that it was better to leave them undisturbed in reaching new feeding grounds whither we ourselves were bound and where the chances were we would meet with them again. Just then P.'s chance arrived. A lane through the bush revealed itself running almost parallel with our course on the downwind side of it. Away he raced as if completely fresh, at a speed about three times as fast as that of the flotilla. This should suffice to bring him ahead although he had farther to go. I, too, made a terrific effort to close the gap between me and the end of the line.

Just as the procession reached a favorable position for an attack, that great fellow P. got in his grand work. The leading files stopped abruptly, heads up, ears cocked toward where P.'s black head could just be seen over some intervening bush dangerously close to the head of the column.

The first shot that presented itself was when the leader swung his head toward P., thereby giving me a chance, albeit a slanting one, at his brain. It was successful and now the next few seconds were hectic enough. The whole bunch broke up in all directions while the nearest to me turned completely round and fell to a frontal brain shot almost at my feet. Two more received body shots and another would have done so had not a head intervened at the very instant of firing, receiving the unintended bullet but not in a fatal place. After making sure that the one nearest me had got it properly, I ran to the leader to make sure he was likewise dead, and finding him suspiciously quiet, I motioned to P. to give him a jab with his spear to the heart. Then we gathered the tails and went in search of our two who had received body shots. We soon came on one standing motionless and sorely stricken. A bullet in the brain settled him. While P. was cutting off the tail, we heard a great crash and knew the other one was down. Reaching him, we found him quite dead. We had a much-needed rest.

It would have been pretty hopeless to follow the now thoroughly alarmed remainder of the herd. Dividing the tails between us, each slinging his on a bush pole, we soon took up the trail for home fairly well satisfied with our day. Instead of revisiting all our victims, we cut straight back to camp, or as straight as the bush would allow. What a weary long way it seemed with nothing to draw one on but visions of rest and drink awaiting us.

It was dusk when we made camp, and how cheering and comfortable everything was as we strode in past the donkey boma now filled with satisfied animals. The cows were being milked, the boys were rested, washed, and cheery, while a merry camp fire was burning in front of my tent with the boys standing by with faces wreathed in smiles at the sight of elephant tails. They are devilish heavy things, these elephant tails, and I was mortally sick of mine by this time. Often we had to reduce them to a mere tip with a few hairs sticking out from it when the bag was heavy.

The boys tell me they got out the tusks of the four in the swamp and that they are being washed. They heard the shots of the morning and a lookout in a tree had seen the whereabouts of the fallen. One of the Masai herders tells me he was chased off by a lioness with young. No other elephant seen. No natives seen. The donkey head-

man says he has saddles soaking ready for the new tusks
and that they will be ready for trekking by the afternoon
of the next day.

And so to bed by the light of the moon midst the hum
of crickets and the roars of a distant lion.

CHAPTER 16

THE next day the chopping-out gang went off with P. to get in the outlying tusks while I took a scour round with Boy Dodinga. It was not likely that anything had drawn into the swamp during the night as the whole area was smoke- and man-tainted by this time. But one never knew.

As we were passing some clumps of thick bush, I was in the lead. Suddenly there was a tremendous racket behind me and this is what met my startled gaze: a large lioness appeared in the very act of striking down Boy Dodinga, who was in full flight toward me. She was reared right up on her hind legs directly over the doubled-up boy while beyond, her two cubs, about the same size as chow dogs, scuttled away. As always, I carried my rifle and it was ready. I instantly crashed a solid into her exposed chest, knocking her right out, for it got the spine. She was probably only chasing him off while her cubs escaped, but why had she let me pass unmolested? Probably my unfamiliar color caused her to hesitate. She was possibly the one seen yesterday by the cattle herder.

We visited the carcasses of the detusked elephant, thinking we might see something of interest, but without result. It is doubtful if lion would touch dead elephant with such an abundance of live game about. It must not be thought that because I only mention elephant that no other game existed. On the contrary, these plains were simply teeming with dry-country buck of all kinds. Giraffe were in scores and oryx in droves of two hundred and more. All our thoughts were bent on elephant and we looked on all else as so much fodder. When we wanted skins for saddlery or meat for the pot, we dipped into the abounding reservoir for our needs; otherwise we paid scant attention to it. As an indication of the extent of our demands on the herds of game, I might mention that it required four hundred skins to ensaddle our donkey-borne ivory when it came to the "Shuka" or retreat, as they called it, when the safari was ended and on its way down country. And this demand could be met just as fast as the buck could be skinned. The .256 was invaluable for this work.

We now had a devilish long and dry trek ahead of us to the natron springs on Murua Akipi. It would not do to bury our ivory here as we might not return this way, especially if the rains broke. Luckily there were no tusks so large as to require to be man-borne. All went to the donkeys. During the whole of this time no natives had been seen. All this country lay under the blight of the Habash, the Abyssinian slave-raider. I often wondered how my twenty .577-bore Sniders firing .450-bore Martini cartridges would come off in an encounter with this highly armed gentry.

When all are rested, the ivory firmly fixed in their hide saddles, and the water bags filled, the signal to break camp is given. The camp chronicler gives a blast on his water-buck horn trumpet, there is a stampede for the loads, and off we go in the heat of the late afternoon to travel far into the night by moonlight. Then the rest till

2:00 A.M. and the rush to reach water with now empty water bags late on the ensuing day.

Crystal clear but deadly bitter stuff, these natron springs, as toward the end of the dry season they become highly concentrated. Far better the most urine-laden, scum-infested, bug-ridden rainwater. And just such a description fits the fetid pool high on the shoulder of Murua Akipi, the water mountain. Chasing off the hordes of baboons, who seemed to think they owned the festering pool, we were soon lowering water gladly into our parched systems but with every pint becoming more and more critical of the hellish brew, until finally weaker gorges rose and rejected the foul stuff onto the burning rock. Then boiling it, passing it through a cloth and finally making tea of it would be tried. That was better but still pretty bad.

After a rest I grabbed a boy to carry the big telescope up the hill. On the way we were surprised to meet on rocky ground, of all unexpected animals, zebra. There must surely be some other source of water than the baboon pool we were using as this was quite inaccessible to such animals. The summit itself was rather too high for our depleted energies, so we slanted up so as to get a view northward as quickly as possible. Here we set up the four-inch glass, fixed the magnification as low as possible —thirty-five—as there was much heat haze about, and then began to sweep the checkerboard of bush and open plain first with plus-six binoculars. Anything of interest picked up by them was fully examined by the big glass.

What a scene it was: in the foreground rolling plains with great lines and whorls of gray bush intersecting in all directions; in the middle distance another hill such as the one we were on but smaller; then more bush and finally a small sugar-loaf kopje jutting abruptly from the sea of bush. That was our objective. That little hill commanded a view unique in my experience of elephant grounds. For it stood directly over extensive flats that reached over the northern horizon and formed one of the sources of the Pibor, I always thought. We hoped to find these flats covered with bull elephant. At the moment haze prevented the four-inch glass from showing whether there were any elephant there or not. One thing we noticed was a thin wisp of smoke from a point on a hill in the middle distance. Pointing it out, the boy said, "Natives, Bwana." But I knew of no native settlement there and surely no wandering Jiwans or Dabossans would dare to flaunt a fire here under the noses of the dreaded Habash. It must be a party of these Abyssinian slavers.

Next day was a daylight trek to end at Pibor Kopje and our route lay directly under where we had seen smoke on the hill. When I mentioned this smoke, P. agreed that it could only be made by the Habash. Orders were therefore given to the askaris to be on the lookout and to allow no straggling. Perhaps we should see our Sniders firing Martini cartridges after all. There was an air of surprised excitement about the safari. It traveled in much closer array than usual. There was less putting down of loads and retiring to the bush. Looking back as it crossed an open plain, I could not help thinking what a formidable appearance it presented. With its eighty or ninety donkeys, its forty porters and its askaris, headmen, boys and boys' boys, it stretched for half a mile or more. I thought any hiding Habash would be terrified unless they were in considerable force.

When I reached the neighborhood of the hill where we suspected the Habash might be, I began to shoot a buck or two with the long .256. There were any amount of oryx about, and it always looks well not only to demonstrate the quality of your armament but it also shows confidence in one's ability to tackle anything. At any rate, when in any sort of jam in Africa and you can kill something in sight, it seems to calm the most turbulent and enterprising feelings in the native breast. After dropping a couple of oryx, I halted the safari at some bare rock at the foot of the hill. Of course our whole performance was visible to anyone on the hill. As we went about our business, skinning and cutting up the meat, smoking, resting or eating, a single Abyssinian was seen coming down the hillside toward us dressed in cotton pants and burnoose with the inevitable felt hat on top. This he doffed as he came to where I was sitting. Calling up an Arab donkey boy to translate, we were soon in conversation with him.

He seemed to be in an awful funk so I guessed it was a very small party out on a slave raid hoping to fall upon some wandering Dabossans. We brewed tea and gave him some, and he asked for meat, which surprised me as I knew these fellows were well armed. Rank bad shots as they are, still no one could fail to kill something from the teeming multitude of game that covered the plains. I suppose they were afraid shots might spoil the manhunt. Giving him as much meat as he could carry away, I indicated I would like to visit his camp and followed him up the hill.

After a short climb we reached their encampment, a perfect little fortress surrounded by a low wall of piled rocks round a natural depression quite invisible from the plain. Here were nine other Habashis and a dozen mules, one very nice one among them, which I determined to buy from them if possible. They made coffee from their meager supply of beans while I looked over their arms. They had two neat little French carbines .256-bore marked "Daudeter," but the rest were the old *fusil Gras* of the French pre-Lebel days. Negotiations were opened for the purchase of the mule. They wanted ivory. So we all descended to the safari.

Now good riding mules run to very high figures in Abyssinia; they are far dearer than horses. Of course the one I wanted would not be a trained riding mule—their price runs to as much as a thousand Maria Therese thalers—but it was a better-class baggage mule worth possibly sixty or seventy dollars. Finally, after much haggling, the mule was saddled complete and one of the "Daudeter" carbines—but without ammunition—passed into our hands while a tusk of 73 pounds passed into theirs. I was interested to know how they would manage to transport a single tusk, but it was a simple problem to such experienced packers. They simply balanced it on the off side of the mule with sufficient gear to counterbalance. Galls mean nothing to these hard-bitten ruffians; in fact, they say a pack saddle is only secure when it sticks to plenty of sores.

While on the subject of those "Daudeter" carbines, I cannot refrain from mentioning a little tale attached thereto. We had "shucked" and were once more in civilization when I happened to meet a traveler at a camp. It appeared he was keenly interested in rifles. In fact he was an employee at the Hythe School of Musketry. He said the school made a point of acquiring every known form of rifle-caliber arm in the world. At once I said he was the very man to tell me more of the "Daudeter" carbine I had got from the Abyssinian.

Sending for it, I placed it in his hands. A look of surprised chagrin spread over his face—he was floored.
Never had he seen one before. Never had he heard of
it. And yet I understand that it is the name of a large
French arsenal.

To resume our tale of the doings at the Pibor Flats,
having parted company amicably with the Habash and
after warning them that they were well inside British territory—which I hoped was true—we had to make all
speed to arrive at Pibor Kopje before sundown. During
all those hot miles not an elephant track was seen except
those made in the rainy season. You would have thought
there was not a beast in the country. Warning the boy
who carried the big 'scope to keep with us, P. and I
hurried on ahead of the safari and reached camp with
enough daylight left for a spy over the flats from the
top of the kopje. It was clad with thorn bush and only
from the very summit could one see clearly, so that the
view burst suddenly on one.

What thrilling excitement as you near the top. One
glance will decide whether the flats are empty or full.
There was never anything half hearted about them. If and
when the conditions were right, they would be full of bull
elephant—or empty if the conditions were wrong. There
was no rival hunter for hundreds of miles. It was instantly settled. The flats were simply sprinkled thickly
with the black dots we knew could only be elephant. No
need to question their sex or size. Every one of them
would be a fully matured bull carrying teeth of from 60
to perhaps 150 pounds each. With a sigh of relief P. and
I glanced at each other; how we wished it was early
morning instead of nearly sundown.

Meanwhile the boy had been mounting the big glass

and I began a close survey of the ivory on view. And a most impressive show it was. Nothing in the 150-pound class certainly but heaps of 100-pounders and over. But the most remarkable thing was that there were no tusks under about 60 pounds. It is when the average is high that real bags are made.

As an example of this, an American protégé of mine, finding he could not stand up to intensive elephant hunting, kept a measuring stick cut to the diameter of a fully mature bull elephant's forefoot. He offered rich reward for news of plantation-visiting elephant, but the claimant had to cut a stick to the exact diameter of the raider's foot and bring it with him. If it equaled or surpassed the standard measuring stick, well and good. But if it fell short of that measure, nothing doing. By sticking closely to this rule, he assembled the most astonishing array of lovely teeth, nothing under about 65 pounds and many over 100 pounds. Not many of them, of course, but about five or six head a month, whereas my average per month over the whole hunting period generally worked out at about thirty.

I well remember meeting up with him on the Ubangi River. He was hunting the Belgian side and had a very nice lot of grand teeth in his forty-foot dugout. His safari consisted of two tough-looking native gunbearers and a native girl cook. Nothing more than that. Here he was drifting placidly along with the stream. That night he told me about the difficulties he had met with in the beginning of his hunting career, how he had tried to carry out the instructions for the brain shot and how he had failed to kill. Then in sheer desperation one day he ran close into an elephant and gave it both barrels of a double .450 in the body and, by gosh, the beast fell. That gave him confidence and he never looked back. I asked him if he did not lose a lot of chances at other elephant. "No," he said. "I hunt single bulls only."

I was much interested in this method of charging into your beast; I gathered from his description that that was what happened, and I asked him to take me with him so as to see the fun. "Yes, but you must shoot too," he said. I explained that I had not a permit for the other side.

"Neither have I," he retorted, "but we will go down tomorrow and see the Chef-de-Poste."

Down we went next day in his canoe and stepped ashore at the Poste. Presently we were ushered into the Chef's office. A spruce officer rose from a desk and shook hands. He spoke no English but my American friend began to talk some kind of rot with a strong American accent as he leaned his arms on the desk top. I gathered that he was explaining that he and I wanted to do a little hunting in his district but without formalities. As he did so, I noticed his hands were playing with a little banker's bag of sovereigns while his features were contorted with strange grimaces meant to express extreme amiability, I suppose. When we rose to go into the Chef's house for a drink, my friend left the little bag on the desk. We had our drink and left after much cordiality. "That's O.K.," said my friend when we were clear of the Poste. "He'd have returned the bag had it not been enough or if he had funked it, under the pretense that it had been forgotten." Rather neat, I thought.

There was no difficulty in finding what we wanted; elephant were feeding nightly in the plantations. When a native brought in a proper measurement, we followed him. We first heard our elephant in dense undergrowth about forty yards away. My friend stopped and took the

.450. Then closely followed by his boys, one of whom carried a cripple-stopper .318, we all started a wild rush toward where we could hear the elephant banging his ears about quite unsuspicious of being attacked.

I never saw anything like it! We fell over tree roots, splashed into and out of mud holes, making a tremendous row. But we covered the ground long before the old fellows—there were two of them, one having joined up unbeknown to us—had decided whether they were hearing a mob of stampeding buffalo or what all the row was about.

The moment the now silent and listening beasts could be dimly seen we all redoubled our speed. My friend, who led, ran right up to one and discharged both barrels of his .450, it seemed to me at random, into the middle of the giant. Then quick as lightning the gun was changed for the .318, the boy being awfully good and right close up. The lunatic was close on its heels as it crashed through the forest, pumping in shots as fast as he could fire. We all followed him as fast as we could.

After about four hundred yards of this sort of thing, during which my friend stayed with his quarry extraordinarily well, we heard a crash. There was the elephant down and so was my friend, dead beat with excitement and effort. He told me he almost always got his beast but that he generally had to rest in camp the next day to recover. He often knocked himself about, too, in these mad rushes. I did not think much of his scheme as I reckoned he should have got the other one as well. He admitted it but explained that it was the only way he had had success. He recounted how once a missionary with ambitions in that line had begged to be taken on a hunt. They found an elephant and the same mad tactics were gone through. After the kill my friend looked round. No

padre. After a while still no sign of the reverend gentle-
man. A search revealed him on his back at the bottom of
a game pit. Asked why he did not come up, he replied
sorrowfully that his back was broken and he could not
move. When they lifted him out with infinite care, he
was found to be quite unharmed, but it took a lot to persuade him of that fact.

After that diversion we now return to a further survey
of the magnificent scene. The furthest confines of the
great green sward—for at this distance the five- or six-
foot grass appeared as a level lawn—stretched away to
the north to disappear over the horizon, and it became
apparent that all the elephant were scattered about that
part of it which was directly terminated by our kopje.
The nearest might be two miles from our perch and the
farthest more like five miles. There were eighty-seven to
be counted in sight, all large bulls as to body but varying
greatly in their show of ivory. One or two very wrinkled
and hollow-looking skulls seemed to bear no ivory at all.
These would prove to have lost their ivory either in prizing up trees, digging salt-lick earth, or in other ways
known best to themselves. It looked good for the morrow.

At 5:30 A.M. the boy presented himself with the customary cup of tea and biscuits—customary as long as such
luxuries lasted anyhow. When they were all finished, a
calabash of gruel made of native flour, milk, and sweet-
ened with wild honey took their place, and a very good
substitute it made. The morning was cold and cloudy and
a misty rain was falling, showing that the rains were not
far away. We would have to make haste if we were to return across those black-soil plains before they became a
sea of clinging mud, a mud so tenacious that heavy buck

such as eland can be run down and speared by native runners, their naked feet apparently affording less adhesion to the mud than the hoofs of their quarry. The swamp grass, too, already five or six feet high, was simply shooting up, while the surrounding dry bush would soon blossom forth. Then it would be all up with swamp hunting and its huge concentrations of those lovely old bulls. In a night they would scatter in every direction, and if you met with two or three together, you would be lucky.

CHAPTER 17

AS SOON as we were ready, Pyjalé and I climbed high enough to give us a view of the swamp. Through the thin rain enough could be seen to assure us that the darlings were still there—not so many as yesterday but still in goodly numbers. P. was shivering in the cold air, his splendid body glistening in the rain. I had the .275 and a full belt of those splendidly proportioned cartridges, each one carefully tried through the action and methodically cleaned.

We made straight for the nearest part of the swamp through the surrounding sea of high thorn bush, there being no apparent wind. P., who was leading, suddenly stopped dead. About ten yards away was a large elephant's head, quite motionless and listening, just visible in the thinner tracery of the upper branches of thorn bush. How extraordinarily well his dull gray hide lent itself to the veiling of the gray branches and festoons of dry thorns. One step further away and he almost disappeared, while one step nearer to him he seemed to be in motion emerging from the bush. Two steps nearer sealed his doom, for then it was easy to direct a .275 to the brain. He dropped kneeling, as he was well balanced on all four feet on level ground when he received the death stroke. At once I ran up onto his back, thinking that possibly I might be able to see at least part of the swamp and note the effect of the shot on the other elephant. The bush however was too high. Then I noted that he had only one tusk, the other being broken off short at the lip. Pity, as the whole tusk was a beauty well up in the 100-pound class.

Pyjalé never mounted these brain-shot elephant for some considerable time after they had fallen. I think he never could quite believe that death could be so swift and complete. This is not surprising when one reflects that such a coup could practically never occur with weapons such as spears or arrows. So he always steered clear of the front end for some time and generally liked to give a lightning spear thrust to the heart just to make sure.

Hoping for the best, we continued our way toward the swamp. As we burst quite suddenly from the bush onto the narrow border of dry grass that ran between the bush and the green of the swamp, this is what met our eyes. Imagine an immense field thickly planted with mealies about five feet high and bounded only by the horizon laid out a few feet below you. Away on either hand stretched the gray wall of bush. Now imagine that field of mealies bashed and blasted in every direction; great patches torn off short by some gigantic grazing; branches leaning drunkenly in every direction; whole sectors trampled flat; pyramids of dung humming with insect life; and permeating everywhere, the strong and delicious odor of elephant.

Although the actual height of the grass, or rather flags would be a better name for it, was not more than five feet or so, the horizon was surprisingly close when one stood on the level floor of the swamp. The soil was now black and friable in contrast to the sandy light soil of the higher ground around. And no elephant were in sight.

Surely we were not to witness one of those sudden and inexplicable flittings so common in this game. Or did that shot in the bush not half a mile away stampede them? With these forebodings in mind we plunged into the scene of devastation. Hardly had we gone four hundred yards, weaving our way through the mangled crop, when we caught a glimpse of the high ridged back we so eagerly sought. Thank goodness, all was well.

Wind was now apparent and the sun was breaking through the morning mists as we rapidly drew in down-wind of our game. The sooner we got him down the sooner we would have a stance from which to view the rest of the field. Indeed, without it our view was restricted to a couple of hundred yards at the outside. On the way in to thirty yards or so I glanced at the .275 to see that the action was all right, then another glance along the open sights and a quick feel along the bases of the cartridges protruding from the belt just to make sure they were not smothered in mud or grit. And then the shot upon which so much depended. A missed brain shot now meant a pricked animal resulting in a headlong flight possibly clearing the whole swamp in an incredibly short time. What damnable excitement seizes one at these early morning moments when one is highly strung and full of beans. Later in the day the opiates of sun and fatigue would steady one enormously. What relief when the shot is finally delivered successfully. If a miss, what a sinking feeling. All is black, bloody, and sour.

However all is well. He drops to the shot and I am up on his back almost instantly. He is kneeling and I have a splendid view from his back, five or six hundred yards in all directions. And are they there! Very scattered and in singles. No bunches here. It won't be so easy to make a heavy killing. But what old, old monsters. Mossy, heavily folded, strongly corrugated hides falling in great ridges into the green surrounding sea. Motionless they stand, almost without life one would think except for the serpent-like trunk busy sweeping in that succulent crop. Not the slightest sign of alarm at the recent shot. Rapidly descending, I glanced once more at the tusks. What beauties! Three and one half forearms outside the lip and a lovely curve. P. had already got the tail. Away we went downwind to work up through the scattered herd, wondering how many of these cracks from the .275 they would stand before striking out for pastures new.

There was one particularly ancient-looking beast far on the downwind side of the viewed space that I thought might carry very heavy stuff. The flags were just high enough to hide the ivory when their heads were in the feeding position. There was difficulty in finding him but when found he was easily got. As I mounted his side—he had fallen on it—I could see that no tusk at all stuck out of the lip. He seemed unnaturally quiet so I gave him a shot in the brain to make certain. This produced the proper convulsions and I gazed around to see how the others were taking all this noise. Sure enough, two of the nearer ones seemed a bit uneasy. There was no sign of panic yet but they were certainly on the move. Further away, however, there were ten or twelve quite undisturbed and feeding animals.

Now what about that other tusk! Not a sign! Both tusks broken off at the lip. Age of this old fellow? Who knows? Possibly one hundred and fifty to two hundred years. Bad luck getting a completely tuskless bull of such age and size. What monstrous teeth they would have been had they stood the hundreds of years of prizing, digging, and perhaps fighting. However, on with the hunt.

Pyjalé and I pegged away at them until we had ten tails in the bag. By this time the remainder were bent on flitting, and our last view of them was as they bunched together toward the far end of the flat preparatory to leaving it for some unknown haunt in the north. Lacking any other means of transport other than legs, we reduced the size of the tails and made for the nearest point of the coast of bush, its thorn-obstructed glades making infinitely better going than did the swamp with its tortured and mangled crop of flags.

Suliemani, the cook, had one of his famous curried trunk and rice dishes ready, and as the day had been such an easy one as well as such a successful one, I had a hearty meal and then climbed the kopje where the big telescope was now mounted with a grass roof built over it. It was too late in the day to start the tusk cutters off, but P. took them to the first elephant we had killed in the bush. He was hardly a mile from camp and the usual crowd went with him to get the fat. These boys never seemed to get enough of it and they used nearly to turn my insides out by drinking pints of it neat.

The big glass showed nothing in the swamp and only a faint dust cloud far away to the north where some fifty or sixty trekking elephant were soaking along under it at that appalling long-step gait of theirs that would probably take them fifty miles to some other green feeding ground known only to themselves. Meanwhile I amused myself trying to pick up the fallen beasts. It was by no means easy, but finally I located them all except the first one we had killed in the swamp. Of course the one in the bush one would not expect to see. Try as I would, I could find no trace of that fellow with the beautiful teeth. Yet he should have been the easiest of all to spot as he was the nearest. Annoyance and doubt began to fill my mind. Then I remembered I had not paid the usual attention to the symptoms of the brain shot. He had been terribly still I now remembered as I had climbed his back. What a fool not to have given him another shot down between my legs as I stood on his neck. I must have been rattled with the prospect of getting among that millionaire herd. How I cursed myself. Even P. had not, as far as I saw, jabbed his spear into him. And yet he had his tail. Surely it must be all right. Perhaps he was hidden by a tall tuft of flags and the boys would get him in the morning.

That infernal bull haunted my dreams that night. P. confessed that he, too, had failed to do anything to him. However the ivory from the morning's bush victim was very satisfactory; it looked like 80- to 90-pound stuff.

At cockcrow next morning I climbed the hill and had a spy through the big glass. As I expected, there was nothing in sight except smoke from the foot of the Jiwé massif away in the northeast, so I determined to go with the tusk gang and make quite sure of the fate of that doubtful bull. P. and I followed our tracks of yesterday meticulously. We found the spot from which I fired and we found the spent case. We found the exact spot where he had fallen to his knees. But he was no longer there. We had his tail, but he was off away in the north as happy as a sandboy. P. and I were filled with fury to be caught napping. Damn! Three and one half cubits outside the lip, too! Thank goodness this sort of happening was rare. In fact only one other elephant was lost in a similar way. About ten per cent of bulls shot in the head received a second shot when using the .275, and this percentage was appreciably reduced when the .318 was used. I put this down to the fact that the 250-grain bullet of the .318 held a truer course than the 170-grain bullet of the .275. I know, too, that in the case of slanting shots from behind where the bullet would have to traverse the immense neck muscles to reach the brain, the .318 long 250-grain bullet was more uniformly successful than the .275. At the same time by far the greater number of my elephant were killed with the .275 and I never had the faintest suspicion of trouble either with rifle or cartridge. I cannot say the same of the .318. In its case the pressures are too close to the danger limit and I had blow-backs, misfires, and extraction difficulties. The shape of the cartridge, too, is not as it should be; there is not enough "bottle" shape about it.

I knew P. would find the others all right so I returned to camp with the pleasant prospect of spending the day with the big glass. I reckoned that any elephant within ten or twelve miles would be visible, unless he were in bush of course. But even then often a light dust cloud would give away their locality.

After a pleasurable rest at the big glass, watching game far and wide and speculating on the natives inhabiting the great rocky mass in the northeast, I returned to camp to find all the ivory in, cleaned, and laid out in front of the tent. Mighty big stuff it looked, old and discolored with very short hollows. And at the end of the row were two immense stumps of a fantastic diameter with scarcely any hollows at all. These were the broken stumps of the veteran beast. Onto the scales with them first: 72 and 76 pounds! Would you believe it! This meant that had they kept their original dimensions, they would have scaled somewhere about 180 pounds or more each.

With the thought of the lost tusker and the one with no teeth occupying my mind so much, I had not given the rest of that day's bag the appreciation it deserved, and it was not until these teeth came off the scales that I began to realize their true proportions. That is a funny thing about ivory. It is not what meets the eye that makes the weight; it is the hollows in the socket. And so in this case it suddenly burst on me that the weights were going to eclipse anything I had hitherto got in a single day. Although I had killed twelve in a day, the highest bag for a single day had stood at 1,340 pounds. Now as I entered the weights in the ivory book, it began to look as if the present lot of nine elephant with one tuskless one was going to top the record lot.

And so it did. The combined weights of the fifteen tusks plus the two stumps totaled 1,463 pounds fresh weights. When, months after, they were sold in London at Hale's auction rooms, they had only lost seven pounds in drying and they realized the astonishing price of nine hundred pounds.

What that herd of some eighty beasts must have carried is nobody's business, but it must have run into many thousands of pounds sterling. In the whole of my hunting career I never overtopped this total of 1,463 pounds. The nearest I came to it was when I killed nineteen bulls in an afternoon in the Lado Enclave, but they totaled only 1,440 pounds on the scales in spite of the fact that they all had two teeth. Two other bags of fifteen each just fell short of 1,400 pounds.

Ruminating on these matters over the camp fire, it seemed to me that contact must be made at all costs with that northward-bound convoy of millionaires. But how far should we have to go, and could we manage it and the return over those black soil plains in the imminent rains with heavily laden donks? Must consult P. first of all. How unfortunate it was there was no farther hill or mountain range to be seen away to the northward where the herd had gone.

Pyjalé of course knew nothing of the country north of us. But he said that where the elephant had gone there was sure to be water. How far away no one could say. They would think nothing of fifty or sixty miles. Now the curious thing was that we had not seen any actual water on the green swamp; there was in fact none at this time of the year. The green growth was entirely due to sub-terranean sources. Whether the elephant were dependent on the juice contained in the cane-like stems of the flags to supply their liquid needs or whether they had some drink-ing place in the neighborhood was a question that would have to be settled before we could move our camp. So we decided that P. and I with a few of the boys would set off on the morrow to see what we could find while the main safari remained where it was. I then repaired to my comfortable camp bed and P. went off to sleep alone by his small fire with nothing but his wooden neck pillow by way of bedding.

Warning the headman to keep a lookout posted on Pibor Kopje in case of wandering Habash, and to build a camp zeriba, I had a spy out over the flats as dawn broke just to make sure that nothing had drawn into them during the night. As I expected, there was nothing in sight. Soon we were heading parallel with the swamp along the dry ridge above it. The slight rains had made no impression and everything was bone dry. All the elephant tracks were windswept and the droppings dried up and almost obliterated by white ants. One would have thought that no elephant had been about for six months.

Owing to a bend in the course of the green strip, we thought to reduce the mileage by cutting across the dry bush country, a dodge we found had been much resorted to by elephant also, their great roads leading ever northward. In the course of a short cut we came out upon one of those inexplicable black cotton-soil plains often found sandwiched between miles and miles of bush. Not a vestige of a shrub and barely any grass seems to be able to grow on them. It was here that we saw the most magnificent sight a hunter could ever dream of—five grand bull elephant in line-ahead traveling majestically along toward the north. Apparently they had emerged from some heavy bush on the southern confines of the plain; they may have been feeding on the flats between Pibor Kopje and the distant hills east of it. At any rate, here they were and it was our job to try to intercept them.

What a hope! They were not to be come up with by anything that I could produce. Pyjalé could have caught up with them doubtless, but they had too much of a start for me. How they moved along with that tireless stride that covers the ground in such an amazing way, their long legs looking quite racy and slender. How very different from their brothers of the forest they looked. We just followed in behind and they proceeded to sink into the horizon ahead while we thought to come up with them somewhere.

We passed some mighty elephant roads, smooth and hard, converging from all directions toward the swamp. They began to narrow as the higher ridges on either side neared each other until finally there was only a narrow green strip to mark the course of what in the rains would be a considerable river. All along this strip we kept a lookout for water holes. We might have followed a huge elephant road running north and along which the great swamp herd had passed, but it diverged so from the course of the green valley that we thought we might miss some water hole by doing so. We began to wish we had some natives with us. Finally, as we had not found water, we had to call a halt. From the tops of such low trees as the bush afforded we surveyed the country ahead. The horizon was just the same level gray bush with no hill in sight as far as the eye could see. There was nothing for it but to return to camp.

Now if we were to break into that strangely flat-looking country lying ahead of us without native assistance, it would mean firstly caching our ivory and secondly relaying waterbags out from Pibor Kopje just as far as would be necessary to make contact with some kind of water or to await the rains while hunting from Pibor Kopje. This would mean that the return to the Dodinga main camp would have to be by the harder dry country away to the west of our outward trek. We were finding it difficult to decide what to do when it was decided for us by the arrival of a change in the weather. All night long thunder could be heard rolling and lightning fizzed all around us. The morning came up cool, refreshing, and smelling of wet earth.

Almost overnight flowers and grass spring up; the parched earth cannot absorb the flow and pools of water form in every depression all over the place. With the arrival of the rains an elephantless landscape would be magically dotted with small lots of bulls. No big herds of course; there was not yet sufficient water for them. But of all the seasons of the year this one of the little rains is the most enjoyable to the hunter. So all hearts were glad at the prospect of the return to base, camping by pools of rainwater at pleasantly reasonable distances instead of the dry season's grinding night-and-day marches.

And so we began the retreat, mentally promising ourselves to return someday and to penetrate the mystery of that flat country to the north, possibly by getting in touch with the Northern Jiwans whose smoke we had seen. About a year later Harry Rayne and I attacked the country lying over the northern horizon by way of Abyssinia. A short account of the hunting was given in *The Wanderings of an Elephant Hunter*, so I will merely say here that we were not disappointed. Great numbers of good elephant were located on the Pibor and tributaries, some of whom might easily have been on the Pibor Flats when we visited them.

From pool to pool we wandered, picking up a number of excellent bulls here and there. No big killings but what easy work. Very often we would see our game miles away across the plains, standing up black above the now green bush, all the dry weather dust, bird droppings, and whatnot having been washed from their wrinkled hides. Often they would be actually bathing, and then it would be necessary to wait until they came out of their baths before killing them so that we might drink the water without the addition of blood and dung to its already foul consistency. And so we went wandering along from puddle to puddle until one day it became apparent that the small rains were petering out. Then it became urgent to reach our askari camp; otherwise we might be caught far from water with drying pools everywhere. With heavy ivory both man-borne and donkey-borne one has to be careful.

One evening we found a pool that still had a good amount of water in it and all round about it were signs that great numbers of elephant were using it albeit much of the spoor was cow. There was a suitable moon for the first part of the night, so I thought it would be interesting to sit up and have a look-see. The surroundings were quite bare of trees so I merely lay back on a sloping bank about fifteen yards downwind of the pool. Nothing much happened and I must have dozed off a bit, for suddenly I was staring at an elephant that had appeared majestically right at the edge of the pool perhaps twenty yards from me. Funny thing was I couldn't see any ivory although the moonlight seemed all right. With only one beast it was hard to determine whether it was a cow or a bull, so I hesitated about firing in case something better should turn up. In a short while the visitor started to glide away in that mysterious way they have in moonlight. Since the moment when I realized its presence there had not been a sound, this showing that he or she quite understood what all the man-taint meant, for of course the safari had been using the pool for the usual domestic purposes.

Fully awake now, I presently saw a ghost-like mass approaching. Exactly as before, it came silently to rest opposite me, remained there some moments quite motionless, and then went off again in the same direction. I must say I was puzzled. Here we were, away back beyond of where elephant were wont to show, but still being treated with the utmost suspicion. And for some two hours this ridiculous business went on. Ever the same beast alone came and drank; at any rate, it appeared to be the same one. Never seeing a glint of ivory, at last I went off to camp as the moon set, determined to solve the mystery on the morrow.

In the morning an examination of the tracks showed that our visitor had been a very large old cow and it appeared that she had been carrying water to quite a little bunch of calves and half- and three-quarters grown animals. There were signs of spillage among the tracks and on the stamped ground where they had waited for the water carrier to return. At any rate that is what it all pointed to. Why these elephant should have shown such excessive caution at this particular locality was surprising.

As the small rains appeared to be definitely over, the subconscious anxiety about water returned. We were pretty heavily loaded by this time—both the porters and the donkeys. There were sixteen tusks of over 100 pounds each being man-borne. One, the biggest, weighed 136 pounds. The best of boys cannot carry these great teeth unless they have water to drink. The water bags would have to come back into use after their holiday while the rains were on. There was no hilltop from which to spy out elephant and, consequently, water pools. In fact we were submerged in the sea of bush; only by climbing a high tree could we see the Kilassa massif in the distance—our one certainty of water.

CHAPTER 18

VERY early indeed were we all afoot. It is strange how circumstances such as ours permeate all hands. Most of the boys were veterans now and knew what it meant to lack water. The march would be orderly and fast, and water would not be wasted. Although the start could not be made until the light came—about 5:30 A.M. —everyone was awake by 2:00 A.M. cooking gruel with a handful of tamarind in it and grilling great hunks of elephant meat. Pyjalé and I set off first, leaving Boy Dodinga to lead the safari on our tracks.

The country now seemed even drier than before the rains. All the greenery brought out then was wilting and dying now and the sun seemed fiercer than ever. We passed many dried-up pools with abundant signs of good elephant around them, great mud baths now cracked and hard as concrete. Once or twice there remained just a little moisture in the mud and great clusters of butter-flies were collected on these patches.

Once we halted to listen to a commotion to our right. A lovely lesser kudu sprang swiftly through the bush followed by hunting dogs. They were right on her tail, but she seemed undistressed and easily capable of throwing off her pursuers. Otherwise I would have lammed into them with a rifle. But I was reluctant to do this as there were sure to be elephant about. So intent were they on their chase that they never even glanced at us.

Presently we came on signs of elephant. First warning was that delightful smell of aromatic dung and crushed vegetation that so entrances the hunter. It means that the great beasts have recently passed, for in that heat all trace of smell is soon dried up. At the first decent tree Pyjalé mounts and looks around while I take a swig at the calabash, the while watching him for signs of game. Out goes his arm and he turns his face down toward me and there is the welcome grin that means he has spotted something. Down he comes and off we go without a word, he in the lead. The rifle of course is always ready, but I silently work open the bolt just to make certain. It is the .275 and I note with affection the bright little cartridges nestling so neatly in the magazine. The feel of the deadly little weapon thrills my arm. Gone is fatigue and sun weariness as we stride swiftly through the bush.

Pyjalé stops to listen. I can hear a rumble, the rumble of giant intestines as they continue their nonstop job of extracting vitamins from masses of vegetation. This sound is particularly welcome as it only proceeds from un-alarmed elephant. Pyjalé's job is done now and mine com-mences. I take the lead and make as straight as the thorn bush will allow toward the sound. We do not come on our game immediately however. It must be traveling. Almost immediately we come on fresh tracks. With re-lief and joy we notice the indubitable bull signs. There are several animals. They are traveling but loafing along between feeding stances. By the number of balls of chewed fiber they must be some way from water, which is a pity considering the loaded state of the safari. However we can always come back for the ivory.

Astonishing how it slows up the pace when tracking has to be done. I put P. in the lead again as no more sounds came over the air, and I determined to rush straight to any further sound we might hear as we could not dally long over this business so far from water. All is well; we bump into the stern of a silent and motionless bull. Extraordinary how such an animal can be so conspicuous at ten yards and yet invisible at fifteen yards. Without waiting to give more than a glance around for others I quickly range out on his broadside and crash him down with a bullet to the brain. He drops instantly and has the death quiver all right. I run toward him to mount when a gigantic head appears through the bush on his far side, swinging toward him with ears cocked and obviously puzzled by the silence of his mate. He presents me with a ridiculously easy frontal shot and he too bites the dust. With a running jump I am up on his back and looking around as the death quiver rocks the great body.

And what should meet my astonished gaze but a solid body of listening elephant, silent and motionless, their top-sides showing well enough above the bush for the brain shot but not enough to show their ivory. One can't go wrong, however, for all are massive bulls, and I whang into the most presentable shots from my unstable perch. The first is down and so is the second, but the third does not receive it properly, slews away, and backs a few steps toward me. The others are now alarmed at last and simply melt from the scene. I dive down and into the bush to-ward the wounded one. If I am really smart I may get another go at him, but it is a matter of seconds as a miss at the brain means nothing to them and once he gets going it is good-by. But my luck is in and I get a broadside shot at his head just as he launches himself into a gait that would have taken him fifty miles off nonstop. This time it gets him properly and he crashes to earth. I rush past him in the general direction the others took, but I soon lose their tracks. My eyes are streaming with sweat and I am far too excited to track properly. So I have to cast around while getting hold of myself and then my beloved shadow, Pyjalé, comes up, cool and collected, but highly pleased and carrying a bunch of tails. He knows I have lost the trail and off he goes straight through the bush. I follow and presently we are back on the trail of the now fleeing herd.

They are by now in single line-ahead formation and beating it for far-distant places. But they make quite a high road through the bush and it is easy to follow fast. We may yet come up with them. Lucky I got that pricked beast; had he been among them we would never catch up.

The pace was plenty hot for some time, but presently there were welcome signs that it was slackening. Instead of the watery spread-out lines of excretion we came on lumps of concise dung showing that our quarry were forgetting their fright. Then more welcome still, we came on heaps and mounds of it showing where they had stopped. We would have them yet. If any water pools still existed, we might even be led to them. It was sincerely to be hoped they would do so, for they were leading us straight into the middle of the ocean of bush well away from any permanent water known to us.

Pyjalé was leading when he suddenly stopped. I knew he had heard something from the way he looked down sideways. I could hear nothing but my heart beating and lungs gasping. He pointed his spears ahead and, turning slightly, smiled. I went in the lead and presently even I could hear the welcome sounds of ears flapping, garglings, and belchings. Just a glance to see the action of the .275 was clear of dust and the sights all right, then adopting a more cautious gait, we drew in.

What a sight meets our straining eyes: a clearing in the bush wth a confused mass of elephant half sunk into a mud pool, everyone enjoying himself, splashing liquid mud over his sizzling hide. Even the ivory has to be searched for as mud covers everything. Our hearts are elated at the finding of water almost as much as at coming up with the game, for we know that the mud will soon settle and there will be enough for the safari.

Now to business. It obviously won't do to kill any actually in the pool as one cannot remove a dead elephant. So we must wait until one comes out. Meanwhile we count as best we can. There appear to be five huge beasts and some of the teeth look heavy, really heavy. That is, 70 to 90 pounds each. What a killing if we could bag the lot. But twice alarmed twice shy, and the chances are much against us. By way of enhancing our chances, we test the wind as we position ourselves so as to command their probable line of flight. What little airs there are seem to be all and every way, so it is anxious work waiting to open the ball.

But very soon there is a concerted move up and out of the bath which is unfortunate as they are too much bunched together for the rifle. The whole muddy crew comes squelching and dripping diagonally toward us. The instant the leader has his hind legs clear of the pool and his body on a level keel I give him one close to his left eye—a very interesting diagonal brain shot. As he is still in somewhat lower ground than where we stand, the shot has to be entered slightly above the line of the eyes. It is easy to visualize the position of the brain as you have both ear roots and eyes in sight at once, although he is only ten or twelve paces distant.

He drops instantly to the shot, disclosing another on his far side and abaft him. Like a fool I drop him before any action can be taken by the others. Now all hell is let loose. Two barge off to the right and one turns tail about and gets going straightaway, thereby saving his hide. That sweet-acting 7 millimeter with its short-travel action gets one of the two in the brain before he reaches bush cover and an oblique body shot into the other. If he is well and truly hit, he too will be ours; if not, there will be nothing the matter with him and no need for us to tear after him immediately, for nothing we could do would ever catch him. Therefore we take a look at the ones we have down. P. is suspicious of the third one and gives him a spear thrust between two ribs, then cuts off the tails. The water looks pretty grim, I must say, and stinks to high heaven, but it will have to do. As long as we don't pierce the carcass of the beast lying in it, it won't be too bad. We must simply leave his tusks to the last.

We can't possibly drink any of the mud as it is too thick from the recent churning, so we divide what is left in the milk calabash. Of course it is now sour and has little balls of butter floating about in it. But how refreshing. Food and drink in one. Like new men P. darts off back trail to find and bring in the safari while I go off on the trail of the body-wounded elephant.

Having no African with me, I have to go much more cautiously or I shall soon be lost. It is easy enough following the trail of an elephant going away from you. Vegetation is bent away from you and reflects light, but when returning it is not so good. Therefore I have to break and leave hanging conspicuous shoots of bush or grass. There is nothing to mark direction except the sun as one's horizon is perhaps fifty yards. All the same it is an entrancing feeling to be on one's very own. Of all the joyous moments that fall to one's lot, those are the sweetest.

After parking the tails in a tree and having a black shag cigarette, I take up the trail with the comfortable feeling that if it is to be, I shall find him within a mile or so, and if not, it does not matter much anyway. The trail is at first dead straight and easy to follow. In that panic rush everything is trodden down. But soon he steadies down and obstacles are avoided. On the sandy parts the spoor is deep and clear but on the harder patches not too easy for northern eyes.

As the trailing goes on I cannot help contrasting my behavior with that of an African savage. I was taut and strung up, imagining elephant in every patch of bush or tree trunk; an African would simply go along imagining nothing because his physical eye saw nothing.

A quarter of a mile perhaps from the pool the trail seems to peter out and I have to search diligently to re-find it, bearing off almost at right angles to the previous course. This is very encouraging. It shows almost certainly that the animal has got a mortal wound, and sure enough, in fifty yards or so I find him lying stone-dead. He has fallen sideways on some heavy bush which no doubt accounts for my not hearing any crash. His tusks I judge to be around about 60 pounds each. Taking his tail, I retrace the trail meticulously back to the battlefield at the mud pool, there to await the coming of the safari.

As it may be any hour when the safari will reach camp,

I begin to look about for something to eat more tempting than a chunk of tough elephant. Given half a chance, my little rifle will provide a meal. I keep a lookout for a dik-dik or guinea fowl and soon have one of the former beautiful little antelope. I carry him by the hind legs like a hare and start a fire where the camp will be pitched. Soon I have his liver and kidneys spitted and roasting. How exquisite the flavor of this priceless dish. When the edges are done I slice them off and they are sweeter than any pâté. Surprisingly salty, too; they require nothing.

I have a good long time to wait so I stroll round viewing the ivory. All have two tusks, I am glad to see. The second beast that fell into the bath had a very fine tooth on top but the under one could only be felt with a stick down in the mire. I thought they should go about 90 pounds. Subsequently they weighed 97 and 101 pounds. All the others were good stuff, too, from 60 pounds upward.

Nowhere else in Africa where I have hunted was the ivory so good as in Karamojo. The average over hundreds of tusks came out at the astonishing weight of 53 pounds per tusk. And the quality was number one. The average over two hundred and ten head of bull elephant killed in the Lado came out at only 23 pounds per tusk, while Ubangi and Lake Chad gave an average of 27 pounds per tusk.

Toward sundown I begin to reckon on having to spend the night alone. It is quite on the cards that the safari may not make the pool in daylight. I therefore begin to get together some firewood. There is no necessity to make smoke to guide P.; should he need any guidance to enable him to make a short cut through the bush instead of following our tracks, he will see the circling vultures now gathering in their hundreds. Now great numbers of sand grouse come flying in thirstily. I take up some of the liquid on top of the mud and am surprised how relatively clear it is. But what a smell. Another few days and it will be bone dry and baked concrete.

At last, with the sun just down, there is a commotion among some perched vultures and here comes the welcome black form of P. closely followed by the safari. Tired but pleased and smiling, they come in with a rush. Weary bodies stretch after dumping loads while glances are directed toward the great carcasses and the meager pool. Suliemani takes over my fire and the dik-dik, and all the merry hum of expert campers rises up with the smoke of new fires while axes ring out as bush trees fall for building the donkey boma. Meanwhile the headman knows exactly what to do about the water pool. Sturdy thorn trees are drawn all round it to prevent our thirsty donks from mobbing it and fouling it. After the humans are served, they will get some in a groundsheet.

Later on it becomes apparent that the pool will not serve for the following day; we will have to trek on for the Big Tree Camp at dawn. Therefore the ivory will have to be chopped out that very night. Poor beggars, the gang is weary enough as it is, but they all know what it means to be caught out in the dry, and everyone sets to with a will after getting some food into themselves. P. has to take some of the gang back to the first elephant we killed, and it is well after midnight when all are finished. The fellow in the bath was troublesome as his mighty head had to be cut off and the whole enormous thing upended so that the tusks stuck up.

In the cool of the morning it was all hands to the safari. None too soon, for the pool was now nothing more than solid mud already beginning to crack at the edges. All out for Big Tree Camp, where we had ivory cached and an unfailing water supply, was the order of the day. After a very long and tiring march we made it and settled for a day's rest while skins were soaked to make saddles for the buried ivory. But first of all we must make certain of the water. One can never really tell in this country, so P. and I strolled down to the river bed to examine the holes in the sand.

It was soon evident that elephant had been at them quite recently. Several new holes had been opened and P. started sounding with his spear, but not as a white man would naturally do by shoving his spear in and then looking to see if it were wet. No, you cannot get the spear in even though it is iron shod at the butt end and sharp. What you do is simply thump the sand and the sound it makes tells a Karamojan whether there is water near enough to the surface to make digging worth while. I myself could never detect any difference in the sound when water was near or far but any Karamojan knew instantly. My other natives, whether Swahili, Masai, Kavirondo, Mganda, or Mnyamwezi were just as ineffective as myself.

Pyjalé soon had an area marked for digging and it was curious to watch the boys waiting on his word to go ahead. Water was abundant, sweet, and still near the surface, so we could all look forward to a day's rest. So we thought until the donkey headman, coming with a gang carrying kongoni, oryx, and topi skins to soak in wet sand, announced that he had not enough. This meant that I would have to get some buck.

After an uneventful night when most of us slept like dead men, I took out the .256 Gibbs Mannlicher. This beautiful rifle had a particularly long barrel and more-over was most meticulously sighted. It used of course in those days the long, parallel-sided, round-nosed bullet with the lead exposed in the nose—a superb all-round killing bullet good enough for broadside or end-on shots. With its weight and good velocity it was at that time the deadliest to be had and was peculiarly suitable to getting buck game. Indeed, even now it is only surpassed by the latest products of American arms manufacturers such as the Winchester .220 Swift with its four thousand feet-per-second velocity or the Winchester .270.

With masses of hartebeest and oryx about, one had not far to go. If in the morning before the heat waves started dancing one got to within two hundred yards and secured a decent stance such as an ant hill, one could bowl over up to ten or a dozen without shifting. I once killed twenty-one hartebeest from one stance. Of course these herds had no knowledge of firearms and were simply plumb stupid. So it was not long before we had enough skins and meat for all hands. It should not be forgotten that the Moslem members of the safari would not eat ele-phant by an order the Prophet made, I presume, not because of any uncleanness of the animal but solely that his followers might not endanger their lives and limbs in trying to cut an elephant's throat while it still lived.

As soon as the "sogis" (saddles) were dry and had firmly gripped their loads of ivory, we started the trek for Kilassa's camp by way of Baboon Pool. We had now a very nice array of ivory indeed, with some heavy teeth carried by porters. There was an air of homegoing about the safari now and everything went with a swing. We would soon arrive at Kilassa's camp, and all were curious to see what that old warrior and his men had done while we were away. I thought that if he had got two or three decent elephant he would have justified the experiment, but Swédé and Suliemani thought he would have far more than that.

CHAPTER 19

THE country was again in the grip of the dry season with its usual mysterious disappearance of elephant. We expected to see nothing now until we reached the base camp. As is so typical of Africa, we were wakened by thunder and lightning, and as no tents had been pitched, all was bustle to get some protection from the storm. Torrential rain arrived in no uncertain manner and soon all was awash, the parched ground being quite unable to absorb the sudden downpour.

This rain was indeed luck. It had no business to come now at all. We knew it would be only local, but it was so heavy that it would fill the ponds everywhere and there would be a rush to this locality from miles around. Elephant seem to scent rain from incredible distances and we knew there would be a great silent trek even now coming on toward us. And here we were right on the spot.

Now on the previous day I had as usual searched the whole countryside with the big telescope from a high rocky stance above the Baboon Pool and had seen nothing beyond the usual show of dry-country game. Certainly no upstanding elephant could have escaped the glass had they been within twenty miles, as all the bush was dwarf although thick enough. As I lay snug and dry in my camp bed under the outer fly of the tent and listened to the drumming of the rain on the taut canvas which, by the way, was being held secure by a dozen devoted boys, my feelings varied between elation at our luck and apprehension of the ridgepole's breaking.

In the cold and fresh of the rain-washed morning air great activity was apparent as the camp reorganized itself for a two or three days' stay. I of course was up the hill with the big glass almost before it was light enough to see. High as were my expectations, what met my goggling eyes surpassed everything ever dreamt of. Apparently the downpour had covered an area of roughly five or six miles of bush with our camp as center, and out of every whorl of bush there stuck up the backs of dark, washed elephant. How could they have arrived so soon? Fourteen hours ago there had not been a single one. Now there were—I counted—twenty-seven great beasts, all bulls. And when you see twenty-seven bulls in an area of a few square miles, believe me, there seem to be far more than the actual number suggests.

Some were quite close and I was immediately scared they would hear or scent the camp, so I sent a boy down to warn the camp to keep quiet and to send up the headman. Telling him to keep a lookout posted and to start off the tusk cutting-out gang when and if we got any down, Pyjalé and I rapidly made out our operations plan and plunged down into the sea of bush. At once all was hidden from sight, our horizon some few yards distant. But today we had the two mountains close aboard and visible above the bush so it was easy to find our way to a group of three bulls we had marked down for the opening of hostilities. It was now hot as hell and the air hummed and buzzed with newly awakened insect life. Especially busy were the huge, inch-long stinging flies that torment elephant so, driving them to the mud baths for protection. There was a nice dry-season breeze blowing. It was as if the rainstorm had escaped control and everything was being done to repair the damage. I determined to make the most of it.

We got down the three elephant without unnecessary noise or fuss, not letting one escape to alarm the countryside. Only the brain shot could have accomplished this. Taking only the tips of the tails, on we went, our only difficulty being in locating our quarry. Occasionally P. mounted a tree high enough to give a view, but trees were few and far between. At other times we found and followed fresh tracks. Soon we began to open the hides of our victims as they became more numerous so the vultures could get at the meat and thereby indicate the locality of the fallen and help the cutting-out gang find them. By about 4:00 P.M. by the sun we had fifteen tail tips and called it a day. There had been but one outstanding incident. That was when I had just killed a bull facing me about ten yards off with the frontal brain shot and there was the most frightful bellow—it seemed in my very ear. Whirling round as I worked the bolt, I was just in time to fell to the ground a high averted head charging through the bush five paces or so distant. Glancing at P., I saw he was straightening the iron neck of his spear. Apparently an unexpected elephant had come right on us from behind and P., seeing I was occupied with the elephant in front, had jabbed his spear into the approaching trunk. The suddenness and speed of it all was amazing. This elephant was only stunned and had fallen sideways. I had to nip smartly up alongside to kill him as he righted himself. They first of all get their hindquarters up, apparently with difficulty, then their front end comes up, then after a second or two they launch themselves into full flight none the worse for their knockout.

I had no idea what the ivory was like from all these elephant. The bush had mostly concealed it from the big glass in the morning, and when at these close quarters one did not delay in looking at the ivory. Rather was it a matter of taking the most favorably presented head. All were bulls anyway and all were mature. But now it was over one could not help speculating on what the result would be. Some of it certainly was big stuff. The morrow would show when it would all come in scrubbed and washed. But the impression on our minds was that it was not particularly heavy stuff.

As we could see our mountain, there was no object in retracing our steps, so it was a case of straight as the bush would allow for home. And what merry goings on here met us. As we were "Shuka" or retreating, everyone wanted elephant fat to take back to base camp to trade for native beer and all the other commodities of bush life. Such a coming and going of bloody imps you never did see. Stripped naked and festooned with fat, they were enjoying themselves to the full.

Some of the ivory was in and looked rather middling. Next day when weighed the average was the unusually low one of 45 pounds per tooth. The total was short of 1,400 pounds and well below that of the nine patriarchs slain on the Pibor Flats. However, one consolation was that it would all transport well on donkeys. In speculating on the smallness of this lot of ivory when sitting at the camp fire that evening, P. mentioned that the Dodossans had told him that away east of us were great herds of cow elephant. That would be in the Turkana country where the Turkwel disappears into the sands and dense thorn bush clothes the country. The elephant we had fallen in with were probably herd bulls from that locality. And so to bed with a great racket from hyenas and jackals.

As there was still some ivory out, P. had to take the gang for it next day while I went very high up the hill with the big glass. From my perch maybe one thousand feet up the view would have been splendid but for the haze. As it was, there appeared nothing but an endless sea of bush right to the horizon to the eastward. Somewhere over the horizon lay Lake Rudolph, but not a glimpse of it could be seen.

We were pretty well loaded up before this last lot of ivory, but now we were seriously overloaded. As soon as I arrived at Kilassa's, I told him to send some of his men to help in the safari. Then I had a talk with Kilassa. All had gone well. They had a fair amount of flour as they had made a trip to base camp. All had been well there. And had they seen any strangers? No, not one. Elephant? Old Kilassa smiled and beckoned me to follow him. We entered his grass hut. K. called someone to bring something and then he started to roll up some skins he had on the floor. He and his mate then started to clear the soil away. They made great progress, the earth seeming to be loose and recently disturbed. In a short time the body of a fine tusk showed. Then others came out. They were passed out and laid in a row. Fourteen of them! All good teeth, nothing under 60 pounds. The experiment had been well worth while and the expenditure of ammunition moderate—about twelve rounds per elephant secured.

There was now terrific bustle apparent in the camp as preparations for the last few treks to base camp went forward. One might have thought we were about to return home. Of course the explanation of much of it was the anticipation of the joys awaiting those who were married while those who had no woman no doubt thought on the beer drinking that awaited them. For me personally these retreats were always accompanied by a certain sadness. One more good hunt drawing to a close. I determined to put in a few good side shows on the way down. Perhaps the Nabwa of Dodosi would be good for a few days' scurry, and then there was Nopak, the never-failing source of one or two good bulls. Then Longellynyung had pressed me to go with him again. There was still hope although we were now ten months out.

In a well-run, well-equipped safari there is no need for the leader to do much beyond pressing on the enterprise when on the way out. Africans left to themselves are prone to long delays between spasms of activity. They are at the mercy of omens, magic, considerations of weather, and also victims to sheer inertia. Swahili-run safaris would sometimes spend a year in preparation and throughout that year think themselves on the point of imminent departure. But when a retreat is decided upon, all objections to immediate action disappear in a most mysterious manner and a sort of rush grips everyone. Starts are made at unheard-of early hours. Halts are called only after two or three of the outgoing stages have been passed. Everyone is offensively exuberant and anxiously eager to be up and doing. But the leader has nothing to do now. Everything runs smoothly, and where one used to be awakened by the terrific cursing of the donkey boys as they loaded up their unwilling beasts, now one heard, if one heard at all, soft-spoken cajolings.

In the course of a quarter of the time we had taken

outward bound we duly arrived at base camp. Of course the entry had to be made in style. The women quickly broke off their clandestine affairs and simulated an eagerness to welcome their bush-weary spouses, secure in the knowledge that any slight lack of passion on their part would remain completely obliterated by the transports of their pent-up husbands. Their last remaining joy-rags donned and their bodies washed with the last remaining scraps of scented soap, out they came to greet us as if they too were about to be delivered from a penance.

What a gallant show the ivory made, all burnished with sand and gleaming in the sunlight. And how fat the condition of those who had remained at base. What gallons of beer were represented by that bloom of skins several shades browner than the dusty black of the bush gang, testifying to several months of sojourn under grass roofs. And what a welcome on all the jolly faces—enough to make even the sour-faced safari leader unbend. I draw a veil over the celebrations of that night, celebrations extending to the native population also. All I will say is that the finest meshed net would have failed to secure an even moderately sober person of either sex within ten miles of that camp.

As a halt would now have to be made to get everything into proper trim for the general retreat, I knew Pyjalé would be eager to be off home. So taking him to the cattle boma, I told him he could have his reward and go off at once. Instantly he was ready. Striking out his chosen beasts, he was set for the trail. He would pass single-handed through two tribes, the deadly enemies of him and his, and that while in possession of great wealth. Yet no hand would be raised against him. He knew it and I knew it. I told him to tell Nopak, Longellynyung, and his people that I was coming and still had some heifer cows for those who found elephant for me.

No sooner had he gone, and I was thinking I would have a good day's rest while reading for the hundredth time the only contact with civilization I ever found pleasurable, *Pickwick Papers,* than I saw a native approaching. He had the sure air of the bush on him: purposeful gait, wrinkled belly, and dull skin. I'll bet he has elephant news, I thought, somewhat regretfully I must confess, for I had not had a day's rest for months. So it was with a much more searching eye that I sifted his evidence, especially on the size of the ivory, than would have been the case had I been fresh and eager. However, there was no flaw to be found, so bawling for the headman, I gave orders for fifteen stay-at-homes to accompany me for a few days' scurry in the bush. Meanwhile the boys got me some food ready and in a little while we were off once more. I took the favorite .275.

We were bound for the Nabwa of Dodosi, a country surpassing all others that I have seen in Africa in its primordial subjection to great game with the sole exception of the ironstone ridges forming the watershed between the Ubangi and Shari Rivers in French Equatorial Africa. Never in the wildest nightmare could one imagine the oppressive feeling conveyed by the desolation and destruction wrought by elephant, rhino, and buffalo. The very climate seemed in league with its ponderous denizens, for you experience there sudden storms of unexampled violence, lightning of a soul-searing brightness, thunder to be likened only to a continuous barrage of heavy guns, and downpours that no tent made by mortal hands could stand against. While all men walk in silence in such a "Nabwa," it undoubtedly holds some of the finest

270

ivory left on the face of the earth. Natives will only penetrate it in pursuit of the highest reward and are reluctant to tarry longer than will secure it for them.

Now the big rains were close upon us and we might expect to be knocked about a bit. Everything happens in a big way in "Nabwa." And sure enough that night there was a terrific storm. We had no tent; consequently we had a pretty miserable time. However, everyone was in prime condition except myself perhaps, and the morning sun soon had us bright and cheerful again. The prospect of meeting with elephant was considerably bettered by the downpour; in fact, a feeling of certainty permeated the little safari as we wound our way like a small black snake along the open spaces of the bush.

Hardly had we reached the "Nabwa" proper when we picked up the fresh tracks of a solitary bull. One glance at the tracks showed that we stood in the presence of something quite out of the ordinary in size. Never had I seen such gigantic pads. Without hesitation and almost without pause we all tailed onto them. With everything necessary for our comfort borne along with us in light little loads and with no anxiety about water, the whole affair was simplicity itself. All we had to do was to follow.

Hardly had we gone a mile or so when we knew we were close aboard. He had plastered himself with mud at a rain pool against a horde of stinging flies that now came out with the rising sun. For although one might think that an inch-thick hide would repel such pests, it must be remembered that this hide is full of tiny blood vessels and nerves. There is a species of elephant fly about one and one quarter inches in length that can drive its proboscis deep into elephant hide. I have watched them balancing and swaying their bodies so as to give momentum to their thrust. Once the mud covering has dried and caked, it is not so easy for these tormentors to get home on their victims. Their presence however adds to the hunter's difficulty as elephant react strongly, become uneasy and restless, and often seek the darkest parts of the bush where one is obliged to approach them much too close for comfort.

In this case we were lucky to view him suddenly in the open. He was quite motionless and resembled a piece of the fantastically contorted rock formation that pierced the bush in all directions. The scene formed a glimpse into the past. One felt awed by the strangeness of it all. Thus probably was the world thousands of years ago.

Certainly this elephant conveyed a sense of great size, but the ivory did not look phenomenally large. That it would weigh well was evident because it held its girth so far out from the head, and one knew that the hollows would be short from the age of the beast. Age was written all over him. His massive head was horny and mossy on top, the skin hung in wrinkled folds, and there was not the slightest sign of movement except the little eye closing wearily from time to time. I never felt so queer as when I gazed on this relic. Usually such stillness on the part of an elephant meant that he had heard some suspicious sound and I would have sprinted silently into position to kill him. But in that case the ears would have been cocked to catch the faintest vibration. Here they drooped forlornly. The whole animal expressed weariness in every attitude. Tired of the century-long struggle, he was probably deaf and almost blind. Burdened with such a load of years, he possibly no longer felt the stings of the swarm of flies that beset him. Indeed, they set up such a hum as to suggest that the living carcass was already far gone in putrefaction.

Although he was ideally positioned for the brain shot and should have dropped poleaxed to the ground, nothing of the sort happened when I fired. To my amazement nothing happened at all. There was no movement whatsoever. Again I fired for the brain. Again there was no response—just a sullen wooden thud of the bullet. One might have been firing into a clay cliff. I can tell you a very queer sensation came over me. I lowered my rifle and gazed thunderstruck. Was he dead on his feet or what? Quickly recovering I gave him a meticulously calculated shot in the heart. Ah! here was some response at any rate. He moved slowly forward so I ran ahead of him and once more tried for the brain, this time the frontal shot. He collapsed, very much to my relief.

I have never understood what happened to the first shot. At this period of my career I had at long last learned the lesson that the first shot must be the best-delivered one. I could not believe that this one had been ill placed, and a close examination of the head showed it to have been properly positioned as far as I could judge. Whether the 170-grain bullet had been deflected by unusually heavy bone or held up altogether remains a mystery.

Turning to the tusks—he had dropped kneeling so both could be examined—it was quite apparent that we had here two that would try our stoutest porters. One boy even suggested that they would have to be slung on a pole and carried by two men. The gang flung themselves upon that moldy head and soon the bush rang to the thud of the axes as they hewed away the great sockets of densest bone. One of our attendant natives was at once dispatched to base camp to bring out a porter gang so we should not be embarrassed by two such huge teeth in our bush prowlings. Visions of even larger elephant filled my mind although I was somewhat sobered by the disturbing memory of those two abortive shots. They linger in my memory to this day.

As soon as we had the teeth out, the boys tried their weight. All conceded they were heavier than anything we had hitherto got. Personally, I was slightly disappointed in them. I guessed they would come out about 125 pounds each. Subsequently they scaled 145 and 148 pounds.

There was something queer about that particular day in "Nabwa." No sooner had we left the scene than I stepped right on a huge viper. As usual it was too lethargic to do anything about it, but the incident added to the queerness. The seeing of these loathsome reptiles was common enough and called for no comment, but to step plumb on one was certainly unusual. They are not hidden in any way and are conspicuous enough.

Then we ran across two great bulls toward evening. I, in my somewhat chastened mood, shot the first one in the body and the second one in the brain. Greatly to my relief the latter fell to the shot while the former was so sorely stricken that before I could give him a quieter he had hove one of his tusks high into the air as he shook his head about in his death throes. At the moment I thought little of this occurrence, guessing that the hollow must be diseased. And so it proved in no uncertain way, for it fairly stank. But the affair had been witnessed by the boys with the gravest misgiving. It was no use inviting them to sniff the hollow tooth; they knew better. It was a clear case of magic, and they warned me that the very next elephant I met would surely kill me. Apparently my estimate of the occurrence was the more correct, for

I killed many elephant after it and so far none have come anywhere near to killing me.

After that one day of queer happenings things resumed their normal course. We flogged the game trails of "Nabwa" for ten days and by that time could move no more ivory. Truth to tell, ten days in "Nabwa" is about as much as one can do with at a time. We were all pretty well battered by the weather and even the boys from base camps soon lost their bloom. One night in particular stands out for sheer discomfort from the rest. It was spent under a slain elephant's ear, sitting in mud, bombarded by lightning, thunder, wind, and rain—and cold as no other country can be cold. So the retreat was sounded and we left that scene of desolation with all the safari gear made into three or four heavy loads and every man thus released laden with ivory. Where weight allowed of it, two tusks would be lashed together.

Some of the rivers were now swollen with the heavy rains of the last few days and we had some nasty crossings to make. Not that they were wide, but the currents were strong. A good rope stretched from bank to bank generally sufficed; where this was impracticable through depth of water, the old safari dodge of a groundsheet stuffed with grass made an adequate raft.

On reaching base, the first thing to do was to weigh the two monster tusks. They scaled 148 and 145 pounds and I was besieged by porters clamoring for the honor of carrying them the three hundred-odd miles to their destination. The headman had everything in trim for a start and it only remained to dispose of our load of ivory from "Nabwa." I must say that when everything lined out, it was an inspiring sight. It certainly looked as if we would have difficulty in accommodating the fine teeth we had left buried in Nopak's village.

Our first camp of the real retreat was at the magic hill of Dodosi where we had so often camped before. It was a short march from base camp and it gave everyone a chance to shake down to safari routine. After so long in permanent camp the boys and animals were soft and fat.

CHAPTER 20

WE WERE now covering two and sometimes three of our outward stages. The two big tusks borne along in the van set the pace. Halfway between Jiwé and Bukora we ran into lion, or rather they ran into us.

It was at sundown as we approached a small stream bed where recent rains might have left water that two lion and a lioness came loping down from the mountain on our left, heading for the great game plains down on our right. Their course would cross ours if they held to it. They did and came within range.

I was as usual carrying the .275 and the magazine was loaded with solids. They were covering a lot of ground and presented a very pretty target, the grass being sparse and short. I fired at the leader, hitting him. He launched into a violent spring forward, at the same time letting out a nasty, angry, snarling roar, and continued on his former course at a flat-out gallop. I thought it was a heart shot and turned loose on the other two. They were now in full flight and presented almost stern-on shots. There was a considerable rise and fall in the target and correct timing was required to hit them. My second shot got one just as it reached the top of the bound and foundered it immediately, but the next one escaped the bullet and was soon lost in the failing light. Meanwhile, the first one was down. We found him stretched out motionless and we thought he was dead. We then went to look at the second one and he too was dead. They were poorish-looking specimens, much raddled by the bush. Manes hardly existed in this country with the constant wear and tear of the thorn bush.

As water was found in sufficient quantities, camp was made quite close to the lion carcasses and some boys were detailed to get the skins. No sooner had they reached the first one than there was a terrific uproar in which unmistakable lion-noise could be distinguished. I seized the rifle and ran toward the sounds, thinking that another lion had fallen foul of the boys. It was now uncomfortably dark but the boys' outcry guided me and I was soon with them. They explained that after they had begun to skin the lion, it had sprung to life, opened its mouth, and attacked them. It sounded very queer to me, especially as they were still quite close to the beast. We were soon beside him and it was quite apparent that he was paralyzed but could just open his mouth. He had been hit a bit too far back.

On reaching Bukora, the news of our arrival spread like wildfire among the natives. By the time we reached our old camp near Nopak's village, Pyjalé came with a very fine fat sheep; its tail must have weighed twelve or fourteen pounds of pure fat. Was there any elephant news was my first question. P. said he had sent a party out as soon as he heard of our coming. I told Nopak we would be digging up the teeth we had left with him.

Next day one of P.'s hunting party came in hotfoot to say that elephant were on Mount Nopak. This was late in the season for them there; rather were they now to be expected in what had hitherto been dry bush. However, P. said the man was reliable, so it was decided to take a

run out to the famous elephant resort while the buried
ivory was got up and ensaddled. In half an hour we were
off, a good many native women going with us—a sure
sign that the chances were good. We could not make
Nopak that day, of course, but we slept near at hand.
Next day early, P. and the news carrier and I set off,
leaving strict orders that no one was to follow until the
sun was well up.

We killed five good bulls near the spring on the northern slope of the massif, and I was for returning as soon
as the ivory was got out, but presently another native
came in to say that he had seen an elephant on the south
side of the mountain. Will wonders never cease, thought
I, as I mentally calculated that if I got that single elephant it would make exactly ninety bull elephant killed in
a circle of ten miles' radius from the summit of the hills
in four years, and not a bad one among them. We found
him and killed him without incident.

Meanwhile the lad who had led us to the recent killing
of the five bulls had to receive his heifer and the one who
had brought us the single bull his bullock because that
was the now well-established tariff. First Nopak chose
his beast and took her off. Then the second lad took his,
and the third was told to choose one of the bullocks. He
seemed reluctant to do so. He wanted a heifer. He knew
perfectly well what the rule was. It was just a try-on. I
resisted it. Had I given in I would have been landed with
everyone who had received bullocks in the past wanting
to change them for heifers. Presently he went off without
the bullock.

Next day there was a tremendous camp. Everyone
came hoping for a bit of the share-out. Dusky beauties
appeared who had been strictly kept away from our

camps hitherto. Affluent giants with hundreds of head of cattle cadged a few beads like poverty-stricken children. And beer flowed in a torrent.

Presently there appeared by my tent our friend of yesterday's little disagreement about the bullock. He was simply simmering with beer, full as a tick. A short way off there was a large fig tree much haunted by green pigeon. I took a .22 pistol I had and strolled over to see if I could pot one or two. Having gone two or three hundred yards, I heard a shout from camp: "Look out, Bwana!" Turning about, what should meet my startled gaze but our friend of the bullock fracas close on me with a spear unsheathed and poised. Instantly I covered him with the pistol and we stood thus a few seconds while behind and beyond him came a melee of boys from the camp.

The drunk was undecided what to do. That nasty-looking little gun evidently daunted him. He had no doubt thought me unarmed. Before he could collect his wits, the boys were close on him, and before he got going, they had him. They hauled him to camp, and there before them all, we flogged him. Might as well have beaten up a rubber tire. After a sound thrashing, I told the boys to give him back his spears and to run him out of camp. They were reluctant to do so, saying he would murder someone. I told them I would look after that, calling for a rifle. Then we turned him loose at the edge of the camp, giving him his spears. Off he strolled as if on normal ploy.

After a while he saw one of our camp followers stooping over something. Like a streak of black lightning he hurled himself straight at the quite unsuspecting boy. There was a united yell from the camp which reached the boy in time, luckily. Giving one glance at the galloping demon bearing down on him, he darted off on a side bias at no mean speed. The drunk never swerved to follow him but continued at undiminished speed, now singing at the top of his voice, spurning the earth, floating as it were on wings of alcohol. Giving a big sigh of relief, I lowered my rifle, for I should certainly have had to take a hand. There was a roar of laughter in camp. Dangerous brutes, these, when in liquor.

CHAPTER 21

ALL was now ready for the real "Shuka" to begin. There was no more buried ivory to dig up and it was not very likely that we would encounter much on the road down as we would be obliged to follow the regular caravan trail owing to the rains having by this time inundated much of our West-of-Dabasian trail, making it impossible for donkey transport.

Now for a trail line-out of everything that had to be moved: three hundred and fifty-four tusks of an average weight of 53 pounds each from one hundred and eighty head of elephant; time spent on the actual hunting, six months; average number of elephant per month of hunting time, thirty; total time of safari, fourteen months; wage bill per month, one hundred and fifty pounds; for the whole safari, twenty-one hundred pounds; bonus to each boy of three months' wages, four hundred and fifty pounds; cost of stock and trade goods, say four hundred pounds; total expenditure, say three thousand pounds. Against this set the value of ivory, all first-rate stuff, salable on the spot to the Indian merchants at seven rupees per pound, say ten shillings per pound, equals nine thousand pounds sterling. After deducting something for drying out, shrinkage, and allowing for extras, the total profit came out at about six thousand pounds, and we still had a full-power safari.

There were thirty-one tusks that required porters to carry them, either because they were too heavy for donkeys or their length and curvature made them awkward when donkey-borne. Of these thirty-one tusks, twenty-nine belonged to the former class and only two to the latter. These two teeth were more like mammoth than elephant tusks, very long and very much curved. Unlike mammoth tusks, they weighed seventy-odd pounds each; all the others were over a hundred pounds each.

A line of thirty tusks does not sound like much, but actually it constitutes a first-class spectacle. When man-borne each tusk requires at least three yards of the line to itself, so we soon have a line a hundred yards long. And when each porter is decked up in elaborately worked garments of many-colored beads, heads bedecked with Karamojan blood red ostrich feathers, and white and black ones too, giraffe manes, lion manes, leopard skins, and baboon manes, the whole thing fills the eye. It is the genuine stuff all right. What glitter and gaud it has it owes to goodness-to-god sunlight and grease. The Hollywood version is far too clean. Dirt is just as much a part of life as anything else and should be given its proper place. It always surprises me when I see a Hollywood hero perform the most prodigious deeds and appear quite immaculate after it all.

Just as we were in the midst of our preparations, who should come drifting across the plain but Longellynyung with a string of women bearing beer pots behind him. He seemed to be pretty well jagged, judging by his shouts. Thank goodness I still had some stuff to give his wives; he never seemed to want anything for himself. Dear old unselfish beggar, he would have given me anything. Of course he was, for a Karamojan, unbelievably rich. Alone of all native men in my experience, riches had not accrued to him through superior cunning or aggressive acquisitiveness. It had come to him solely by light of courage in battle. Even in his cups—the final test—he was innately modest. He would not tell of his exploits, but all his people did. His character was such and his generosity so great that his wealth caused no envy in the hearts of his neighbors. He always reminded me of a bull terrier, rushing to meet battle with genuine joy.

There was a tremendous gathering of natives present and a big gathering of bald heads round the beer pots. Speeches were freely spouted, all about how friendly they felt toward the "red man"—myself—and how he—the "red man"—could beat his children—themselves—as much as he liked, and how he would give them tobacco and trade goods, cows and sheep, and so forth, without end. As long as the beer held out, at any rate. I warned them not to kill any traders while I was away and not to kill any enemy women. I told them that I would soon be back among them and that if I saw anyone freshly tattooed on the left side I might be unable to resist shooting him. And so on; the usual palaver.

The first march was a short one, just to get everything into running order. After that the safari rolled along from day to day until the final camp before entry to civilization once more. Terrific preparations went on all that night. Visitors from Mumias came to camp, both male and female. Long before dawn the dressing-up began. A local band of drums was engaged by runner to meet us outside the town and play us in. As we neared the town, strings of women in the latest product of Manchester cotton mills began to meet us. A great concourse lined the main street to see the safari parade in. It was a great event in the life of a small town like Mumias. Safaris lasted at least a year and sometimes two or three years, and when they returned there would be thousands of rupees to be sharked from beer-sodden boys. The ivory buyers were in great force, too. Only those who had a large sum of hard cash would stand much chance, for I always liked the pay-off at once.

After the interminable parade down the main street, camp was made about a mile from the town. A visit would be made with Swédé to the shops, and some fearfully unwholesome tinned stuff, long since condemned, would be bought together with some liquor.

Barring the haggling over ivory prices, the clashes of our lit up porters with the local police, the thieving of our boys' quickly acquired goods, and all the usual money troubles appertaining to a return to civilization, there is nothing further to relate. The safari was ended.

APPENDIX

NOTES ON BIG GAME SHOOTING

NOW that licenses to kill elephant cost so much and the numbers allowed are so few, it behooves the inexperienced sportsman to avail himself of the experience of others who have been lucky enough to have had opportunities in the past that are now impossible. It is in the hope that these notes will prove useful to the novice that I pen these lines. They may save him bitter disappointment and help him to avoid wounding with all that that entails.

THE NOVICE

First of all, it will be absolutely necessary to make sure that:
1. You possess, or can borrow, a suitable rifle.
2. You have available suitable cartridges and bullets.
3. You can use the weapon in a proper manner.
4. You know where to place the shot.

1. Suitable rifles. Any of the modern military caliber rifles will kill elephant provided they are used with the proper ammunition. For elephant, rhino, buffalo, and hippo the bullets must be of the blunt-nosed solid type. I don't say you cannot kill with the more modern pointed type, for I know you can, but they are unreliable in their course and should be avoided altogether for big stuff.

Lots of elephant have been killed with the .256, .275, .300, .303, 7.9 mm., .318, 9 mm., .350, .375, .400/450, .416, .425, .450, .465, .470, and so on up to .600. It is far more a question of where the bullet is applied than of the diameter of that bullet.

All have sufficient penetration when used with the solid round-nosed type of bullet. With this wide field to select from, the novice will surely find something to suit the occasion.

A note of warning against long-travel bolt actions. Some very long and powerful cartridges have been evolved for use in the Mauser action. This action has been so well designed and is of such high quality steel that almost any charge may be safely burned ahead of it. This, and the cheapness of the action, has led gun-makers to produce rifles using cartridges much too long for fast repeating action. The travel of the bolt backwards in ejecting the fired case is so long that in moments of extreme tension one is inclined to cut it off before the empty shell has been ejected and to begin the forward thrust of reloading too soon, so that the fired case becomes reinserted into the barrel instead of a fresh cartridge from the magazine. Into this category fall the .350, .375, .425, and the .416.

If one is bound to one of these particular rifles, something can be done about it, but it takes a lot of practice. You must constantly handle your rifle, snapping it off at anything and everything, without cartridges of course. Each time you go through the reloading motions, shove the rifle away from you with the left hand as you draw back the bolt with the right hand. Do this over and over again, aiming the rifle each time at some object and always in the standing position; it is seldom in Africa that you will have any other. Never mind if people think you are crazy; stick to it; it is worth it.

2. *Suitable bullets.*   There is only one form of bullet for use against heavy game: the solid round-nose. What you require from your bullet is that it continues on a straight course after entering the animal and does not break up.

In all these large animals the vitals lie a long way in. The hide is strong, thick, full of sand and grit, maybe mud-encrusted. The muscles are hard and tough, the bones massive and, in the old males, dense. All this mass of obstruction must be penetrated and the vitals reached. This object is best served by a long, parallel-sided, heavy, and strong-coated bullet traveling at a moderate velocity, say two thousand twenty-four hundred feet per second.

Of course an expert will kill with any bullet. As an instance of what can be done, I have seen twenty-three West Coast buffalo laid low with twenty-seven shots from a .22 Hi-Power "Imp," all soft-nosed bullets, the operator having no other kind. What he did was to take a tip from the old American bison hunters' technique used in the days when they were killing bison for their tongues and robes. He inserted his tiny 70-grain soft-nosed pellets into their lungs—nothing but hide, a little flesh, and an odd rib to obstruct—and so got them blowing blood about, thus enraging the unwounded into that extraordinary bovine state known as "ringing." I don't suppose the whole stricken herd covered a tennis court in area.

Broadly speaking, the best bullet for killing elephant is one which combines a good weight (it will not be easily deflected), long parallel sides (this will help it keep course), good sectional density (not too much diameter to length), and a good but not excessive velocity. In my opinion the 250-grain .318, although far from perfect, approaches most nearly the big game hunter's ideal bullet, followed by the 7.9 mm. or 8 mm. Mauser.

3. How to use the weapon. Now that we have touched upon the mechanical side of the business, we must tackle the human element, by far the most difficult one.

It really is a problem. You cannot go and practice on elephant; they don't like it. You have paid one hundred pounds, or thereabouts, to kill one elephant in a year.

Doubtless you will be advised to take a heavy double-barreled rifle, say a .465 or a .470. If you feel you would like this—that is, if you feel that the formidable weight of the rifle itself and the more formidable appearance of its cartridges give you confidence— well and good. Decide on it. But you must train yourself to it.

First of all, make sure of a decent supply of cartridges, say one hundred; two hundred would be better. Now see that some of them are of the proper solid type of bullet. These will be for actual use against game. The others are for practice only and may be soft-nosed.

Above all, see that you get a pair of dummy cartridges with the rifle. These are cases with spring-loaded caps or primers, as they are more rightly called. The spring-loading is to take up the thrust of the strikers when you snap off the rifle during practice. Strikers have to be tempered hard so that they will not flatten or burr over when brought into sharp contact with the anvil inside the primer. Unfortunately, this hardening produces brittleness, and if you snap off with no cartridge in the chamber, you are very likely to cause the fine point of the striker to break. In my opinion this constitutes one of the many faults of the break-open action. It means that there is always a certain reluctance to practice with the rifle at inanimate objects for fear of damaging something, whereas one can bang a military bolt action about anyhow and snap it off a million times without fear.

When you have got your arm muscles used to throwing the weight of your heavy double about and find you can hold it moderately steady in the standing position, you may commence the second and most important part of the battle: the elimination of flinch. This is without doubt the greatest obstacle to decent shooting ever invented by Providence to bring to naught the ingenious efforts of the human brain. There is no doubt whatever that the modern rifle is far ahead of the man behind it.

Try a few shots, in the standing position of course, at a fairly large mark—say a circle or square six inches wide and about fifty yards distant—and see how you like it. If all goes well, try from eighty or one hundred yards. You'll be surprised how difficult it is to be certain that your *first* shot will be within six inches of where you wish it to be. And remember it is the *first* shot that counts usually. You cannot have a "sighter" when you come face to face with your hundred-pound shot.

It is that little fact that is so easily overlooked, and yet it is so important. It is well worth your while to go to extreme measures to get yourself into such a condition of familiarity with the unpleasant part of firing these heavy rifles in cold blood. But if you persevere, you should finally reach a stage when you feel fairly confident that you can put your bullet within six inches of any selected object the *first* time.

On the way to your hunting ground you should take every opportunity of firing your heavy rifle at guinea fowl or whatnot. If you hit you won't get much meat, but you will be one step nearer that sublime state when you feel you can put your bullet exactly where you want to. Most people are reluctant to fire these heavy weapons except at heavy stuff; that is why we hear of so many failures.

With the small bores this essential practice is very much easier and pleasanter. For one thing, the rifle is lighter to carry. During your approach to the actual moment you should aim and snap-off your rifle at any and every object you see. Dwell on your aim after the shot and you will see how it goes. Practice with both eyes open always. Never mind which eye is the master one. Use a good-sized foresight. After ten thousand snap-offs you will do it all automatically. Then and not until then are you ready for your trial, the hundred-pound shot.

It is a very good thing to fire one shot at a selected target—anything will do, say a tin—every morning over a series of days and jot down the results. If some of the famous hunters would do this —especially the heavy brigade—they would be surprised at the result.

Should you happen to be of a severely self-critical nature and you find your first shot not what it ought to be, or rather not where it ought to be, there is still hope for you. You can go closer.

If you cannot count on your first shot being in at fifty yards, try what you can do at thirty yards. If still no good, try twenty yards, at the same time disciplining your mind to the fact that you must tackle your game at close range. Get accustomed to the idea of doing so. After all, in heavy stuff you may most likely have to approach to ten yards even to see your game. Presumably you will be clad in some neutral tinted stuff, khaki or what will you, and remember that it is *movement* that catches the eye of game. Therefore reduce all your motions to the very minimum when approaching game. You will be astonished how close you can go, even in full view, if you avoid all abrupt movements. Of course if the wind is wrong you are up against it and you cannot prevail.

4. Where to place the shot. By this time you will most probably have done one of two things: either you will have thrown this handbook onto the fire or you will have tried to bring yourself into such a state that you think you can deliver a bullet where it is most required. In the latter case the following notes may help you in deciding where your bullet will do most harm to the game and most good to yourself.

As I have remarked before when dealing with bullets, the vitals of all large animals are stowed away as far from danger from outside sources as possible. They are protected by heavy hide, tough muscle, and large bones. Such protection, while effective against spears and arrows, utterly collapses when opposed to modern metal-jacketed bullets.

Let us first consider the so-called heart shot, more properly called the body shot.

The Heart or Body Shot

This so-called heart shot is certainly the one that the novice should select for his first effort. Not that the heart itself is so much larger than the brain but because it is surmounted by—not surrounded by—a large deadly area wherein are to be found a network of arteries and a great vulnerable expanse of lung. Very, very few elephants' hearts are ever pierced by the bullets that lay them low. There are several reasons for this.

First, the heart in all four-footed animals is situated in the most inaccessible position, right down in the chest cavity. It is closely invested by the almost impenetrable bone forming the anchorage for the rib ends. In addition to this, the huge bone of the foreleg stands guardian over its charge when the animal is at rest and the nearest foreleg bearing its share of the weight. It is only off guard when the foreleg is extended forwards, as in walking.

Another reason why the heart itself is so seldom hit is due to its low position in the body of the living animal; when dead and lying on its side, the heart occupies a considerably higher portion of the chest cavity than when the animal is alive and upright. For this reason the heart is seldom hit because it is so often obscured by bush or grass. It would almost seem as if African vegetation had been designed for the express purpose of hiding this vital organ. On the other hand, the aforesaid lung area is very conspicuous and very often an unobstructed view may be had of it.

Hitherto I have been considering the tyro's problem as consisting in killing his game from a position at right angles to the body of his quarry. He would be well advised to confine his first effort exclusively to this position. Of course the experienced shot will kill from any angle and from the front. There is a very easy path for a bullet into the chest cavity from dead in front if only the victim will be co-operative enough to hold his head up and his trunk aside for a moment or two. The bullet has to enter with the windpipe—more like a huge hose than a pipe—but woe betide it should it encounter either wall of the passage. Definitely not a shot for one's first effort.

When selecting a position from which to fire that first all-important shot, be careful that your animal is really broadside-on. In the blinding light of an African noon or in the obscurity of heavy bush it is not easy to judge where the fore and aft line of the animal's body is. Yet this is quite important because the vitals lie some distance in from the exterior covering of hide, and allowance must be made for this fact. If one is lucky enough to see the leg of the far side, the position of the vitals will become clear at once. Always try to visualize the course your bullet will take after entering the body.

The Brain Shot

While this is not a shot for the tyro's first effort at elephant, it may transpire that it is the only one offered, as for instance in the case of an elephant launching itself straight at one, or, as will be more common, should you wish to finish off an animal wounded in the body and bleeding to death.

Here the ability to follow the course of your bullet after its entry will help. If you can see any indication of the locality of any of the features on the far side, this will help enormously. Very often a piece of the far ear can be seen, and if you identify it with the corresponding piece of the near ear, you can form a judgment of the locality of the brain. Eyes and ear holes are all pointers to the location of the brain. But it is of no use shooting at them; they are only the outward ends of invisible lines radiating from the brain.

Now let us see if common sense will help us here. It is obvious when looking at the enormous bulk of an elephant's head that tremendously strong neck muscles must be required to support the weight. Roughly speaking, the spine or vertebral column will be found in the center of the muscular column of the neck. Where the vertebrae end in the skull will be found the brain. Now that is a valuable indication. It means you have to shoot for the *center* of things whether from the side or from the front.

The Frontal Brain Shot

There is nothing serious for your bullet to overcome on its passage to the brain provided it follows the course of the air passages into the skull and then leaves them to break through a quite thin wall of bone into the brain itself. No respectable bullet that had been correctly launched could be diverted sufficiently from its course as to miss the brain. But you will notice that the air passages run up the forward face of the heavy bone carrying the tusks and joining them together. This bone is not ordinary bone. It is of a dense cellular construction full of oil and extremely resistant to bullets and axes. Only saws make any impression on it. A sharp ax flies back from it while a high-velocity bullet is brought to a standstill in an incredibly short distance. This bone wall must be avoided at all cost.

Luckily for the shooter and unluckily for the elephant this formidable barrier is lowered in the middle so as just to allow a bullet to reach the brain. The eyes are the external markers for this shot. Draw an imaginary line between the eyes and put your shot a little above this line according to the position in which the head is held.

There is a boss, or raised part, covering the cartilage that shields the hollow giving access to the air passages into the skull. This boss is very conspicuous on the living animal and should be looked for. Then watch that the head is not in any unusual position, that it appears to be facing exactly toward you, and get your shot in. But no flinching or you may be wrecked on that bony barrier.

The best general advice that I can think of is to keep your bullet directed toward the center of things, neither high nor low.

BUFFALO AND RHINO

Just as in elephant, the heart will be found tucked away in the most inaccessible place low between the forelegs. If there is grass, about ten to one it will hide that vital organ. In this case the old hunter's advice of "a shot behind the shoulder" is quite good although somewhat vague.

But there is a better one. Unlike the elephant, where it is very short and much obscured by the enormous ears, the neck of the buffalo and of the rhino is comparatively long. Nearly all of it is vulnerable, and is a large target. All the nerve channels pass through it and they are of necessity closely grouped together. The vertebral column need not be touched to insure a kill, but it is as well to aim for the center of the neck. It is a clean, deadly, and humane shot. Furthermore, it is often clear of interfering bush. It does not enrage the animal as a shot too far back in the body might. And it does not result in one of those unpleasant follow-ups occasioned by a lightly pierced lung. Moreover, it can be used with success from a variety of angles; it is not essential that it be broadside-on. I don't know why the neck shot has been so neglected. In all the deer and bovine animals the neck presents the largest vulnerable area of the whole body.

It is remarkable how often a clear view of the neck can be got when a similar view of the body vitals is obscured *once you have trained your mind to look for the neck shot.*

Apart from that, a solid of any caliber will soon lay low any of these animals when directed toward the *center* of the vital body area. Just as in elephant, ignore the outward marks except as indications to the whereabouts of the life spark far in the interior of those capacious barrels.

LION

It is quite impossible to lay down any rules for shooting the big cats. The almost infinite variety of position they may present themselves in makes any precise rules ridiculous in practice. As a general rule, however, the vitals are to be reached by a centrally directed bullet just as in the case of elephant, rhino, and buffalo.

You cannot walk about and select your position when dealing with lion as you often can with elephant. More often you have to take what offers or leave the chance altogether. Fortunately, here again a true-flying bullet of any caliber directed toward the vital area will accomplish wonders even when fired up the stern, should it be a solid. If you must use soft-nosed bullets, you should be more selective and perhaps await a broadside shot.

Whatever you do, try to avoid any of the high-velocity, pointed, soft-nosed type of bullet. Although you may have only one lion to get, you have likewise only one life to lose.

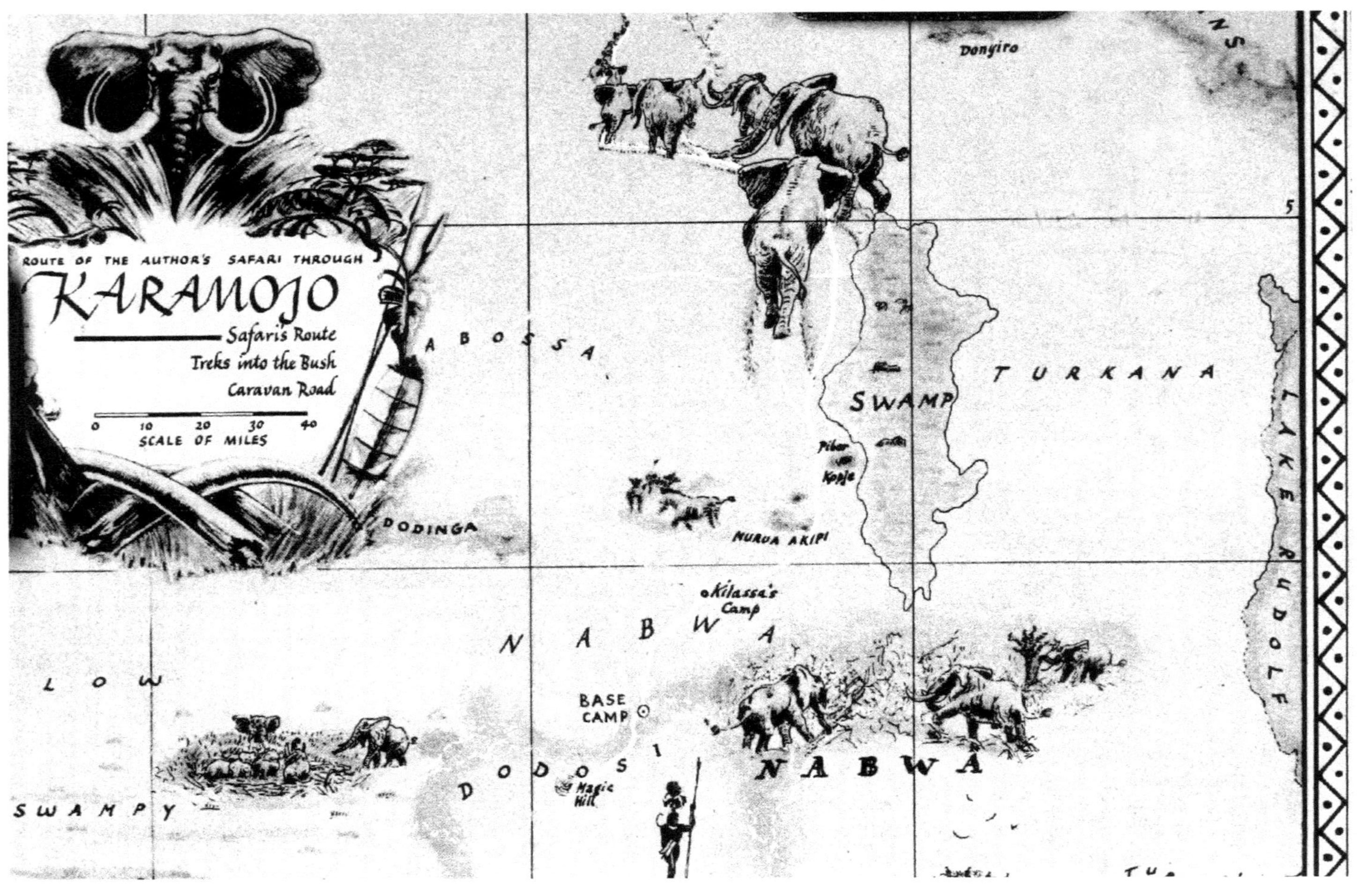
ROUTE OF THE AUTHOR'S SAFARI THROUGH
KARAMOJO
Safari's Route
Treks into the Bush
Caravan Road
0   10   20   30   40
SCALE OF MILES
ABOSSA
DODINGA
Donyiro
TURKANA
SWAMP
Pibor Kopje
NURUA AKIPI
LAKE RUDOLF
Kilassa's Camp
NABWA
NABWA
LOW
BASE CAMP
DODOSI
Magic Hill
SWAMPY

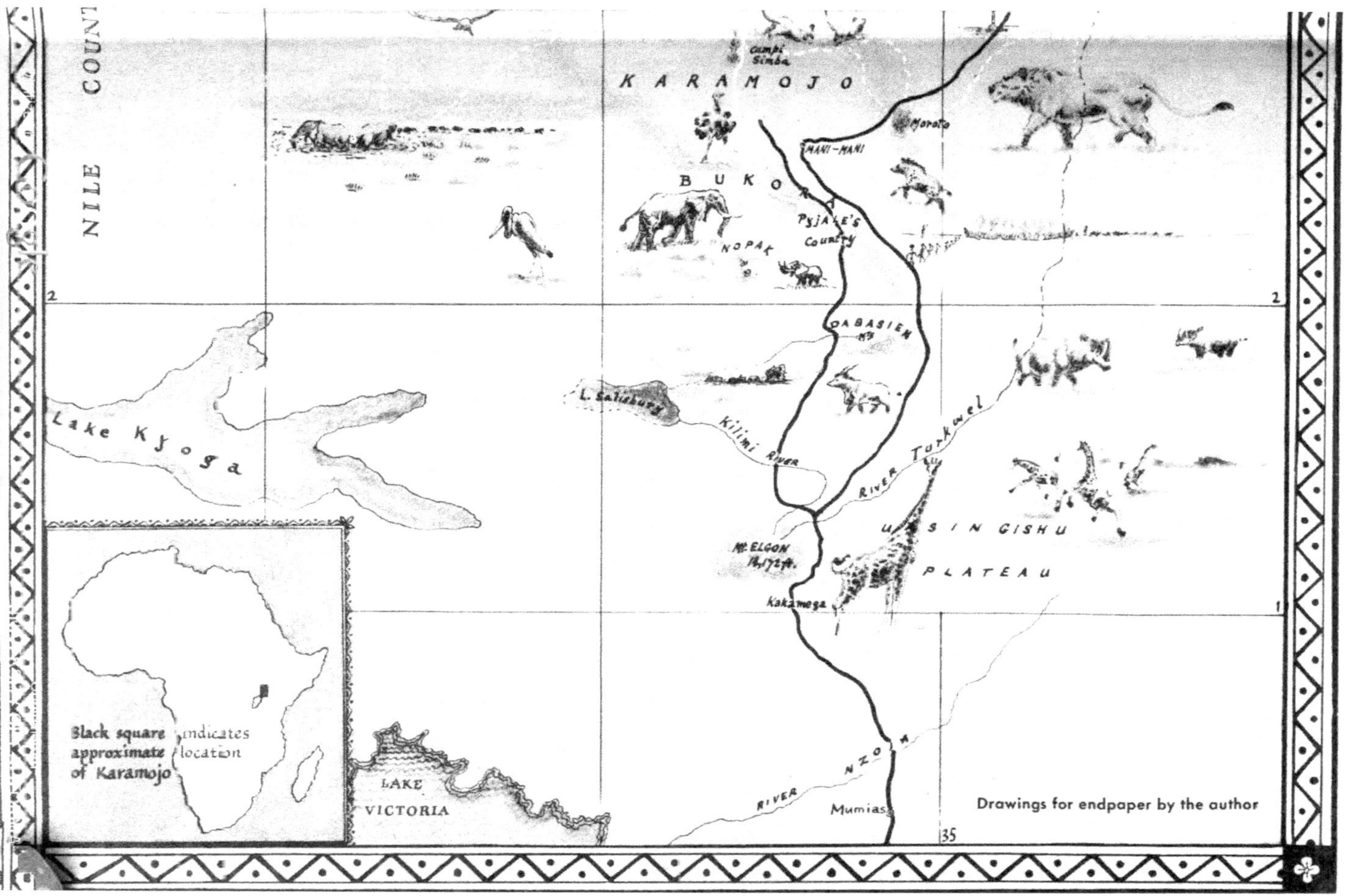

NILE COUNT
KARAMOJO
Campi Simba
Moroto
MANI-MANI
BUKO
Pyjale's Country
NOPAK
DABASIEN
L. Salisbury
Lake Kyoga
Kilimi River
River Turkwel
U A SIN GISHU
PLATEAU
Mt ELGON 14,172 ft.
Kakamega
RIVER NZOA
Mumias
LAKE VICTORIA
Black square indicates approximate location of Karamojo
Drawings for endpaper by the author